Managing Equity Portfolios

Managing Equity Portfolios

A Behavioral Approach to Improving Skills and Investment Processes

Michael A. Ervolini
Foreword by Terrance Odean

The MIT Press
Cambridge, Massachusetts
London, England

MIT Press books may be purchased at special quantity discounts for business or sales promotional use. For information, please email special_sales@mitpress.mit.edu

This book was set in Stone Sans and Stone Serif by the MIT Press. Printed and bound in the United States of America.

Library of Congress Cataloging-in-Publication Data

Ervolini, Michael A., 1955–
   Managing equity portfolios : a behavioral approach to improving skills and investment processes / Michael A. Ervolini ; foreword by Terrance Odean.
     pages cm
 Includes bibliographical references and index.
  ISBN 978-0-262-02834-9 (hardcover : alk. paper)
1. Portfolio management. 2. Investments—Psychological aspects. I. Title.
  HG4529.5.E78 2014
   332.63′22—dc23
2014013234

10 9 8 7 6 5 4 3 2 1

To Carol, for filling my life with Joy.

Contents

Foreword

Terrance Odean

In 1995, Don Keim and Ananth Madhavan published a study of 62,000 equity orders placed by 21 institutional investors. Three of the institutions were indexers. Of the remaining 18 active managers, 15 sold stocks that, on average, had outperformed the market the week before the sale. This finding was hardly puzzling if managers used price targets to trigger trades. What surprised Keim and Madhavan was that "some traders appear to adopt different strategies on the buy and sell sides." Six of the managers who were selling recent winners were also buying recent winners, and two of the three who were selling recent losers were also buying recent losers. Keim and Madhavan wrote: "The asymmetry between buy- and sell-side behavior is difficult to explain. This could reflect the use of complex, nonlinear trading strategies that are not readily apparent from an examination of the data."

The dominant academic paradigm of the time was that economic agents—especially professionals—always behaved sensibly. If money managers bought stocks very similar to the ones they sold, a good—if not obvious—explanation had to exist. Even today, normative corporate finance theories are confirmed by showing that corporate behavior is consistent with the theory. When the two diverge, the presumption is that the theory is wrong rather than that the behavior is suboptimal.

At the time that Keim and Madhavan's paper was published, I was analyzing the trading records for 10,000 individual investors at a large discount brokerage. I found that, like the institutional investors who puzzled Keim and Madhavan, individual investors have a strong tendency both to sell and buy stocks that have outperformed the market over the previous week (or month, or year). I was, though, trying to test behavioral theories of investor behavior and thus was not surprised by apparent inconsistencies in buying and selling strategies. I wrote, "While theoretical models of financial markets often treat buying and selling symmetrically, for most investors the decision to buy a security is quite different from the decision to sell." Buyers face a huge search problem: in equity markets alone, there are thousands of stocks to choose from, and yet sellers—especially individuals—usually choose from the few stocks they already own. In other respects, though, selling is more complicated. Buyers care only about future performance, yet sellers must consider not only the future but the past. Selling a past winner may trigger a tax bill; selling a past loser may cause regret. For many investors, buying is a forward-looking activity and selling is backward-looking.

The tax consequences of selling create an opportunity to pit normative economic theories against behavioral theories based on research in psychology. Tax theory predicts that investors will usually sell losing stocks so as to minimize taxes. Psychology predicts that investors will hang on to their losers and sell winners, a tendency that Shefrin and Statman (1985) term "the disposition effect." I found that the individual investors in my dataset tended to sell winners and hold losers. Only in December did tax-loss selling dominate.

We've learned a great deal about individual investors in the past 19 years. Studies have found that individual investors exhibit a disposition effect for many different assets and in many different countries. (See Barber and Odean 2013 for a review.) Individual investors trade more than is in their best interests. The stocks they buy subsequently tend to underperform the ones they sell. The more actively they trade, the worse they do. Men, who tend to be more overconfident about investing than women, trade more actively than women. Active trading reduces portfolio returns for both men and women, but men lose more because they trade more. The cost of excessive trading can be substantial. Including commissions and taxes, the aggregate trading costs of individual investors in Taiwan from 1995 through 1999 were equivalent to 2.2% of GDP!

Individual investors underdiversify. They pay too little attention to fees. They chase past performance. They buy attention-grabbing stocks. They purchase stocks they've owned before if they made money the first time and if the stock has gone down since they sold it. They tend to buy the same stocks as each other and sell the same stocks as each other. They prefer stocks with lottery-like distributions and trade less when they can buy lottery tickets and when the lottery payoffs are high. Investment performance goes up with IQ and down with age. And investors who get more speeding tickets also trade more.

One reason that we've learned a lot about individual investor behavior is that researchers have found many rich sources of data, including brokerage firms in China, Germany, Israel, the United States, and Sweden; stock

exchanges in Australia, China, Finland, Norway, India, and Taiwan; and
government agencies in Finland, Sweden, and Norway.

So far, the psychology of institutional investors has been studied less
than that of individual investors. While fewer sources document the trading activities of institutional investors, a lack of data is not the only impedi-
ment to understanding the behavior of institutional investors. Individual
investors who trade without professional advice make decisions about their
own money, whereas institutional investors make decisions about other
people's money. But these same decisions will, in many cases, affect the
institutional investor's own compensation and future employment opportunities. So an institutional investor's behavior depends both on what is
best for the client and what is best for the investor himself or herself.

Thus, a money manager's behavior will be influenced by how his or her
performance is measured, monitored, and rewarded. And these incentives
sometimes lead to unintended consequences. For example, fund managers
engage in window dressing—selling poorly performing stocks prior to being
monitored by plan sponsors (Lakonishok, Shleifer, Thaler, and Vishny
1991); managers increase risk in the second half of the year when their performance is below a benchmark and decrease it when above (Brown, Harlow, and Starks, 1996); and hedge funds that have built up less reputation
value take more risks than their peers and are more likely to fail (Brown,
Goetzmann, and Park, 2001).

While incentives play a large role in explaining money manager behavior, so too do the biases and limitations of human decision-making. Money
managers, like the rest of us, are prone to biased estimates of probability, to
overconfidence, and to loss aversion. They, too, have limited attention and
emotions that distort decisions. Managers who are unaware of their own
biases are likely to make trades that enhance neither their own welfare nor
that of their clients.

How can we use research from behavioral finance to improve investor
behavior? Advice for individual investors as a group abounds: diversify;
trade less frequently; pay attention to commissions and fees; don't chase
performance; when selling in a taxable account, sell your losers; look at
stocks that are out of the news. Of course, not every individual investor is
going to make the same mistakes. And if it were critical to improve the trading of specific individuals, we would want to study their personal trading
patterns. Fortunately, the long-term investment performance of the vast
majority of individual investors can be greatly improved by simply buying and holding well-diversified, low-cost mutual funds—either open-end
funds or exchange-traded funds.

"Buy-and-hold mutual funds" may be good advice for an individual investor, but it isn't going to satisfy a professional money manager. Nor do the lessons learned from the study of individual investor behavior necessarily apply to professionals. Most—though not all—professional investors do diversify. Trading turnover does not predict the performance for professional investors as it does for individuals. Indeed, high-speed trading can be quite profitable. Even performance chasing can be a successful strategy for professional investors (as long as they know when to get out). Furthermore, as is also true for individuals, professional money managers vary greatly in their strategies and behavior. Changes that may improve the performance of one manager may hurt the performance of another.

How can professional investors identify biases and behavior that hurt their performance? That is the topic of this book by Mike Ervolini. As Mike points out, improving performance depends critically upon feedback. To improve your golf swing, you need to know whether the ball is going too much to the right, too much to the left, too far, or not far enough. Without such feedback, learning will be slow or nonexistent.

Markets generate a lot of data, but they don't generate a lot of clear feedback. Outcomes are noisy. Good decisions may have bad outcomes. Bad decisions may have good outcomes. Long-term horizon investors must wait months or years to see how an investment works out. Markets are difficult environments in which to learn and are conducive to many learning biases.

For example, an old Wall Street adage warns, "Don't confuse brains with a bull market." We all have the tendency to take credit for our successes while blaming our failures on bad luck or other people. This tendency is known as self-attribution bias and can lead to biased learning. In the paper "Learning to Be Overconfident" (2001), Simon Gervais and I explored the theoretical implications of self-attribution bias for markets. Traders in our model differ in ability, but before they start trading they don't know whether they are more or less skilled traders. When traders are successful, they overweight the probability that their success was due to skill and not luck. More successful traders are wealthier and, on average, more skilled than unsuccessful traders, but they tend to be less skilled than they think they are.

In actual markets, not only are successful money managers likely to be overconfident, but their assets under management are likely to increase greatly due to the tendency of investors to put money into recently successful funds.

Another bias that leads to distorted learning is confirmation bias. Once people have made up their minds about something, they tend to look for evidence that they are right and ignore evidence to the contrary. Most money managers will focus on examples of when their investment approach succeeded rather than examining their failures. Doing so reinforces their current behavior and passes up an opportunity to learn.

Yet another source of biased learning is the disposition effect. Many institutional investors exhibit the same tendency as individuals to sell winning investments and hold on to losers (Jin and Scherbina, 2011). Thus, relative to opportunities, more stocks are sold for a gain and fewer for a loss. This behavior does not improve performance, but it could impede learning. Suppose a manager who is trying to evaluate her own strengths and weaknesses focuses solely on whether previous decisions resulted in a realized gain or loss. She will see a record distorted by her own selling decisions. Counting winners and losers could also lead a manager to ignore valuable information about what tends to happen to stocks after he sells them. Successful portfolio selection requires not only knowing when to buy but when to sell.

How can money managers improve? In a market in which good decisions can lead to losses and bad decisions to gains, analyzing individual trades usually won't help. As Ervolini points out, regardless of investment style, a manager who wants to learn needs to take a rigorous look at many decisions and many outcomes. Learning requires feedback, but not all feedback is equal. Feedback based on small samples and interpreted with bias is like the mirror in a funhouse. It distorts. If you want to take a good hard look at your trading behavior, you'll need a better mirror.

References

Barber, Brad M., and Terrance Odean. 2013. "The Behavior of Individual Investors." In *Handbook of the Economics of Finance*. Vol. 2, ed. George M. Constantinides, Milton Harris, and René M. Stulz. Amsterdam: Elsevier Publishing.

Brown, Keith C., W. V. Harlow, and Laura T. Starks. 1996. "Of Tournaments and Temptations: An Analysis of Managerial Incentives in the Mutual Fund Industry." *Journal of Finance* 51:85–110.

Brown, Stephen J., William N. Goetzmann, and James Park. 2001. "Careers and Survival: Competition and Risk in the Hedge Fund and CTA Industry." *Journal of Finance* 61:1869–1886.

Gervais, Simon, and Terrance Odean. 2001. "Learning to Be Overconfident." *Review of Financial Studies* 14:1–27.

Jin, Li, and Anna Scherbina. 2011. "Inheriting Losers." *Review of Financial Studies* 3:786–820.

Keim, Donald, and Ananth Madhavan. 1995. "Anatomy of the Trading Process: Empirical Evidence on the Behavior of Institutional Traders." *Journal of Financial Economics* 37:371–398.

Lakonishok, Josef, Andrei Shleifer, Richard Thaler, and Robert Vishny. 1991. "Window Dressing by Pension Fund Managers." *American Economic Review* 81:227–231.

Shefrin, Hersh M., and Meir S. Statman. 1985. "The Disposition to Sell Winners Too Early and Ride Losers Too Long: Theory and Evidence." *Journal of Finance* 40:777–790.

Preface

Portfolio management is tough business. Each day, managers face the challenges of an ever-changing and unforgiving market, where strategies and processes that worked yesterday suddenly stop producing alpha. Generating lackluster portfolio performance and explaining it to disappointed clients takes an emotional toll no matter how strong prior performance has been or how many years the manager has been in the business. This kind of stress makes individuals feel vulnerable. Persevering when the results are disappointing and criticisms are being hurled requires realistic confidence in one's ultimate ability and more than a little courage.

As my salute to those of you with the heart to dare greatly, I offer the words of Theodore Roosevelt:

> It is not the critic who counts; not the man who points out how the strong man stumbles, or where the doer of deeds could have done them better. The credit belongs to the man who is actually in the arena, whose face is marred by dust and sweat and blood, who strives valiantly, who errs, who comes short again and again, because there is no effort without error and shortcoming; but who does actually strive to do the deeds; who knows great enthusiasms, the great devotions; who spends himself in a worthy cause; who at the best knows in the end the triumph of high achievement, and who at the worst, if he fails, at least fails while daring greatly, so that his place shall never be with those cold and timid souls who neither know victory nor defeat.[1]

Note

1. Theodore Roosevelt, from his speech "Citizenship in a Republic," the Sorbonne, Paris, April 23, 1910.

Acknowledgments

I owe a great deal to the many scientists and investigators who have pioneered and developed the fields of psychology, neuroscience, behavioral finance, and now emotional finance. Their work, particularly as it relates to decision-making, has greatly advanced our understanding of the choices that shape portfolio performance.

I am deeply indebted to my friend and business partner Hal Haig, without whose support and intellectual guidance this book would have fallen far short of the final manuscript. Among his many contributions, Hal has been and continues to be the driving force behind the analytic innovations Cabot Research uses to serve its clients, many of which are described in this book. I also owe a great deal of thanks to Terry Odean for the helpful advice he has provided to Cabot over the years, for the good-natured honesty he brings to every conversation, and for writing the foreword to the book. I want to thank Walter D'Alessio for being a superb mentor early in my career and a terrific friend to this day. I learned numerous lessons about business and leadership from Walt that have served me well. My sincerest appreciation also goes to David C. Evans Jr., without whose sage advice and support my career would surely have taken a lesser trajectory. Dave and I have grown to become great friends and I especially enjoy trying to outfish him whenever the opportunity presents itself. To my friends Sidney and Sheila Siegel, thanks for the fun, the friendship, and being there every time. My thanks also to John Cafarella for innumerable laughs, many shared experiences, and a deep friendship. It is with great affection and immense respect that I thank Susan C. Peters for being a world-class friend and for her willingness to traverse some of life's most challenging terrains together.

I want to thank all of my colleagues at Cabot Research for their energy, hard work, and dedication to our vision of helping portfolio managers achieve their best. It is a pleasure to spend my days with each of you. And a special thanks to Peter Baldwin for making the initial introduction to the

MIT Press and to Elaine Bresnick for her expert editing of several drafts of this book. Thanks also to our many clients who have taught me a great deal about portfolio management and other aspects of their business. I especially cherish the friendships we have formed. My thanks to the members (past and present) of Vistage 140 for their advice and caring over the years. You are a terrific team and I am fortunate to share the second Thursday of every month with each of you. Thanks also to Jane A. Macdonald of the MIT Press for taking a chance on a first-time author and for smoothing out the lumps in an earlier draft.

No words can adequately express my appreciation for the love and support of my family and friends. You've been there through the successes and disappointments over the years, and it is because of you that I find the courage to strive toward exciting and challenging goals.

Finally, a tip of the hat to all of the professionals engaged in equity portfolio management, for you have chosen to enter the arena and dare greatly.

Introduction

Is there anything new to say about equity portfolio management? Yes, and it has to do with improving. Not the usual stuff about developing your strategy, staying within your style, doing better research, and trading more efficiently. These things are important, of course, but they don't get to the heart of improving. And that is what this book does. It lays out a new framework that enables you to improve confidently, simply, and deliberately. But I'm getting ahead of myself, so I'd better back up and explain why I wrote this book.

The Improvement Dilemma

Cabot Research LLC has been helping equity portfolio managers to improve for over nine years, building groundbreaking analytic software and serving scores of funds around the globe. As part of my work at Cabot, I have talked to hundreds of equity portfolio managers about their businesses. Our conversations have touched upon a wide range of topics, from the 2008–2009 market collapse, to the struggles of reversing outflows, to ideas regarding how best to communicate skill and process to clients. Each manager spoke with energy, confidence, and clarity when describing his or her investment philosophy, portfolio strategy, buy process, sell discipline, and even marketing message. Invariably, at some point the conversations would touch upon the manager's desire to improve. And then the whole tone of the conversation changed. The energy levels fell off, the confidence retreated, and the clarity hazed. This shift in the dynamics of our discourses never failed to occur. These inflection points in our conversations exposed a pervasive weakness within active management: Professional money managers aren't sure *how* to improve.

This shortcoming is not due to a lack of motivation or trying. To the contrary, the idea of becoming better is of paramount concern to these professionals, but making it happen is problematic. Three facts came through repeatedly from these conversations.

1. Managers want to improve. Most believe that becoming better is an essential part of their professionalism and a duty to their investors.
2. Managers work hard to improve. Each year they invest vast amounts of time, energy, and other resources in hope of becoming better at their jobs.
3. The results are disappointing: Managers report realizing little to no payback on their improvement efforts, and this experience is nearly universal. Try as they do, improvement remains elusive, whether the manager is currently above or below his or her benchmark, and regardless of strategy or style.

Can't Improve What You Don't Measure

Active equity management exemplifies the validity of this keen observation attributed to the father of continuous improvement, W. Edwards Deming. The feedback in this industry is focused 100 percent on measuring outcomes, with zero attention given to measuring the skills needed to generate those outcomes. How, then, can we expect managers to improve their skills when they aren't being measured? According to Deming, we can't— and this inability is at the root of the problems plaguing active portfolio management, as is described more fully in chapter 1. Equally absent are rigorous calibrations of investment process and behavioral tendencies. The combined effect of not understanding skills, process, and behaviors is what makes improving impossible today, as detailed in chapter 2.

The New Science of Improving

Improving demands looking well below the surface of returns and other measures of outcome to learn what it is that the manager does well and what needs fixing. It requires new analytics that isolate the types of decisions the manager makes and then use this granular data to quantify how much alpha comes from buy, sell, and sizing decisions as independent skills. A conceptually straightforward and well-tested framework for doing just this is presented in chapter 3. This framework is then extended to show how investment process and behaviors can be analyzed, using the methods shown in chapter 4. More important than establishing the framework is demonstrating evidence that it actually helps managers improve. Examples of how the new science of improving is helping managers to enhance their self-awareness and become better investors are delivered in chapter 5. Chapter 6, which concludes Part One of the book, considers how the emotions experienced by the manager go well beyond affecting skills and behaviors, right into influencing portfolio risk.

Smart Thinking

We know very little about how our brains actually work. In fact, most of what we know about the way we think is either grossly incomplete or simply wrong. For one thing, the vast majority of mental processing and formation of choices occurs not as the result of conscious deliberation, but as the result of automatic unconscious processes. And the dominance of this unconscious thinking in shaping choices is equally true when buying and selling stocks as it is when mindlessly scanning through radio stations while driving on the interstate.

We now know that portfolio managers cannot reach their personal best without greater knowledge about their own thought processes, including those in which biases and unintended choices are likely to dominate. A deeper look into how thinking really happens, including the enormous role of the unconscious in shaping perceptions, analyses, and choices, is taken up in Part Two of the book. This includes a series of essays presented in chapters 7 through 40 that investigate topics from psychology and neuroscience, relating various scientific findings to the challenges of portfolio management. The essays will help professionals build their knowledge about the many hidden forces that shape investment choices and how to harness these forces for greater success.

Just Do It

The ultimate value of this book depends upon whether or not it helps you become a better investor. That is the purpose of Part Three, which offers seven ideas for learning and improving more deliberately. The projects, as they are termed, range from suggestions about maintaining an investment diary, to describing how to perform rudimentary calculations that quantify basic skills, on through to investigating skills on a more granular level. Each project helps you gain a deeper understanding of your strengths and shortcomings and then use this knowledge to improve.

The precise way you go about improving must be bespoke to you and your business. The methods for improving presented here are already being used to support a rapidly growing number of managers whose portfolios represent a wide range of strategies and styles, and whose processes include everything from traditional, bottom-up research to those that employ some analytic and quantitative screening. Possessing the desire to improve is common, but choosing to improve scientifically is not, and consequently it offers one way you can differentiate and grow your business.

Part One: Game Change

He that will not apply new remedies must expect new evils; for time is the greatest innovator.

Francis Bacon, "Of Innovations"

1 Industry Challenges

Introduction

The debate over skill within the active equity management industry is alive and robust. Proponents point to portfolios that have beaten their benchmarks for three, five, seven years or more as ample evidence that skill exists. The opponents harrumph that the majority of actively managed funds underperform year after year. The truth, as with so many topics that arouse strong emotions, lies somewhere between these polar positions, as will be explained.

This chapter provides a sobering look at the state of the active equity industry, particularly regarding investment performance. Rather than being presented as an indictment of active management, these data are offered to challenge industry practitioners to begin thinking about improvement not merely as an aspirational goal, but as an activity that can be pursued deliberately. You will also be introduced to the two greatest stumbling blocks preventing managers from improving today—the lack of quality feedback, and a weak understanding of how their emotions run roughshod over their intentions.

Under Siege

If ever there were a time for active equity managers to take a hard look in the mirror, it is right now. The vast majority of actively managed equity portfolios are underperforming and have underperformed for many years. The result has been a decline in assets under management, dramatic fee compression, and other stresses reflecting investor disappointment. A closer look at historical performance and capital flows is presented below.

Industry Scorecard

Standard & Poor's has been collecting and analyzing mutual fund performance data for over a decade. Compiled and released as the S&P Indices Versus Active Funds (SPIVA) scorecard, this report includes a look at the proportion of funds that underperform their respective benchmarks annually. In the 2013 mid-year SPIVA report, active equities showed disappointing results for the past one, three, and five years and longer. And while some styles did a little better and others a little worse, actively managed funds were mostly surpassed by their benchmarks.

Table 1.1 shows the proportion of U.S. funds beaten by their benchmarks in the past five years. An impressive 80.5% (5 years, averaged) of all actively managed U.S. funds underperformed over this time period. Levels of underperformance within the major style groups of large-, mid-, and small-cap stocks was 79.46%, 81.98%, and 77.88% respectively.

SPIVA reports slightly better results for global/international actively managed funds, as presented in Table 1.2. The majority of these funds also underperformed their benchmarks, although the five-year averages were stronger than for U.S. funds. One particularly noteworthy group is international small-caps, where 81.97% outperformed their benchmarks.

Disappointing as these results are generally, they merely hint at the longer history of actively managed equities' underperformance. An earlier SPIVA report states, "As we noted previously in the 10th anniversary SPIVA report, one-year figures fluctuate wildly and can favor either active funds or benchmarks depending on the market environment. However, the trend of a large percentage of managers failing to outperform their benchmarks over a longer-term horizon remains consistent."[1]

The effects of relatively poor performance are being experienced by active managers as higher allocations to passive equity products, fee compression

Table 1.1

Proportion of U.S. Mutual Funds Beaten by Their Benchmarks

Funds	One Year	Three Years	Five Years
Large-cap	59.58%	85.95%	79.46%
Mid-cap	68.88%	85.78%	81.98%
Small-cap	64.27%	80.19%	77.88%
Multi-cap	63.41%	84.31%	82.57%
Real estate	56.83%	95.07%	80.56%

Source: S&P Dow Jones Indices, SPIVA Scorecard, Mid-Year 2013, McGraw Hill Financial, page 3.

for active management, and a more challenging environment for winning new allocations. Another reaction to poor performance is the disappearance of underperforming funds, as mentioned in the SPIVA report: "The continuing volatility in the equity and fixed income markets over the past five years resulted in nearly 27% of domestic equity funds, 24% of international equity funds and 19% of fixed income funds [having to] merge or liquidate."[2]

Reallocating Investments

Investors have been steadily moving capital away from active equity management and into passive alternatives. This shift reflects a response to continued disappointing performance coupled with the lure of lower fees and greater liquidity. Figure 1.1 vividly depicts this reallocation from active to passive equity products. These data describe the cumulative flows within the active management industry (i.e., mutual funds) and passive products (i.e., ETFs and index funds) over the period 2006 to 2013. As can be seen, the flows to active and passive equity products were positive and of comparable size in 2006 and 2007 but began to diverge in 2008. By 2009, active management was experiencing net outflows, while passive products continued to grow. In just the past eight years, U.S. passive equity products have grown by approximately $1 trillion, seemingly at the direct expense of actively managed funds. Both institutional and retail investors have participated in this sizable reallocation from active to passive equities.

Commenting on this decade-plus trend, Vanguard founder Jack Bogle reflects, "Well, if you saw the curve, with the rise of index funds, including ours and Fidelity's in particular, and the fall in actively managed fund assets, including particularly Magellan's and then American Fund's growth

Table 1.2
Proportion of Global Mutual Funds Beaten by Their Benchmarks

Funds	One Year	Three Years	Five Years
Global	60.78%	70.72%	62.59%
International	54.18%	58.81%	65.86%
International small-cap	13.43%	11.11%	18.03%
Emerging markets real estate	54.81%	55.77%	74.53%

Source: S&P Dow Jones Indices, SPIVA Scorecard, Mid-Year 2013, McGraw Hill Financial, page 10.

$ Billions

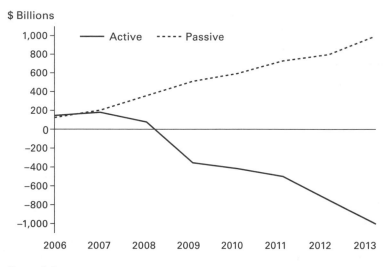

Figure 1.1
Global active and passive equity flows, 2006–2013. The graph portrays worldwide cumulative flows in and out of "actively managed" and "passively managed" equity funds by year, from January 2006 through January 2013. "Active" includes actively managed open-ended equity mutual funds and not indexed funds; "passive" includes open-ended equity funds that are passively managed (index funds) and passive ETFs (electronically traded funds). *Source:* EPFR Global, Boston, MA, September 30, 2013

fund, you'd see that … probably 80 percent of the cash flow now is going into the index funds and only 20 percent into the active."[3] Speaking more to today's dynamics, Sanford Bragg of Integrity Research comments, "A bigger worry for us [active industry] is the shift toward passive management and ETFs. ETFs are at $13 trillion in assets [globally] and growing 22 percent a year."[4] This trend could become even bleaker should the lower allocations to equities now being discussed begin to take hold. "Nearly one-quarter of the institutional funds participating in the most recent Greenwich Associates U.S. Investment Management Study [2013] say they plan to further reduce domestic equity allocations in the next three years,"[5] reports Bragg.

Mounting Unpopularity
Investor advocates, financial advisors, journalists, and academics are increasingly urging investors to shift their equity allocations from active to passive instruments. Beta is close to free, they say, so why pay a fee for merely benchmark or subpar returns? Bogle has long recommended that investors eschew actively managed funds in favor of passive products. His consistent

message has been that most managers do not outperform, and identifying which manager is likely to outperform is beyond the ability of most investors. He makes this point himself more colorfully: "The chances you will do better playing that game [picking the right funds] are infinitely small. If I want to put a number on it, let me just say [off the] top of the head that maybe you have 0.1 of 1 percent chance of beating the market over time."[6]

Similarly disenchanted with the results of active equity management is John Authers of the *Financial Times*. He encourages his readers to sidestep active management in favor of passive products. He writes, "It will help everyone if active investors can work out what they are doing wrong."[7] He goes on to say, "But for now, investors are best advised to pull money out, and switch to ETFs or index funds. That will put pressure on active funds to sort their act out."[8]

Summary

Active equity management is hurting. Approximately four-fifths of actively managed funds have underperformed their benchmarks for the past five years, with chronic underperformance being the case for decades. Investors are responding by reallocating their equity holdings away from active management and toward passive alternatives. This trend has accelerated in recent years and shows no signs of abating. The current trajectory portends a bleak future for active portfolio management. It will take more-active managers delivering stronger and more consistent results to nudge the industry back onto a brighter path. Two impediments now preventing the much-needed improvement by equity managers are discussed next: confusion about skills, and emotional interference in decision-making.

Skill versus Luck

Considerable time and vast amounts of capital have been invested to determine just how much skill exists among equity portfolio managers. The quest for appropriate metrics to quantify manager skill has resulted in hundreds of journal articles, scores of doctoral dissertations, and more than a few Nobel Prizes along the way. Amateurs and professionals alike involved in everything from playing bridge to sequencing DNA know that measuring a skill is essential to achieving higher proficiency. Yet there is no consensus over whether equity manager skill even exists, let alone how it should be measured.

Efforts to uncover investment skill have primarily involved looking for persistent alpha generation. Behind this is the thought that if a manager possesses skill, he should be able to deliver risk-adjusted excess performance consistently over many years. Intuitive as this approach appears, its greatest weakness is that it infers skill from outcomes rather than measuring skill directly. And while this shortcoming does not appear to have dampened the interest of academics or manager selection consultants, it has at least two obvious drawbacks. First, it is useless in helping managers themselves become more self-aware and improve; and second, it has not proven reliable in helping capital sources to identify managers who are likely to deliver outperformance going forward.

CAP-M

Rigorous investigation into the skill question began with the formulation of the capital asset pricing model (CAP-M) introduced by William Sharpe in 1964, for which he was awarded the Nobel Prize in 1990. Building upon the earlier work of Harry Markowitz, another Nobel laureate, CAP-M describes the relationship between risk and expected return, and it serves as a model for the pricing of risky securities and assessing portfolio performance. Regarding the latter, CAP-M separates systematic risk (beta) from nonsystematic risk, or the idiosyncratic risk of a particular portfolio. It further supports the quantification of alpha, or the amount of excess return that cannot be accounted for merely by taking on extra risk. The notion that excess risk must be accounted for in assessing excess return is fundamental to understanding the quality of a portfolio and the skill of its manager. Not doing so would make a 10% return from an investment of modest risk equally desirable as the same return from an extremely high-risk venture. Pointing out the importance of measuring risk-adjusted performance, William Sharpe is commonly credited to have said, "But the fundamental idea remains that there's no reason to expect reward just for bearing risk. Otherwise you'd make a lot of money in Las Vegas."

CAP-M is commonly referred to as a single-factor risk model in that its alpha assesses risk-adjusted performance relative to the broad market (i.e., its single factor). Positive alphas indicate that active portfolio management has contributed returns over and above the market, after compensating for the portfolio's relative riskiness. A negative alpha points to the opposite conclusion. Advances in the understanding of market cycles, systematic risks, and themes that periodically drive asset performance have led to the use of multiple factors in attempts to further tease out manager skill over and above not only the overall performance of the market, but also after consideration of specific market dynamics that may have helped or hampered a particular portfolio.

Fama and French

A generally accepted method for computing alpha within academia today is the three-factor model introduced by Eugene Fama (2013 Nobel laureate) and Kenneth French. The Fama-French model quantifies excess risk-adjusted performance by analytically resolving for the amount of portfolio return that cannot be attributed to three sources of systematic risk: the market overall (beta), and the two prevalent style tilts (i.e., the relative performance between large and small capitalization companies and the relative performance between growth and value companies). For a manager to be viewed as delivering alpha within this framework, the portfolio must deliver risk-adjusted returns that surpass the market's returns and that outperform the style tilts that are reflected among the portfolio's holdings. Since the addition of momentum as a fourth factor by Mark Carhart in 1979, many academic studies of equity portfolio performance have provided results using both the three- and four-factor alpha models.

Fama and French have investigated manager skill extensively. Their conclusions have not been encouraging. Philosophically their approach begins with the premise that before fees, at least half of active management must underperform, and that this proportion grows as fees and expenses are layered in. They refer to this concept as equilibrium accounting, which they describe as follows: "Suppose that when returns are measured before costs (fees and other expenses), passive investors get passive returns; that is, they have zero alpha (abnormal expected return) relative to passive benchmarks. This means active investment must also be a zero sum game—aggregate alpha is zero before costs. If some active investors have positive alpha before costs, it is dollar for dollar at the expense of other active investors. After costs, that is, in terms of net returns to investors, active investment must be a negative sum game."[9] Disheartening as this picture of the market seems, it nevertheless does leave the door open for a portion of active managers to demonstrate skill by outperforming.

Fama and French tested their hypothesis by examining the performance of thousands of mutual funds from 1984 through 2006. Their results are rather sobering, as they explain: "For fund investors the simulation results are disheartening. When alpha is estimated on net returns to investors, the cross-section of precision-adjusted alpha estimates, α (alpha), suggests that few active funds produce benchmark adjusted expected returns that cover their costs."[10] Offering a faint flicker of hope, Fama and French acknowledge that a few funds in the large group studied do show skill as defined by their methodology. And that is where the skill versus luck debate begins to turn.

Active Share

Martijn Cremers and Antti Petajisto have investigated skill in relation to manager conviction. They use a measure termed "active share" to quantify a manager's willingness to deviate from his or her benchmark or to make bets. Here's how they define active share: "[W]e can decompose a fund's portfolio into active and passive components. Whenever the portfolio weight of an individual stock exceeds the stock's index weight, the fund is taking an active long position in the stock; similarly, a position less than the index weight implies an active short position in the stock. The sum of the active positions then indicates how active the fund is."[11]

Looking across the mutual fund landscape, Cremers and Petajisto's investigations show that "[t]he active share of 'active' all-equity mutual funds in the US ranges from 30% to 100%, with an average of 66% for large-cap funds."[12] Relating this measure to performance, their research finds that higher active share is correlated with continued outperformance. They note: "Funds with the highest active share exhibit some skill and pick portfolios that outperform their benchmarks by 1.51%–2.40% per year. After fees and transaction costs this outperformance decreases to 1.13%–1.15% per year."[13] Their results further show that the highest active share group delivered the strongest results: "[T]he most active funds have outperformed their benchmarks by about 2.7% before expenses and 1.4% after expenses. This group has an active share of 95% or higher."[14]

Cremers and Petajisto also found that the stronger performance of the higher active share funds was not simply the result of taking greater risk. They write, "Interestingly, the tracking error of a fund has no predictive power for future returns—if anything, high tracking error is related to lower future performance. Even though both tracking error and active share measure active management, they capture somewhat different aspects of it. Tracking error emphasizes systematic risk a fund may take relative to the index, while active share emphasizes individual stock selection. Apparently the stock selection dimension of active management is rewarded in the market while systematic risks are not."[15] In other words, many fund managers are able to reliably pick and overweight stocks that help them outperform. This conclusion offers strong support for the existence of skill—just not enough for many managers to beat their benchmarks.

High Conviction

In their paper "Best Ideas," Cohen, Polk, and Silli drill down a little differently to the concepts of conviction and stock selection skill. They analyze the largest holdings in funds over time. These high-conviction positions typically generate considerable performance; as they note, "We find that the stock that active managers display the most conviction towards ex-ante, outperforms the market, as well as the other stocks in those managers' portfolios, by approximately one to four percent per quarter depending on the benchmark employed."[16] Cohen and colleagues found similar results in other high-conviction positions: "The results for managers' other high-conviction investments (e.g., top five stocks) are also strong. The other stocks managers hold do not exhibit significant outperformance."[17] The authors suggest that "even the typical active mutual fund manager is able to identify stocks that outperform by economically and statistically large amounts."[18] Their research suggests that if most managers were to hold more concentrated portfolios composed of their higher conviction names, the performance of such funds would reflect greater skill and higher returns.

Separating Skill from Luck

Further complicating the identification of skill is the fact that luck plays a role in investing. In his highly informative book *The Success Equation*, Michael Mauboussin provides a framework for considering when luck or skill is likely to dominate outcomes. He writes, "here's the distinction between activities in which luck plays a small role and activities in which luck plays a large role: when luck has little influence, a good process will always have a good outcome. When a measure of luck is involved, a good process will have a good outcome but only over time. When skill exerts the greater influence, cause and effect are intimately connected. When luck exerts the greater influence, cause and effect are only loosely linked in the short run."[19]

Separating skillful decisions from lucky ones is something at which individuals are not adept, according to Mauboussin. He explains, "Part of the reason is that few of us are well versed in statistics. But psychology exerts the most profound influence on our failure to identify what is due to skill and what is just luck."[20]

Summary

The future of the active equity industry is intrinsically linked to manager skill. As obvious as this statement may appear, skill is a completely unknown quantity. The majority of analytic work over the past six decades merely infers skill from portfolio outcomes. Recent studies of portfolio holdings have improved the granularity of skill investigations, although they continue to quantify skill inferentially. Ignorance regarding what skill is and who possesses it is exacerbated by the unavoidable forces of luck and unconscious motivations shaping portfolio performance. The challenges to investment decision-making posed by psychology and emotional struggles are taken up in the next section.

Loving and Hating Investing

What does managing emotions have to do with active portfolio management? The answer is everything—or, more precisely, it has everything to do with delivering top performance. This is what leading scholars such as Daniel Kahneman and Amos Tversky began to uncover as they advanced the understanding of decision-making under uncertainty, leading to the development of behavioral finance. Chief among their numerous contributions is the repeated demonstration that individuals rarely act as purely analytic economic agents, but instead make choices that often satisfy some unconscious need rather than maximizing wealth. This insight alone challenges many of the bedrock assumptions underpinning neoclassical finance and helps explain why nonoptimal choices flourish within professional investing and elsewhere.

Best known for their formulation of prospect theory, Kahneman and Tversky showed in several studies that individuals experience a one-dollar loss two to three times more intensely than they experience a one-dollar gain. Such asymmetry in the way individuals internalize losses versus gains underpins a host of more specific behavioral tendencies such as the disposition effect, loss aversion, the endowment effect, regret aversion, risk aversion, and many more. Their pioneering work has been advanced by scores of scholars, including Nicholas Barberis, Terrance Odean, Hersh Shefrin, Robert Shiller (2013 Nobel laureate), Andrei Shleifer, and Richard Thaler, to name just a few. The collective works of these and other finance academics have been building steadily since the early 1980s, giving new and important insights into how investment decisions are really made, why they are commonly counterproductive, and how it is possible to better align the choices we make with our conscious intentions.

Emotional Finance

David Tuckett and Richard Taffler of the United Kingdom are leading the way in the study of what they have coined "emotional finance." This new branch of academic finance is deeply concerned with the role that emotions and feelings play in shaping and misaligning financial decisions. As they put it, "Barring a very few exceptions, such as passing references to greed and fear and more extensive discussions of the wish to avoid loss, emotions in investment have tended to be treated as dangerous signs of weakness, embarrassment or anxiety in both academic and professional circles."[21] They continue, "Cold rational calculation is idealized. This approach contrasts with that widely used in modern psychology and neuroscience, which has revolutionized the accepted academic understanding of emotion and its ongoing dynamic role in human behaviour. Emotion ('gut feeling') is central to all thinking and experience and is particularly important for reliable and accurate decision-making."[22] Tuckett and Taffler point to the propensity of academic finance to study markets, with a corresponding paucity of research into individual portfolio managers and the role that emotions play in their investment decisions. Discussing this point, they suggest, "Individuals have not really mattered. There has therefore been no systematic study of their thoughts, fantasies and fears or how they cope with their experience and its stresses."[23]

Manager Interviews

In their CFA monograph *Fund Management: An Emotional Finance Perspective*, Tuckett and Taffler detail findings from a series of interviews with over fifty fund managers globally. At the broadest level, they observe, "every professional investor knows that their everyday experience is dominated by uncertainty and informational ambiguity and that investment is an inherently emotionally arousing process."[24] Yet, the researchers go on to note, by and large the portfolio managers they interviewed were not comfortable openly discussing fear, anxiety, or other emotions they experienced daily. Instead, these professionals preferred to describe their process as one of stoicism and cold, calculating objectivity. When these same professionals related detailed examples of their investment triumphs and disappointments, however, their narratives were packed with emotional content.

The stark contrast between how portfolio managers describe their processes and how they experience specific assets they owned or did not own underscores an important fact that, by silent consensus, has been steadfastly avoided: Portfolio managers are emotional beings who often pretend not to be, and this sweeping under the rug of feelings that permeate every waking moment of life contributes to underperformance. Overplaying objectivity as if it were a permanent condition one must attain to be a professional investor not only is wrong-minded but invariably undermines one's ability to achieve one's personal best. Or as Tuckett and Taffler have so nicely summarized, "Any attempt to bypass or ignore feelings is likely to lead to poor decision-making outcomes."[25]

Inherent Struggles

The study of emotional finance further points out that not only are individuals innately emotional, but the business of portfolio management brings with it specific emotional conflicts with which each professional must wrestle. A glimpse into a few of the nonanalytic challenges identified by Tuckett and Taffler is offered below.

Exceptionality   The active manager proposition is this: The portfolio will deliver above-benchmark returns without taking on excessive risks (that is, it will deliver alpha). Achieving this has been difficult for most managers, as described above. Being cognizant of how difficult it is to deliver excess returns, while also convincing yourself and others that you will be among the rarified group that does this, creates stress, anxiety, pressure, and fear— all of which find their way into the portfolio.

Intrinsic Uncertainty   Comparing today's price for an asset to the analyst's estimate of intrinsic value is one of the cornerstone activities of portfolio management. Yet this comparison and many other investment processes require establishing expectations for future outcomes which are, by definition, unknowable. Individuals overcome the uncertain choices they must make regarding financial assets with the help of an emotional charge—one that nudges them toward either low or high expectations, strong or weak likelihoods, go or no-go decisions. These emotional impulses often reflect the individual's unconscious desire to either seek pleasure (from a needed winner) or avoid pain (by sidestepping a possible loser). Emotions, therefore, help individuals resolve the angst of making judgments regarding the future about which clarity, never mind certainty, is impossible.

Time Factor   The emotional relationship that portfolio managers form with assets begins prior to their purchase and often lasts well past the time they are sold. Assets considered for purchase may result in intense relationships even if never bought, especially if they go on to be notable winners, thus fomenting painful regret over a missed opportunity. Owned assets provide seemingly endless moments of emotional connection: the initial buy (which invariably represents hope), then the decision about how and when to size and resize as optimism and pessimism alternately occupy one's mind, and ultimately the assessment of whether the asset is achieving its thesis or drifting. Unlike buying, selling is more often associated with negative feelings—the position did not perform, or the position is tired and can't be counted on any more. Each day these choices are played out over numerous candidates considered and positions held, with the result that the manager encounters boundless opportunities for experiencing elation and disappointment.

Shorting the Long Term   Both retail and institutional investors tend to allocate their capital based, in good part, on the manager's long-term investment strategy. Then they quickly revert to evaluating these supposed long-term allocations based on quarterly, monthly, or daily performance. Believing in and selling a long-term proposition only to defend your portfolio's performance at each market twist and turn places managers in an emotional no-win situation.

Although their clients sign up for a bold strategy that they hope will deliver excess returns over time, these same clients quickly lose their composure when they experience more than timid risk-taking. With investors holding such inconsistent desires, managers must do their best to implement their long-term strategies while being prepared to defend themselves against onslaughts of second-guessing from clients and their consultants, who unconsciously desire smooth and steady performance from a market that is inherently volatile. Seeking alpha through high-conviction investing is thus risky with regard to manager-client relationships, and its pursuit is often reined in by concerns over managing tracking error. Fear, anxiety, and frustration are understandable emotional responses by managers to such conflicting mandates.

Viewed from this more expansive perspective, the role of the portfolio manager, then, is to harness self-awareness of his internal emotional struggles together with research, knowledge, and judgment about financial markets and individual assets to make informed decisions. Emphasizing the importance of emotions within investing, Tuckett and Taffler make the following point: "Our fund managers can thus be considered to be in the emotional front line of the asset management industry and, as such, to have to carry with them on one level not just their own anxieties and concerns but also those of their clients and employers among others."[26]

Broader Motivations

Emotional finance offers what seems a natural extension to behavioral finance. The two are similar in that they directly challenge conventional ideas about objective decision-making, but emotional finance further expands upon the mechanisms for systematic error-making beyond biases and cognitive shortcomings, to fully embrace the notion that emotions are ever present and need to be accounted for within investing. Put succinctly, rational thinking cannot be separated from emotions, and believing otherwise overlooks what modern psychology and neuroscience now understand about how individuals make decisions. Relating this idea to investing, Tuckett and Taffler suggest "the need to abandon what we consider the highly misleading rational-irrational distinction in finance and ... the importance of replacing the similarly misunderstood but widely held notion of investment activity being driven by greed, fear and hope with a much richer and more realistic understanding of what investment professionals are doing and the emotions that actualize them. Based on the evidence of our research interviews, we argue that investment activity is, in fact, far more accurately characterized as motivated by the emotions of excitement, anxiety and denial."[27]

Summary

Managing money is inseparable from managing emotions. Nevertheless, managers tend to regard the presence of emotions as a weakness rather than as a valuable component of human intelligence that can be harnessed. Denying the existence or importance of their own emotional needs has undoubtedly contributed to managers' struggles in delivering top performance. Learning to become a better investor will necessitate the dual practice of developing skills and managing emotions, as further described in this book.

Conclusion

Active management is being challenged as never before. Investors are increasingly diverting their equity allocations into passive alternatives and away from traditional, actively managed products. Those managers fortunate enough to capture and retain assets often face intense pressure to reduce the fees they charge. The reductions to overall industry revenues are resulting in business consolidations and the disappearance of many funds, as achieving profitability becomes ever more difficult.

Driving this industry dynamic is widespread chronic underperformance. The vast proportion of funds are being beaten by their benchmarks, reflecting a trend that has existed for a decade or more. Any chance of stemming this tide will come from more managers delivering stronger performance. Improvement at the scale needed, however, will require the honing of skills and management of behavioral tendencies to levels not seen to date.

One significant obstacle to skill improvement is poor feedback. After decades of refining ways to infer skills from outcomes, virtually all managers are still clueless about their strengths and shortcomings in buying, selling, and sizing positions. Overcoming this industry-wide inadequacy is essential if enough managers are to improve to make a difference.

An equally important obstacle to improving is the often negative influence that emotions and the unconscious have on investment decisions. It is now well understood that emotions play a role in the choices we make and the judgments we form. Little practical use has been made of what behavioral finance and now emotional finance teach us. Harnessing intuition, impulses, and emotions will be a critical part of helping more managers beat their benchmarks.

Notes

1. SPIVA Scorecard, Mid-Year 2012, contributed by Aye Soe, *S&P Dow Jones Indices/ McGraw Hill Financial*, http://www.spindices.com/resource-center/thought-leadership/ spiva/.

2. SPIVA Scorecard, Mid-Year 2013, contributed by Aye Soe, *S&P Dow Jones Indices/ McGraw Hill Financial*, http://www.spindices.com/resource-center/thought-leadership/ spiva/.

3. John Bogle, "The 'Train Wreck' Awaiting American Retirement," interview with *Frontline*, November 12, 2012, transcribed at http://www.pbs.org/wgbh/pages/ frontline/business-economy-financial-crisis/retirement-gamble/john-bogle-the-train -wreck-awaiting-american-retirement/.

4. Sandy Bragg, "Greenwich: No Relief for the Weary," *Integrity Research Associates*, June 25, 2013, http://www.integrity-research.com/cms/2013/06/25/greenwich-no -relief-for-the-weary/.

5. Ibid.

6. Bogle, "'Train Wreck.'"

7. John Authers, "Quest for Test of Investment Skill Persists," *Financial Times* (London), January 11, 2013, http://www.ft.com/cms/s/0/8df368a4-5bd7-11e2-bef7 -00144feab49a.html#axzz2iNzqxh2U.

8. Ibid.

9. Eugene F. Fama and Kenneth R. French, "Luck versus Skill in the Cross-Section of Mutual Fund Returns," *Journal of Finance* 65, no. 5 (October 2010), 1.

10. Ibid., 2.

11. K. J. Martijn Cremers and Antti Petajisto, "How Active Is Your Fund Manager? A New Measure That Predicts Performance," Yale School of Management working paper (2006), available at http://www.som.yale.edu/Faculty/petajisto/.

12. K. J. Martijn Cremers and Antti Petajisto, "How Active Is Your Fund Manager? A New Measure That Predicts Performance," *Review of Financial Studies* 22, no. 9 (2009), 4.

13. Cremers and Petajisto, working paper, 1.

14. Ibid.

15. Ibid.

16. Randy Cohen, Christopher Polk, and Bernhard Silli, "Best Ideas," draft dated March 15, 2009, Social Science Research Network, http://ssrn.com/abstract=1364827, 1.

17. Ibid., 1.

18. Ibid., 1.

19. Ibid., 19–20.

20. Michael J. Mauboussin, *The Success Equation: Untangling Skill and Luck in Business, Sports, and Investing* (Boston: Harvard Business School Press, 2012), 3.

21. David Tuckett and Richard J. Taffler, *Fund Management: An Emotional Finance Perspective* (Research Foundation of CFA Institute, 2012), 2.

22. Ibid.

23. Ibid.

24. Ibid., 3.

25. Ibid.

26. Ibid., 6.

27. Ibid., 8.

2   Why Johnny Can't Improve

The shortcomings of economics are not original error but uncorrected obsolescence. The obsolescence has occurred because what is convenient has become sac-
rosanct. Anyone who attacks such ideas must seem to be a trifle self-confident and
even aggressive.
John Kenneth Galbraith, *The Affluent Society*

Introduction

Equity portfolio managers have every incentive to beat their benchmarks,
yet few are able to do so. In attempting to do better, managers spend several billion dollars each year on enhancing their stock screening, refining
portfolio construction, tightening position sizing and risk management,
achieving stronger trade execution, and so on. Yet consistently delivering benchmark-beating results remains elusive for many managers. This
chapter considers why improving is so difficult for active managers, with
particular focus on the inadequacies of traditional portfolio analytics,
the importance of harnessing intuitions, and the need to use a scientific
approach to improving.

Mediocre Metrics

Chronic dissatisfaction with the use of return and alpha to gauge investment ability has long fueled the search for better measures of manager
skill. Unlike active share and best buys discussed in chapter 1, the more
traditional efforts to quantify ability are, by and large, extensions of conventional portfolio analytics. While their purpose is to shed light on what
portfolio managers do that helps or hurts performance, the fact is they fall
far short of this goal. And while these metrics offer little in the way of

disentangling skill from luck, they have nevertheless wormed their way into becoming part of the orthodoxy of portfolio analysis, review, and management. Five such analytic concepts commonly used today and their shortcomings are discussed below.

Hit Rates

The hit rate is obtained by summing the number of successful or desired outcomes and dividing by the total number of attempts. According to conventional wisdom, the higher the hit rate, the higher the ratio of successful outcomes and, all other things being equal, the greater the skill that can be inferred. One example for equity management is the hit rate for new buys, which can be computed as the number of new buys that go on to outperform divided by the total number of new buys over the same time period. Accordingly, if a manager purchased 40 new stocks for the portfolio during a calendar year and 21 of them outperformed, then the hit rate for that year would be 21/40, or 52.5%. Hit rates greater than 50% tend to be admired, while those below 50% are often viewed as disappointing. These general notions about hit rates have numerous flaws, as further discussed.

Hit rates, of course, are computed to capture the impacts of numerous subtleties for various purposes. To begin with, hit rates can be computed for different activities within portfolio management, including buying (as in the example above), selling (where successes are those positions that underperform after being sold), and holding (where a successful holding is one that outperforms over some time interval). When computing the hit rate, we must also choose how to define success. Within portfolio management, the common approach is to measure a stock's success based on its relative performance. This can be done by comparing the total return of a particular stock to the broad market, to the portfolio's benchmark, or to the return of the stock's sector within the benchmark. Defining success as the stock's total return might also satisfy a particular inquiry. Yet another consideration is the length of time over which the success of the position is measured. For example, when analyzing buys, two common choices are (a) measuring relative performance over the position's entire life in the portfolio, from initial purchase until its final sell date, referred to as its "holding period"; or (b) measuring relative performance from the date of the position's initial purchase through some arbitrary length of time, which might be a month or two, a quarter, a year, etc.

Hit rates that examine buying focus on the initial purchase and ignore subsequent adds, which are more appropriately thought of as belonging to sizing skill. Hit rates may be computed for all portfolio positions or only for those positions with a non-zero active weight (i.e., overweight and underweight). Since actual position sizing is ignored in computing the buy hit rate, the relative returns used in the hit rate calculation reflect equally weighted positions. This has the benefit of focusing the result squarely on name selection, while ignoring the performance impacts of decisions about when or how much to size each position or when to sell. Despite their broad acceptance as proxies for skill, hit rates measure outcomes but really say nothing about skill. In fact, hit rates, while satisfying an emotional need to understand skill, may actually obfuscate what is really occurring. This obfuscation encourages hopeful but inaccurate assessments of skill and makes improving even more difficult. Consider this example.

Funds ABC and XYZ are managed by different individuals. They both have the same annual hit rates of 55% over the most recent five years. Both funds have similar turnover rates and hold the same average number of positions, so their hit rates are based on a comparable number of observations. Outperformance is measured as the relative return of each stock over its entire holding period. Some positions may have outperformed throughout their holding periods, generating positive relative returns consistently. Others may have outperformed initially and then succumbed to underperformance later in their holding periods, with only some of these delivering a net positive relative return. And still other stocks may have performed poorly initially and then achieved stronger performance later in their holding periods, with the same result that only some of them realized a net positive relative return. While it is clear which stocks delivered a net positive relative return, the hit rates describe neither the duration nor the timing of strong versus weak performance over each stock's holding period. Why is this important? Because a stock's relative return over its holding period includes the success of both the buy and sell decisions. Let's consider this in more detail.

Suppose that the manager of Fund ABC is an above-average buyer and a below-average seller, and the manager of Fund XYZ is a below-average buyer and an above-average seller. In our example, they both achieve the exact same hit rates, yet their skills at buying and selling are opposites. The manager of Fund ABC makes lots of good buys and mismanages the selling of more than a few. The net effect of his buying and selling is that slightly more than half of the positions owned deliver a positive relative return over their holding periods. The manager of Fund XYZ, on the other hand, makes fewer good buys but sells them much more effectively. The net effect of her buying and selling is also that slightly more than half of her positions delivered a positive relative return. The manager of Fund XYZ achieved the same hit rate as the manager of Fund ABC even though she picked fewer good names to start with. Since the hit rates for both managers are above 50%, each might conclude that his or her buying is above average. Why wouldn't they? Hit rates, as applied in this example, are purported to identify buying skill. Yet we have seen that neither manager really understands the quality of his or her buying. While both managers will conclude that their buying is strong, one of them will be severely mistaken.

If the manager of Fund ABC concluded that he is a good buyer, but got there by overinterpreting the hit rate, that would not be the worst outcome. He would benefit from luck, obtaining the right insight for the wrong reason, although he'd still be clueless about his selling. Alternatively, if the manager of Fund XYZ concluded that she too is a good buyer, she would be wrong, and this might lead her to inappropriate improvement efforts. For example, she might decide to change her sell discipline in hopes of doing better, when in fact, she'd potentially be damaging a skill that works well. She might also choose to leave her buying alone since, as the hit rate indicates, her buying is above average.[1] This simple example underscores the fact that hit rates provide results whose meaning is vague at best and often confounding. Their use is as likely to misdirect one's understanding as it is to provide useful self-awareness.

Even when buying is assessed over shorter time periods (i.e., more granularly), the results can obfuscate the truth while playing to emotional satisfaction. One particularly troubling way that misinformation can result was pointed out by an experienced portfolio manager. He explained: "A high hit rate might very well be a bad thing. Suppose that I am a generally good buyer, but I sell every name as soon as it has an unrealized gain. I'm racking up lots of winning positions that can push my hit rate well above 50%. Yet I'm throwing away valuable alpha by selling my winners much too quickly. My terrific hit rate disguises the fact that I'm engaging in risk aversion. My portfolio would be better off if I let my winners run and accepted a lower hit rate."

Selling   There are shortcomings in the application of hit rate analysis to selling as well. The usual measure of a successful sell is when a long position goes on to underperform (say for two months or so) after it has been eliminated from the portfolio. Such a sell decision in effect has improved portfolio performance by pushing out a stock that was bound to drag down the portfolio's returns the longer it was kept. Using this measure of success, a hit rate analysis would compare the number of stocks sold that went on to underperform (i.e., successes) to all stocks sold over an evaluation horizon, perhaps the most recent twelve months. What does such a hit rate indicate about the portfolio manager's skill at selling? The answer is far from clear. One reason is that this approach analyzes only sells that were executed and completely ignores positions that should have been sold but were not.

Consider this example: A stock is purchased and it outperforms for the initial 15 months but is held in the portfolio for 25 months, underperforming during the final ten months. If, after it is sold, it continued to underperform (months 26, 27, etc.), then it would be a successful sell in hit rate parlance. However, we know that it ran out of steam at month 15 and was dragging down portfolio performance during months 16 through 25. Holding this stock for an extra ten months once it began to underperform constitutes a bad sell: It should have been sold when it stopped delivering excess return. Yet, even though the manager held on to this position far too long, it will actually *raise* the hit rate of his sells. For this manager, hit rate computation not only yields a false-positive sell skill, it also fails to reveal her strongest or weakest selling decisions (i.e., those not taken).

Hit rate analysis can provide feedback that is easily misinterpreted, suggesting unqualified success when the manager's decisions actually hurt performance. While the hit rate does serve up outcomes more thinly sliced than return or alpha, it does not provide meaningful insight into skills. Attempting to develop self-awareness or to improve based on hit rates is a bit like throwing darts while blindfolded. You might get lucky and occasionally hit the bull's eye, but you're betting much more on luck than skill.

Win/Loss Ratio

The win/loss ratio compares the average return of successful decisions to that of unsuccessful ones. Its purpose is to shed some light on the magnitude of impact that the winners and losers have had on portfolio performance, an approach slightly different from the hit rate. The most common unit used when computing the win/loss ratio is again the relative return of individual positions over their holding periods. All of the subtleties discussed above for computing hit rates also apply to the calculation of this ratio.

The win/loss ratio essentially measures the asymmetry of performance within winning and losing positions. Ratios above 1.0 indicate that the average relative return for all winners is greater than the average relative return for all losers, also termed a "positive asymmetry." Ratios below 1.0 indicate that the average relative return for all losers is greater than the average relative return for all winners, also termed a "negative asymmetry."

The simple averages of relative returns used in the numerator and denominator effectively assign an equal portfolio weight to all positions.

What does the win/loss ratio say about a manager or his portfolio? It indicates whether, on average, the portfolio's winners taken as a group outperformed its losers similarly aggregated. If the win/loss ratio is above 1.0 or, better yet, far above 1.0, then the performance of the manager's good picks will outweigh the performance of his bad ones and should lead to better outcomes. Positive asymmetry leads to two common misinterpretations: (a) the manager is skilled at buying, and (b) such portfolios are likely to outperform. Both interpretations reflect considerable hope but are not supported by this performance metric for reasons similar to those that dampen the usefulness of the hit rate, as discussed below.

Metric Mash-up Managers often deliver returns that are above their benchmarks with either a low hit rate, a negatively asymmetrical win/loss ratio, or both. Let's consider some examples.

Low Hit Rate, High Win/Loss Ratio A portfolio such as this that outperforms might be indicative of a strategy that involves high risks and high upside. Some small-cap strategies, for example, might possess these characteristics. Picking which small capitalization company will execute its business plan brilliantly and deliver its full promise by increasing dramatically in value involves making choices that are very risky. A manager of such a portfolio might pick many companies that display great potential, meeting or exceeding investment guidelines, only to find them beset by one or more issues after purchase and either stalling or falling upon hard times. The few companies that do hit their marks may deliver tremendous growth and provide returns of five times or more, easily offsetting the disappointing performance of the weaker picks. Such a portfolio can have a low hit rate and a high win/loss ratio, and can outperform if the positions are sized and otherwise managed well. This same portfolio can also underperform if too much capital is tied up in underperforming stocks while the winners are starved.

High Hit Rate, Low Win/Loss Ratio A portfolio reflecting these characteristics might be observed from an investment strategy described as low to moderate risk and generally bounded upside. This combination might be found within some large-cap strategies, where picking many reasonable bets among large capitalization companies might be easier than finding a few with tremendous growth potential. Implemented well, a strategy based on a high hit rate and modest win/loss ratio can allow relatively strong positive performance from a broad group of companies that provide stable growth and that can offset a handful of underperformers, ultimately delivering above benchmark returns. This strategy can underperform when too little capital is invested in the winners, or if the losing positions linger in the portfolio for too long.

Low Hit Rate, Low Win/Loss Ratio   It is eminently possible for a portfolio with low scores in both metrics to deliver performance above its benchmark consistently. This can be achieved, more often than not, by having most of the portfolio's capital invested in those few stocks that are outperforming at the moment. Accomplishing this implies that the manager is very good at a number of granular skills such as selling losers promptly once they are determined to be hopeless, allowing strong winners to run as long as they can generate excess returns, building up young winners sufficiently to capture their full alpha potential, trimming back on stocks entering a lull, and so on. Substantial expertise at these and other granular skills enables portfolio managers to deliver strong results with a low hit rate and low win/ loss ratio. The reverse is also true, in that poor to average management of a portfolio composed of low hit rate and low win/loss ratio positions is a formula for underperformance.

And therein lie the shortcomings of these two metrics. Even when the hit rate is above 50% and the win/loss ratio is above 1.0, success is not guaranteed. For one thing, poor position sizing can drag such a portfolio's results down below its benchmark. When one of these metrics suggests lots of ability and the other indicates little ability, actual portfolio performance can range from well above its benchmark to severely underperforming. Even when both metrics suggest weak skills, the portfolio can outperform its benchmark regularly. These various combinations of high and low metric values with either high or low performance call into question just what insight, if any, hit rates and win/loss ratios really provide.

Vacation Report

The vacation report (more correctly, the vacation report comparison) investigates the effect of active management decisions on portfolio performance. The basic idea is to discern whether a particular portfolio benefited from the actions taken by its manager over a specified time period, or whether it would have been better off had the manager done nothing (i.e., taken a vacation). Employing the vacation report comparison begins with constructing a hypothetical portfolio that mimics what would have occurred had the manager left the portfolio alone. The vacation portfolio includes exactly the same assets that are in the actual portfolio on the first day of the analysis period (say, January 1). These assets then remain in the vacation portfolio until the end of the analysis period (say, December 31).

Performance of the vacation portfolio is based on the positions owned in the actual portfolio on day one, ignoring the manager's buys, sells, trims, and adds throughout the year. Next, the performance of the actual portfolio is compared to that of the vacation portfolio to assess the impact of active management. To take the example of return, if the return of the actual portfolio is greater than that of the vacation portfolio, this suggests that the actions taken by the manager were, on balance, helpful and added to performance—and vice versa. It should be clear that the goal of the vacation report comparison is to indicate whether the portfolio manager's active decisions were skillful or not. Let's examine exactly what can be learned from this report, in order to see whether this goal is achieved. Consider the case where the actual portfolio underperforms the vacation portfolio. This tells us that the changes to portfolio composition resulting from the portfolio manager's actions actually hurt performance. But which decisions were most detrimental to performance? Was every one of the portfolio manager's decisions a mistake? Did a few actually help, only to be overwhelmed by a few poor decisions? Did the new buys work, while the sells lowered performance? Were winners pushed out too quickly, while losers were allowed to stay in the portfolio? Did the portfolio manager inadvertently build up the size of losers, while shrinking the size of winners? Accurately inferring any of these specifics from the results of the vacation report comparison is impossible. Yet this analysis is used both to inform and to evaluate managers.

The vacation report comparison merely measures the difference between the portfolio's actual performance and what might have occurred if the manager had left the portfolio composition alone for a period of time. And while it is possible to modulate the construction of the vacation report to gain more granular insights about which active choices had the largest impact on performance, the results will always be of limited utility because they do not quantify skill.

Attribution Analysis

Attribution analysis, as its name suggests, attempts to attribute portfolio performance to the different types of choices reflected in a portfolio's composition. Perhaps the best-known use involves attributing portfolio performance between stock selection and sector selection. The basic data used to perform the analysis are portfolio holdings, based on daily, weekly, or monthly observations. The more frequent the holding information, the more granular the analysis and the clearer the result.

Stock selection return measures how much of the portfolio's performance is attributable to picking strong names, relative to their sectors. Given that some sectors will outperform and others will underperform, the idea is to quantify whether the manager holds those names that tend to outperform their respective sectors. This sector-relative or "level playing field" approach means that holdings with a positive return add to stock selection return only if they do better than their sector peers. Holdings with negative returns can also add to stock selection return as long as they are among the best performers within their depressed sector.

Sector selection return measures the portfolio performance resulting from the manager's allocation of capital across sectors, independent of the specific names owned. A positive sector selection return indicates that more capital was invested in the strongest-performing sectors and less within sectors that underperformed.

Attribution analysis is widely used in conventional portfolio analysis and seems particularly helpful in comparing the results of a portfolio against its stated style. For example, one might expect a bottom-up manager whose explicit strategy is to pick great stocks to deliver more return from stock selection than from sector selection, at least over time. This portfolio manager's fundamental research and conviction should be reflected in the strength of the names held in the portfolio. Conversely, a strategy purported to be very strong at sector rotation might be expected to show superior sector selection returns as a core ability. The use of attribution analysis results beyond style confirmation is limited, as demonstrated in the following example.

A portfolio delivered substantial performance from sector selection and underperformed on stock selection in the current year. Yet the results were the opposite during the previous twelve months. What do these results say about skill? The answer is nothing. They do describe a possible change in style, which may be worth discussing with the manager. Twenty-four months is, however, a somewhat short time period, and the observed differences in performance attribution may be explained with or without style drift as a cause.

Attribution analysis results are, as we've seen, weakly linked to skill. Their real value seems to be in assisting investors and consultants as they drill deeper into what has happened, a sort of forensic analysis of past performance. In addition to investigating name selection and sector allocation, attribution analysis is also used to deconstruct performance based on risk factors (e.g., How much performance came from interest rate exposure?). Useful as these results can be, attribution analysis provides a poorly delineated road map for manager improvement.

Transaction Cost Analysis

Transaction cost analysis (TCA) is the study of trade patterns and prices to determine whether stock trading was executed at favorable prices for the portfolio (i.e., lowest prices for purchases and highest prices for sales). TCA is based on the measure of the difference between two prices for a stock. The first price is the prevailing price at the time the portfolio manager decides to execute a specific buy or sell. Alternatively, this initial price can be the daily volume-weighted average price for the stock (VWAP). The second price is the one actually realized by the transaction, including the stock's trade price, commissions, and other costs. Portfolio managers use TCA to assess whether their brokers/traders are providing them with the best execution possible. Capital sources use TCA to understand whether the portfolio managers they have engaged are fully capitalizing on their ideas by obtaining effective execution.

Trading effectiveness can be very important to portfolio performance, especially in highly competitive markets where excess return is scarce, in markets where liquidity is thin, or when a portfolio needs every basis point it can get. But TCA is of unclear value in understanding portfolio manager skill. One reason is that trading is often viewed as a tactical skill, whereas knowing when to buy or sell is thought of more as a strategic skill. Portfolio managers will sometimes generate trade orders and then hand them off to internal or external traders for execution. In other words, while TCA is important, it is commonly outside of the manager's direct control. Thus, while transaction effectiveness needs to be managed, its measurement says a lot about trading but potentially nothing about the decisions being made by the manager.

Interestingly, the underlying analytics of TCA are being used by several consultancies to understand portfolio manager skills and behavioral tendencies. Knowledge obtainable from such efforts is limited in that skills can only be grossly inferred through metrics like hit rates and win/loss ratios, whose shortcomings are now clear. Similarly, behavioral tendencies are only guessed at by performing "what if" analyses around buying and selling. The extension of TCA into quantifying skills and behaviors, while of modest value, does underscore the pressing need for a more formal and better-grounded approach to helping portfolio managers gain greater self-awareness and improve.

Summary

Conventional portfolio metrics help explain past performance but offer no help in assessing skill. As innocuous as these lackluster metrics might seem, they do have a downside: They may be satisfying an emotional need to understand skill while either obscuring what's actually going on or encouraging incorrect conclusions. Portfolio managers, for their part, have a clear need to understand their own skills and shortcomings. Without this understanding, they can neither learn correctly nor improve. Similarly, capital sources and their consultants are driven to understand the strengths and shortcomings of the portfolio managers whom they engage to manage money. Better analytics for discerning and quantifying persistent skill would benefit portfolio managers and their clients alike. In an almost desperate desire to obtain answers, the industry is now depending upon metrics that offer the illusion of insight but don't really deliver.

Uncalibrated Intuitions

A portfolio's success depends a great deal upon the choices made by the manager. Managers often describe these choices as rigorous, disciplined, objective, analytic, by the numbers, rational, and so on. Investment choices do reflect these qualities, but only to the point where the correct choice is not obvious and therefore requires professional judgment. This is the point when intuition or unconscious processing intervenes or simply takes over. When you are exercising professional judgment, your choices reflect motivations you are oblivious to and feelings you are not aware you are experiencing, all of which work to filter how you perceive events, shape what information you'll recall from memory, and determine the connections among ideas that you'll have available as you proceed toward a solution. Consequently, the choices you make are influenced greatly by the direction in which your unconscious nudges your deliberations, to the point that an opportunity under consideration might be viewed as either a buy or a sell with no change in facts, just a shift in how you perceive them. Improving necessitates understanding unconscious motivations and aligning them with intent, as discussed below.

Automatic Reasoning

Successful investing requires thinking. However, we know precious little about how we actually think. For the most part, we presume that those thoughts of which we are consciously aware constitute the dominant way we think. Yet brain scientists estimate that well over 95% of all thinking actually occurs unconsciously—outside of conscious awareness. This means that the majority of thoughts you have, conclusions you arrive at, judgments you form, even choices you make, are the result of unconscious processes and not conscious deliberation. Robin Hogarth, a psychologist who has delved deeply into how thinking occurs, explains: "It is not hard to make the argument that most information processing in the human organism occurs at a subconscious level even though goals may be articulated at a conscious level, for example, to catch a ball that has been thrown to you."[2] It is, of course, natural to reach out our hands and try to catch the ball or, if surprised or unskilled at catching a ball, to deflect it away. Either way, our hand movements are both instantaneous and largely involuntary.

These same automatic processes control our thinking regarding critical and complex choices as well. Hogarth explains:

> It is clear that our intuitions affect most of the small decisions that we make on a daily basis. As such, their cumulative effect on what we experience across our lifetimes must be huge. However, our intuitions can also affect how we view and deal with major decisions—in at least two important ways. The first is how we may feel about the underlying issues even if we are unable to articulate these feelings; the second is the manner in which we approach problems. If we have developed intuitive habits for making small decisions across time, these are unlikely to be suppressed just because we are now facing an important decision.[3]

Noted brain researcher George Lowenstein finds that conscious thinking may play an even smaller role in daily deliberations vis-à-vis intuitions: "Rather than actually guiding or controlling behavior, consciousness seems mainly to make sense of behavior after it is executed [by the unconscious]."[4] The bottom line is that it is natural for us to feel that our investment decisions are deliberate and reflect intent when, in fact, they are frequently motivated by unconscious urges whose origins are not known and whose power is often irresistible.

Adaptation Gone Wild

Unconscious mental processing is one of many human characteristics resulting from the struggle for survival. Consider early man. Here he is walking down a secluded path, when his brain registers leaves rustling. Is this the result of a slight breeze, or a clue that a predator is about to pounce? What action did our protagonist take? One possibility is that he looked around 360 degrees to try to identify an animal lurking behind a bush or up in a tree. Another is that he performed a quick mental calculation based on the probabilities of the noise being either a nonpredator or predator and their respective outcomes on his safety. Having thus computed his answer, he then made his decision to either continue on his walk or to flee, based on the resulting expected value and where it fell on the live-or-die continuum. A third option, however, seems more likely. When his unconscious detected rustling leaves, he ran! And those who ran the fastest went on to become our ancestors, while the others ... well, let's just say they became the *plat du jour*. The ability to respond instantaneously to potential danger and to make quick decisions with limited information thus became important adaptive behaviors essential to man's survival, a point underscored by Hogarth: "It is not hard to generate evolutionary arguments for the existence of automatic, intuitive responses. When survival is at stake, the ability to make decisions quickly is critical. Organisms that make speedy decisions in daily activities, such as the gathering of food, also increase their chances of prospering relative to rivals who are slower."[5]

But there is more to the story of our ancestral protagonist. When this fellow's brain registered the leaves rustling and alerted him to potential danger, a series of events were set off. His endocrine system pumped hormones into his blood stream. In response, his blood pressure elevated and his pulse quickened. At the same time, nonessential body functions were halted and blood flow was diverted to the large muscle groups he might need to call upon—legs, arms, and upper body. He was pumped and ready for action. These temporary physiological changes are what we now refer to as the "fight or flight syndrome." And one more thing happened: He acted. As his body was preparing for fight or flight, his brain was sorting out the best course of action. Not sensing the need to fend off an immediate attack, his brain went on to approximate the direction of the noise and compelled him to run in the opposite direction. And there he was, running at full tilt, away from a potential predator and toward safety, well before his conscious brain even registered that there might be danger lurking. The point is that through a vast number of survival challenges not unlike this one, humans developed the capacity to process stimuli and react automatically, faster and more effectively than is possible when using conscious deliberation. Today our automatic responses are not always effective, because most learning occurs automatically and the accuracy of such learning is highly dependent upon the quality of feedback available.

The Practice Paradox
The old adage that practice makes perfect is well meaning but wrong. A more correct phrasing is that practice makes permanent, turning what you do repeatedly into intuitions and habits that will spring forth automatically. Good habits can keep you aligned with your intended goals and propel you

further toward successful outcomes. Bad habits, from which most of us suffer to some degree, make us feel as if we're doing the right things, only to wind up off target and disappointed.

The selling or substantial trimming of young winners is a clear case in point. Many managers tend to harvest their winners as they achieve an attractive gain, say up 15% or 20%. The sell disciplines for these same managers typically include rules like these: We sell when a stock hits its price target, or when its thesis is no longer valid, or when we identify a more opportunistic use of the capital. For the most part, however, regularly selling young winners has more to do with taking gains off the table than with portfolio management. The manager has developed an emotional connection with the stock being a winner and doesn't want to risk having this feeling evaporate if the stock's price declines. Selling and locking in gains provides a positive and pleasurable experience, eliminating any need to understand whether holding these positions might have proved superior, and reinforcing a habit that feels smart but whose true efficacy is unknown.

Alignment

When the unconscious is aligned with conscious intent, marvelous feats of physical and intellectual achievement are possible. To illustrate this point, consider a typical golf swing. Consciously you know you want to swing the club. You grip it and then begin your back swing. Then somewhere along this path, control is handed off to your unconscious. The reason the unconscious takes over is that in each swing you are using almost every muscle in your body from your fingertips to your toes. As soon as you contract in one direction, it's time to uncoil and reverse all the movements and then some. Your conscious brain simply is not capable of orchestrating all this activity. Yet it is a piece of cake for the unconscious brain. It winds you up, stops you at the end of your backswing, and then releases and delivers all the kinetic energy you've developed squarely onto a sphere less than 1.7 inches in diameter. Watching a fully grown person focus so much power directly onto a tiny ball, all through the extension of a roughly four-foot clumsy club, is an amazing sight. When all works well, you make a great shot. It goes just as you'd hoped, matching your intentions. When it's a poor shot, however, you hit too long, too short, or off in the wrong direction. The experience is frustrating and not what you intended at all.

The difference between good and bad golf shots is all about how well the unconscious is aligned with intent. The same is true for investing. When unconscious motivations, urges, and intuitions push you toward success consistently, they are part of your skill set. When these same forces push you toward persistently faulty choices, they are behavioral tendencies. Learning to harness the unconscious deliberately, the way other top-performing professionals do, is of obvious value. But professional investors have never done this before, and it will require retooling how managers go about the tasks of developing self-awareness and improving.

Summary

While our intuitions make us feel as if we're deciding and acting in conformance with our intentions, this is often not the case. Unconscious drives can nudge analysis and judgments away from intention and well into faulty choices, also called behavioral tendencies. Relying on uncalibrated intuitions can be dangerous to portfolio performance. Building greater self-awareness and learning to harness intuitions is a clear differentiator that enables managers to achieve their best.

Improving Deliberately

After years of investigation and rigorous analysis, we now know what's making improving nearly impossible for active portfolio managers: It's poor feedback, pure and simple. Unlike other high-performance professionals, money managers lack feedback that helps them understand their skills, their shortcomings, and how they can improve. They live in a world where outcomes are measured ad nauseam, but virtually no metrics are available for quantifying actual skills. The contrast in feedback available to money managers versus other high-performance professionals can be illustrated with another example from the sport of golf.

Sue plays twenty rounds of golf at night in pitch darkness. A flashlight illuminates the ball for each stroke. Once she hits the ball, she can't see its flight or how it lands, bounces, and rolls. At the end of each round, she is told her score. After all twenty rounds she knows the scores of each game, her average score, high and low scores, standard deviation, etc. What Sue doesn't know is which of her skills helped her the most. Was it her drives off the tee, her irons on the fairway, or her putts on the green? She has no way of telling, with only the scores to look back on and memory to provide calibration. Nor will she have a handle on what part of her game held her back the most. In fact, she will be totally clueless about the one change she might implement today that would help her improve the most.

Of course, golfers receive considerably more feedback than just their scores, but if they were limited to this paltry level of information, they would find it nearly impossible to improve. This is precisely the position that portfolio managers find themselves in today: They receive plenty of feedback on outcomes but none on skills. Portfolio managers are inundated with measures of beta, return, relative return, information ratios, alphas, hit rates, risk, and attribution analysis. Although these are important and useful metrics, they are nothing more than scorecards. They describe how the portfolio performed over a period of time. And to a lesser extent they provide basic insights into the sources of that performance (e.g., asset selection versus sector selection; excess return versus excess risk). But they don't say anything about specific investment skills; they only suggest their presence if the returns are above the benchmark. Sure, a manager who delivers performance above her benchmark for three, five, or more years in a row has skill. But what are her skills? How does she protect or improve them? How does she know which skill is underdeveloped and precisely what action to take to rebuild it? The answer is, she can't know. That lack of knowledge is a huge problem, one that limits the success of tens of thousands of investment professionals and contributes substantially to the overall difficulties of active equity management.

Advantage, Feedback
In contrast, elite athletes have access to tremendous amounts of data that help them improve. Consider a professional tennis player who is world class at hitting serves and returning shots from the baseline. He can place either type of shot wherever he wants with any kind of spin. He hits serves and groundstrokes not only well but very consistently. Unfortunately, he has no net game and mishits most volleys. His competitors quickly identify this weakness during play and then use it to their advantage, bringing him to the net as much as possible, pushing him into his area of vulnerability. Consequently, he loses more often than he wins, resulting in a win/loss ratio of less than 50:50. Put in financial terms, his tennis game is under the benchmark. If he were evaluated using the same metrics applied to money managers, he would be dismissed as having no skill. Yet we know that he has skill; his serves and groundstrokes are exceptional. The problem is just that his net game is undermining his chances at winning, at beating his benchmark. Spectators—those investing their money, time, and energy to watch him play—can appreciate his serving and groundstrokes, while being disappointed by (or even empathetic to) his weak net game, because individual skills are readily observable in tennis.

Deliberate Improvement

To borrow a phrase from Oldsmobile, deliberate improvement "ain't your father's way of improving." It is, instead, a highly disciplined approach to learning and becoming better at essentially any activity or profession where skill can be developed. In an article about deliberate improvement, journalist Geoffrey Colvin offers this definition: "It's activity that's explicitly intended to improve performance, that reaches for objectives just beyond one's level of competence, provides feedback on results and involves high levels of repetition."[6]

Practically speaking, deliberate improvement involves the implementation of a four-part process: (a) possessing fact-based self-awareness of current skills and shortcomings; (b) defining a very specific plan to improve one or two skills; (c) implementing the plan with lots of reminders about where change is desired and what that change should be; and then (d) receiving feedback about how well the plan is being implemented and whether the results being achieved are those expected.

In sports, an athlete like our tennis player can deliberately improve by watching videos of his games and hiring a coach. He can then break down his game into what works and what doesn't. Before long, he begins to focus on his net game as the source of his underperformance. He arrived at that focus objectively, not based on memory, a feeling, or simply guessing. Next, he rigorously assesses the elements of his net game: backhand and forehand, cross court and down the line, defensive shots or put-aways. Then he ranks each element based on how significantly it hurts his game. When this player is ready to change, his improvement plan isn't simply to be a better tennis player, or even to be better at volleying. He will choose the one shot among all his volley shots that, if turned around, would most help him win matches. He'd pick the one that today is most persistently costing him points.

He'd practice getting better at this single shot until he improved. He'd then incorporate this new, refined shot into his competitive game and make sure it was delivering the level of improvement expected. And, again with the help of a video and a coach, he'd get steady, objective feedback on how well his new volley shot is doing in competition. Is the new shot being executed as intended, or is it being thrown off by old behaviors that are hard to overcome? Discipline and clear feedback will enable him ultimately to replace the old shot completely with the new one. At that point, he will have improved this one specific skill.

Eventually he'd rebuild other net shots using the same process. The more volley shots he rebuilds, the stronger his net game will become. As his net game improves, over time he will better capitalize on his original skills at serving and groundstrokes. He'll begin to win an ever-increasing percentage of his games. Eventually his win-loss ratio will edge above the 50:50 level, and he'll be above his benchmark. His outcomes will be positive and reflect his combined skills—his newly acquired skills at volleying plus his continuous skills at serving and groundstrokes.

Deliberate improvement is used by top performers in all types of professions. Elite athletes use their off seasons to rebuild their skills and then bring their enhanced talent into competition. Surgeons adopt the latest microsurgical techniques through simulation and observation and then use them to achieve better outcomes for their patients. Professional musicians practice, practice, and practice throughout their careers, seeking ever-improving technique and sound. One extraordinary example of deliberate improvement was Captain Chesley Sullenberger's safe landing of a US Airways plane on the Hudson River—an accomplishment that occurred not only because he is brave and a great pilot, but also because he, like the vast majority of his colleagues, never stopped improving. What made the difference is that Captain Sullenberger had practiced making emergency landings just like the one he executed in the winter of 2009. He did it countless times through simulation, learning what a cataclysmic engine failure feels like and ingraining the appropriate skills to assess and react effectively. When the Canada geese took out his jet engines and his aircraft was incapable of gliding to the nearest airport, Captain Sullenberger drew upon a very specific skill that he had perfected through extensive practice, and this enabled him to stay focused and to land his plane safely. Other pilots might be excellent at flying jet aircraft and be brave as well, but without this one specific emergency landing protocol deeply etched in their skill set, they likely would not have been as effective in the same situation. Captain Sullenberger made deliberate improvement a life-long practice, and it eventually enabled him to save the lives of himself and the 154 passengers and crew for whom he was responsible. Or, as he put it, "One way of looking at this might be that for 42 years, I've been making small, regular deposits in this bank of experience, education and training. And on January 15 the balance was sufficient so that I could make a very large withdrawal."[7]

Summary
The challenge, then, is for equity portfolio managers to learn and improve as effectively as top performers do in other professions. Accomplishing this requires feedback that is more rigorous and granular than the industry currently depends upon, or to which its many practitioners have ready access.

It requires information that will enable portfolio managers to develop self-awareness about their current strengths and shortcomings based on data and not hunches. And this new higher level of feedback needs to connect skills to processes and behavioral tendencies. It needs to enable managers to understand their individual emotional drives, align them with conscious intent through clearer investment processes, and apply intuition and judgment where these unconscious abilities can skew outcomes more toward skill and repeatable performance.

Conclusion

Becoming and remaining a top performer requires the ability to improve regularly throughout one's career. This is certainly the behavior observed in every high-performance profession save one—active equity management. Professional investors work hard over their careers and, if they are very fortunate, earn the opportunity to become portfolio managers. Once achieving this lofty position, however, their further efforts to become better commonly produce more disappointment than actual improvement. Poor feedback is, without question, the single greatest obstacle managers face when attempting to improve. It begins with the mediocre metrics that compose today's portfolio analytics. While these metrics provide measures of portfolio performance and some insights into its sources, they say nothing about what the manager does well or how she or he might improve. More alarming is the fact that the active management industry currently embraces these metrics as meaningful measures of skill, when in fact they tend to be ambiguous and to completely misinform, rather than to deliver helpful insights.

Another element that makes improving difficult is the general lack of understanding of how individuals make decisions. The common misconception that choice reflects mostly conscious deliberation is not only wrong, but also tacitly supports the prevalent notion that judgment and, heaven forbid, the emotions are not topics that serious-minded professional investors should be discussing. Yet when a manager ignores unconscious processing, he never understands or harnesses his intuitions, which then leads to underdeveloped skills, weak adherence to investment processes, and ineffective behavioral tendencies.

Finally, improving is the output of a rigorously implemented process, not a desire. The best improvement processes are built on the key elements of the scientific method. These include capturing and analyzing accurate data at the right level of granularity, attention to all aspects of the performance environment including intuitions, just-in-time reminders of when to up your game, and feedback on how well the improvement goals are being achieved.

The choice is clear. More active managers can learn to deliver better performance, or the industry can sit on its hands and watch assets continue to flow elsewhere. Fortunately, the vast majority of managers have both the ability and the heart to meet this challenge. What they have lacked is a scientific method for learning and improving. This void has taken a mighty toll on managers and their clients alike. All this can now change, as discussed in the following two chapters.

Notes

1. In fairness, hit rates are often computed over arbitrary time frames that may be shorter than the actual holding periods. Shortening the period over which investment decisions are evaluated helps to isolate success at making buy and sell decisions independently and thus lessen, although not eliminate, the types of confusion discussed above.

2. Robin M. Hogarth, *Educating Intuition* (Chicago: University of Chicago Press, 2001), 43.

3. Ibid., x.

4. George Lowenstein, "The Creative Destruction of Decision Research," in Gerald Zaltman, *How Customers Think: Essential Insights into the Mind of the Market* (Boston: Harvard Business School Press, 2003), 10.

5. Ibid.

6. Quoted in Geoffrey Colvin, "What It Takes to Be Great," *Fortune*, October 19, 2006, http://money.cnn.com/magazines/fortune/fortune_archive/2006/10/30/8391794/

7. Chesley "Sully" Sullenberger, in an interview with Katie Couric, *60 Minutes*, broadcast February 8, 2009.

3   New Analytic Framework

A fact is like a sack—it won't stand up if it's empty. To make it stand up, first you have to put in it all the reasons and feelings that caused it in the first place.

Luigi Pirandello, *Six Characters in Search of an Author*

This chapter sets out a new analytic framework for isolating and quantifying investment skills. Rather than working backward from outcomes to infer what happened, the new framework builds insights from the bottom up by using each decision that goes into a portfolio to compute skills. It provides both rigor and granularity in investigating which decisions are consistently adding alpha to the portfolio and which are not. In chapter 4, the same framework demonstrates both how investment processes can be rigorously defined, codified, and improved, and how to identify, quantify, and overcome behavioral tendencies. The framework can be implemented robustly as described below, or using simpler methods as explained in Part Three.

The new framework identifies and measures precisely what generates portfolio outcomes, rather than simply measuring outcomes themselves. To accomplish this, we need to step back and look at portfolio management afresh, and rethink which metrics would help portfolio managers develop greater self-awareness and learn to improve deliberately. This chapter begins with a conceptual description of the portfolio manager's information advantage, followed by a definition of individual investment skills and how they can be quantified. The chapter concludes with a discussion about the common perception of buy and sell decisions as paired choices and why this viewpoint undermines improvement.

Information Advantage

A useful construct for thinking about investment skills is the information advantage. That is, for a portfolio manager to generate alpha, his

investment decisions have to be better than average: They must capture
excess returns. This outcome implies that his decisions reflect some sort
of insight, knowledge, or know-how capable of identifying opportunities
not generally known to others. This ability to ferret out and capitalize on
good ideas ahead of the crowd embodies what is referred to as the portfolio
manager's "information advantage."

Hypothetical information advantage curves are presented in figure 3.1.
The curves describe conceptually how two portfolio managers' new buys
perform on average, from the day of initial purchase and for months thereafter. The y-axis denotes performance and the x-axis time. The higher the
curve lies above zero, the stronger the information advantage. The more
time that the curve is above zero, the longer the information advantage
lasts. These curves are, of course, idealized and present the information
advantage as a smooth and continuous line. While no single buy is likely
to perform in exactly the same way as the information advantage curve, it
is nevertheless a useful way to think about how a manager's buys tend to
perform when considered in aggregate.

Curve A represents an information advantage that delivers very high
performance almost immediately after purchase and then subsides within a
few months, ultimately becoming negative as the stock's alpha is exhausted.
Curve B shows an information advantage that starts out slowly, builds up

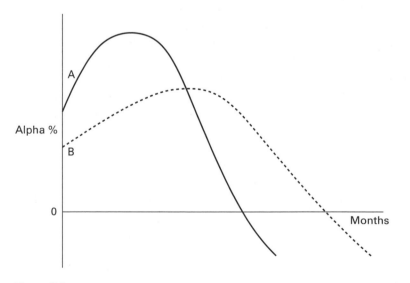

Figure 3.1
Hypothetical information advantage curves.

over time, peaks, and then slowly drifts down over the next couple of years. The difference in the curves suggests a strong difference in the information advantages for these two managers. It also provides useful feedback that can inform the sizing regimes and sell disciplines of each manager. The curve for portfolio manager A describes a process whose buys generate tremendous levels of excess return quickly, but for a somewhat short duration. A manager with this type of information advantage can be very successful if, along with her strong name selection, she realizes that she must (i) build her buys up to full size quickly in order to capture the maximum alpha that they deliver, and (ii) start to challenge holding these positions as soon as they begin to get tired. The curve for portfolio manager B indicates a different information advantage. His buys take a while to build up steam and then go on to deliver excess returns that are typically lower than those of manager A but longer lasting. Portfolio manager B, therefore, can take his time building up to full position size and can frequently let his winners run much longer than portfolio manager A.

It would be very difficult, if not impossible, for these two portfolio managers to understand their unique information advantages accurately by using conventional portfolio analytics. Should they nevertheless choose to try to improve, without benefit of accurate insights into their individual strengths and shortcomings, they might decide to implement changes that they hope will lead to improvement, only to find either that little has changed or that they are doing worse than before. Portfolio manager A, for example, might be tempted to wait until new buys have experienced a meaningful price movement prior to purchasing more and building them up to full weight. Test-driving a new stock like this is an approach used by many managers. The downside of such an approach if undertaken by manager A is that she will unknowingly leave considerable alpha on the table, as her best names are likely to outperform substantially, but with too little capital invested. Knowing that her new buys typically take off dramatically right after purchase is the kind of feedback that can help this portfolio manager sharpen her sizing skills. Portfolio manager B, on the other hand, might be tempted to wring out a little extra performance from his older winners by leaving them in the portfolio. This might seem helpful, since many of these positions outperform for a long time. However, the downside is that his average younger position far outperforms his typical older winner. By leaving capital tied up in older positions and not recycling it into more vibrant, younger ones, this manager is missing significant alpha year after year.

The point is this: By depending upon conventional metrics like return, relative return, alpha, and hit rates, portfolio managers are perpetually stuck in the dark, groping for ways to improve. All too often, the ideas for improving that they chance upon seem reasonable but don't help at all, or actually even hurt future results. Approaching improvement in a more scientific manner begins with defining precisely what skills are and how they can be observed.

Skill Framework

Portfolio management involves three basic investment skills: buying, selling, and position sizing. Portfolio managers use these skills as they make choices about which names will be in the portfolio and what size or portfolio weight each will be given. Although these three basic skills may seem obvious, they have, for the most part, only been alluded to in the literature and have never really been defined or quantified. For example, the term "buying skill" is recognized universally, but what precisely does it encompass? Does it focus primarily on the identification of new names? Should it include adds to an existing position? This section posits definitions for the three primary skills and presents an analytic framework for measuring the strength or quality of each. Although this discussion focuses on long investing, the framework is equally applicable to analyzing shorts.

Sizing Skill

In concept, effective sizing suggests that on any given day, the manager generally maintains most of the portfolio's capital invested among the highest-performing stocks owned, all other things being equal. Examples of skilled sizing actions include strong buys built up before they hit their peak performance, adds made as stocks continue to rise or resurge, and trims occurring as positions enter a lull. The challenge, then, is to measure whether this is actually what the portfolio manager is doing, and to quantify to what extent it is happening over time. The approach employed in the framework is both analytically robust and intuitively appealing. It involves comparing the performance of the actual portfolio to a second or adjusted portfolio in which all of the manager's active sizing decisions have been eliminated, and all positions are instead sized using a straightforward, passive rule.

Analytically, this is accomplished by creating an adjusted hypothetical portfolio that contains all of the portfolio manager's active buy and sell decisions but none of her active sizing decisions. This adjusted portfolio buys new positions whenever they are initiated in the actual portfolio (i.e., initial buys) and exits them whenever they are ultimately removed from the actual portfolio (i.e., final sells). Thus, the adjusted hypothetical portfolio possesses exactly the same names as the actual portfolio on each day over the entire history under analysis, but the sizes of the positions on any given day do not reflect the active sizing decisions made by the manager. For the convenience of reference in this discussion, this particular adjusted portfolio is termed the "Name Portfolio."

The passive sizing of positions within the Name Portfolio can be approached in a number of fashions. They can receive an equal weight on their first day in the portfolio; they can be periodically resized to equal weights over time; or they can be initially sized in relation to their benchmark weights. One approach that is simple to implement and provides useful results is called "equal active share." Here the term "share" refers to the weight or proportion of portfolio capital invested in a position. An equal active share includes a stock's benchmark weight plus its *pro rata* amount of the active bet in the total portfolio. Let's consider an example of how equal active share is determined for a new position involving stock XYZ.

Before the manager purchases stock XYZ, the Name Portfolio contains 50 positions whose aggregate benchmark weights total 12%, indicating a current active bet of 88% (i.e., the total portfolio, or 100%, minus the aggregate benchmark weights of 12%). On the day that the actual portfolio purchased its first shares of stock XYZ, XYZ is also added to the Name Portfolio. The size given to stock XYZ in the Name Portfolio is, again, the sum of its benchmark weight plus its *pro rata* of the active bet, adjusted for the benchmark weight of stock XYZ. If the benchmark weight of XYZ is 0.75%, then its equal active weight will be 2.46%; that is, 0.0075 + [(0.88 − 0.0075)/51]. Thus, 2.46% is the weight given to stock XYZ on its initial day in the Name Portfolio. From then on, its weight can increase or decrease depending on whether stock XYZ outperforms or underperforms the average return of the Name Portfolio. If the new position outperforms, its size will increase, and vice versa.[1]

Equal active share enables the Name Portfolio to reflect the performance of the manager's buys and sells while disregarding all of the manager's active sizing decisions. Next, the returns for the Name Portfolio are computed. The performance of the actual portfolio can then be compared to that of the Name Portfolio. If the actual portfolio outperformed the Name Portfolio, this indicates that the net effect of the manager's active sizing decisions was positive. Conversely, should the Name Portfolio outperform the actual portfolio, this means that the manager's active sizing decisions were less effective than the passive rule. In either event, the manager's sizing skill so far has been examined only at a gross or aggregate level.

Further investigation is needed to identify specific sizing strengths and weaknesses in order to support deliberate improvement. For example, it is common to investigate whether the manager's adds to losing positions actually help or hurt performance. "Doubling down" is a typical practice across the money management industry and reflects the notion that if a stock is a hold at its original purchase price, then it should be a buy at a lower price, all other things being equal. The framework can be used to construct an adjusted portfolio wherein all of the manager's sizing decisions are included in the Name Portfolio except those involving adds to losing positions. Comparing the results of this adjusted portfolio to those of the actual portfolio would quantify just how effective adding to losers has been over time. This type of analysis can be further refined by adjusting only adds to those losers that reflect a particular attribute, such as high price to intrinsic value, or low earnings growth. Such granular analysis supports a deeper understanding of where sizing skills are helping and where improvement is required. The application of this framework to hundreds of portfolios yields the following broad observations:

• Slightly over half of the portfolios analyzed reflect a negative sizing skill. This means that, in aggregate, the managers' active sizing decisions underperform a passive equal active share rule. Granular analyses enable these managers to improve deliberately.

• Despite the adage that encourages investors to "feed their winners and starve their losers," professional managers seem to prefer doing the opposite. They more commonly add to positions that have an unrealized loss, while hesitating to build up younger positions that start to take off. Sadly, these contrarian activities usually don't work, as too few underperforming positions successfully rebound, and too many winners continue to run undersized.

Buying Skill

The buy skill can also be computed by constructing and analyzing an adjusted portfolio. This adjusted portfolio contains only the manager's active buy decisions, and neither her actual sizing nor her actual sell decisions. Constructing this adjusted portfolio begins with the Name Portfolio, which already has had the manager's active sizing removed. The next step is to remove the manager's active sell decisions with yet another passive rule. The resulting adjusted portfolio buys positions whenever they are initiated in the actual portfolio and then sizes them using a passive rule and sells them using a passive rule. Since this adjusted portfolio contains only active buy decisions, it is called the Buy Portfolio.

There are many ways to formulate a passive rule for selling. Using a first in/first out rule that maintains position count is one approach, and simply selling buys after a fixed holding period is another. Selling based on a fixed holding period is easy both to implement and to explain; this is the approach I used below.

A sell rule based on a fixed holding period means that each position is sold a specific number of months after its purchase date. A common initial value is the portfolio's average holding period. There is no important analytic reason for using the average holding period, although it is somewhat intuitive and its use has the benefit of maintaining the level of turnover in the Name Portfolio equal to that of the actual portfolio. Implementing the sell rule involves adjusting the holding periods for just about all positions relative to when they were actually sold, with some sells being advanced and some being delayed.

Consider a portfolio where the average holding period is 16 months. Among its many positions, this portfolio contains stock ABC, which was held for 24 months. Selling it passively by using the first in/first out rule requires advancing its sell in the Buy Portfolio. This would be accomplished by selling (or eliminating) stock ABC after it has been in the Buy Portfolio for 16 months, and then reinvesting its sell proceeds across all remaining positions in the portfolio on a *pro rata* basis. This one adjustment would produce a Buy Portfolio in which the selling of stock ABC is advanced based on the application of a passive rule. Similarly, if the actual portfolio also contained stock JKL, which had been sold just 9 months after purchase, its sell date would be delayed in the Buy Portfolio until month 16. This would be accomplished analytically by repurchasing stock JKL back into the Buy Portfolio on the day it was sold, thereby extending the holding period of stock JKL to 16 months. To make room for this repurchase of stock JKL, all of the other positions then in the Buy Portfolio would be reduced *pro rata*, essentially selling a slice of the portfolio to create the liquidity to repurchase stock JKL. Finally, stock JKL would be sold when its holding period reached 16 months, and these proceeds would be redistributed *pro rata* across the positions then in the Buy Portfolio. After this second adjustment, the Buy

Portfolio would include two positions (ABC and JKL), whose sells reflected the passive rule and not the manager's active sell decisions.

It is easy to see that by making such adjustments to all positions in a portfolio's history, the resulting Buy Portfolio would include all of the actual buy decisions but none of the portfolio manager's actual sell decisions. In practice, when applying such adjustments to a multiyear portfolio history, dozens if not hundreds of positions are modified to support a specific investigation. This can lead to several positions being modified on any single day. Implementing such multiple adjustments requires careful accounting of the intricate interplay across all positions in the portfolio, as the sells of stocks are extended or delayed.

Once the complete Buy Portfolio is constructed, its daily returns are computed, reflecting the portfolio manager's actual active buy decisions and the passive sizing and selling rules. The performance of the Buy Portfolio thus directly defines the buy skill of the portfolio manager, since it contains only active buy decisions and no active sell or sizing decisions.

A series of such Buy Portfolios can be constructed with varying holding periods (e.g., 4 months, 8 months, 12 months, 16 months, 20 months, etc.). Computing the buy skill as described for each such adjusted portfolio enables the manager to better gauge the strength and duration of her information advantage. Once again, this initial measure considers only the aggregate or gross buy skill. This same analytic approach can be used to investigate more granular buy skills, such as buying effectiveness across sectors, across countries, or based on recommendations of individual analysts. A few observations regarding buy skills:

• Information advantages vary considerably and have more to do with the portfolio manager's unique strategy, research, and buy process than style. No discernible buy skill commonalities are observed among value, growth, small-cap products, or large-cap products.
• Great success does not equate with perfection. Individuals with strong buy skills can regularly stretch outside the disciplined part of their process and make buys that, as a group, tend to underperform. Eliminating pockets of unproductive buys enables managers to improve an already successful skill.
• Poor buy skill is reversible. While a portfolio manager's overall buy skill may be negative, she nevertheless may possess one pocket or more of buying that is adding alpha. Building upon these granular skills together with avoiding unproductive buys can enable a portfolio manager to improve deliberately and reverse poor buying.

Selling Skill

Successful selling means that the portfolio manager effectively captures the information advantage contained in each buy. This means that, on average, positions are held as long as they add to portfolio performance and no longer. In contrast, ineffective selling includes pushing out young winners before they have given their full alpha to the portfolio; capitulating and selling off young losers and locking in the loss, only to have these stocks rebound and deliver excess performance; hanging on to older losers that continue to drag down portfolio performance; and allowing older winners that have become tired to remain in the portfolio, tying up capital that could be reinvested in younger, more vibrant positions. Just as in measuring sizing and buy skills, the sell skill is computed based on adjusted portfolios and reflects many decisions over a multiyear time frame.

Computing the sell skill is relatively straightforward. It involves the use of an identity based on the Name Portfolio and Buy Portfolio described above. The Name Portfolio contains the portfolio manager's active buying and active selling decisions, while the Buy Portfolio contains only the portfolio manager's active buy decisions. The difference between the Name Portfolio and the Buy Portfolio, therefore, describes the portfolio manager's active sell decisions. Consequently, the sell skill is computed as the performance of the Name Portfolio minus the performance of the Buy Portfolio.

This computation measures the sell skill in aggregate. More granular investigations can peel back selling in order to learn where selling is strongest and where improvement is required. Types of granular sell investigations include examining how effectively the portfolio manager sells younger versus older positions, or how well he sells winners versus losers.

What makes this method for measuring selling skill particularly valuable is that it considers both stocks that have been sold as well as those that have not. This distinction is important, because poor selling among professional money managers is heavily skewed toward sells not taken. The strongest evidence supporting this observation is the fact that one in four portfolios analyzed exhibits the endowment effect. This is a behavioral tendency to hold on to winners well past their productive lives, or after their information advantage has waned. Not only is the endowment effect the single most common behavioral tendency found among professional money managers, it also typically costs portfolios over 100 basis points in lost performance year after year. The ability to rigorously and appropriately assess actions not taken as well as those that were taken is just one of the advances of the new framework over hit rates, win/loss ratios, and other traditional analytics.

Alpha versus Returns

The new framework enables portfolio managers to understand their skills accurately and objectively. They receive rigorous feedback regarding which skills are adding to performance and which need improvement. Implementation of this framework presents several choices that trade off simplicity and accuracy. One such choice is the measurement of skills themselves. In the simplified examples above, I used portfolio return to illustrate how the framework generally works. A rigorous implementation of the framework would benefit from the use of alpha over returns, wherever adequate factor data are available.

The preference for measuring skills using alpha over returns is twofold. The first reason is to eliminate noise or confusion within results. A major source of noise is market cycles. A growth manager would be expected to exhibit high buy returns during a growth cycle, in contrast to expectations for a value manager during this same period. Regressing portfolio returns against the Fama-French three- or four-factor models mentioned in chapter 1 significantly dampens the noise that market cycles introduce into returns, offering a clearer view into skills. Alpha, therefore, expresses persistent skill independent of market cycle, regardless of whether the manager was fighting a headwind or benefiting from a tailwind. The second reason for using alpha is related but concerns the nature of adjusted portfolios. If by advancing or delaying certain actions the analysis inadvertently moves such decisions into a more or less favorable market cycle, this unintended impact needs to be eliminated. The use of the Fama-French three- or four-factor alpha does this nicely. It is the superior clarity about skill provided by alpha over returns that causes alpha to be the preferred metric in academic studies.[2]

The Siren of Paired Choices

Results based on this analytic framework have been shared with hundreds of portfolio managers over the past few years. The majority find it both analytically robust and intuitively satisfying. Some, however, find it difficult to shift their perspective regarding how they do their jobs and what type of feedback might help them improve. One such bump in the road toward greater self-awareness is the insistence that all buy/sell decisions are paired choices—that is, that the manager is buying stock ABC only because he is selling stock XYZ and must redeploy the capital. Or, he is only selling stock KLM in order to fund the purchase of stock NOP. The belief that these choices are inexorably paired often arises, ironically, from managers of fundamental, long-only strategies, not long-short strategies or quantitatively driven products. Why is it, then, that some traditional, bottom-up portfolio managers see their investment decisions as paired choices?

Naturally, there is no single answer to this question. A host of cognitive errors or behavioral tendencies may explain why managers view decisions as paired choices. One possibility is that pairing buy and sell decisions enables the individual to sidestep ambiguity, which can arouse unpleasant feelings. When managers see only paired transactions, each buy is supported by an offsetting sell, and each sell fits neatly into a new buy. The alternative is to make a high-conviction sell and then worry about how to invest the proceeds, and vice versa.

Timing transactions so that they become paired trades can work brilliantly. Formulating and executing the buy and sell at the same time may allow the manager to obtain maximum efficiency and effectiveness from research and trading. It may also reinforce risk management and portfolio thinking generally. Yet even with these benefits, the buys and sells can be evaluated separately. They may be paired for convenience, but they reflect two separate skills and need to be understood as such. Assessing these decisions retrospectively as paired choices makes learning extremely difficult, if not impossible.

For those who may require further convincing, consider this option. A new buy can be funded by selling a thin slice of everything in the portfolio, rather than pushing out an existing holding. Likewise, the proceeds from a sell can be allocated *pro rata* across all the remaining holdings, rather than used to fund a new buy. Pairing may be useful in motivating managers to do their best, but it is an inferior way to assess skills. Cleaving to the notion that buying and selling must be evaluated as paired choices will keep you from seeking out and benefiting from the right feedback. You'll be perpetuating one of the many practices that have poorly served active equity management for decades. Instead of building your buying and selling skills independently—improving deliberately—you'll be following the siren's song, and we know how well that worked out for the sailors in Homer's *Odyssey*.

Conclusion

The new analytic framework presented in this chapter enables portfolio managers to isolate and quantify their investing skills. This rigorous and objective information allows them to then develop deeper self-awareness and to improve deliberately. The framework uses a portfolio's actual history to uncover the manager's information advantage, including how effective she is at buying, selling, and sizing of positions. Key to the new framework is the use of adjusted portfolio histories. The adjusted portfolios are used to support bespoke analyses that lead to actionable opportunities for improvement. The new framework can be implemented to varying degrees of thoroughness, with a modestly rigorous method described in this chapter and a less rigorous approach presented in Part Three.

The new framework investigates skills in a manner that challenges some traditional views on portfolio management. One such notion is that buys and sells are paired choices. While it is true that buying and selling can be executed together, each choice relates to a different skill that can and must be measured separately. It is only through studying and improving these skills distinctly that portfolio managers can improve deliberately and begin to move toward the level and consistency of outcomes they desire.

Notes

1. This method can be refined so that outperforming positions do not become excessively large and underperforming positions maintain a minimum level of portfolio weight.

2. For more information on the use of alpha and its benefits in clarifying skills independently from market cycles, the reader is referred to "Understanding Risk and Return, the CAPM, and the Fama-French Three-Factor Model," a Case Note by Adam Borchert, Lisa Ensz, Joep Knijn, Greg Pope, and Aaron Smith, Tuck School of Business, Dartmouth University, 2003.

4 Process and Behaviors

The calculation of intrinsic value ... is not so simple. ... [I]ntrinsic value is an estimate rather than a precise figure, and it is additionally an estimate that must be changed if interest rates move or forecasts of future cash flows are revised.

Warren Buffett, *The Essays of Warren Buffett: Lessons for Corporate America*, 3rd ed.

This chapter builds upon the new analytic framework developed in chapter 3, providing robust methods to investigate, quantify, and improve investment processes and behavioral tendencies. The primary method introduced for supporting investment processes is context analysis. Context analysis supports codifying the processes being used and identifies clear opportunities for improving. This section concludes with an example of how to improve the buy process. The new framework is then applied to analyzing behavioral tendencies using the adjusted portfolios that were introduced in chapter 3. The analytic framework is extended to introduce out-of-sample simulations to confirm the persistence and statistical significance of observed behaviors. Descriptions of the five most common behaviors observed within professionally managed portfolios are also provided.

Codifying and Enhancing Process

Process is one of the most discussed and least understood aspects of active portfolio management. The term shows up in every pitch book, has its own checkbox on manager search consultant review forms, and surfaces in essentially every discussion between clients and managers. But what does it mean for a specific portfolio? How complete is a manager's process? How faithfully is it followed? Does it really help? These fundamental questions cannot be answered today with any confidence.

Flow charts and other diagrams are used to help explain the process as managers envision it. Stories about specific buys and sells then commonly accompany the schematics, lending credence to how process is put into action. While sincere and well intentioned, the graphics and narratives are notional, describing what is intended but not accurately portraying ideas generated, possibilities entertained, and analyses applied. Actual decision-making is much messier, and often constrained, based on incomplete information and fraught with emotional urges. Yet when it comes to presenting one's investment process, a few artistic graphics and a couple of anecdotes represent current best practices.

Even in the absence of a written policy or PowerPoint® slide, every portfolio manager follows some sort of process when making buy, sell, and sizing decisions. And though it may not be codified, or the portfolio manager may not be able to articulate it easily, process is there nevertheless. We know this because individuals gravitate toward rules and heuristics to manage complex and highly repetitive choices. Rules that are intentional and whose efficacy is known compose the successful elements of an investment process. Unconsciously triggered heuristics and those rules whose results have not been calibrated may engender in managers the same feelings as the successful process, but more often than not they deliver disappointing outcomes.

While managers typically recall only those few large choices made in a quarter or perhaps a month, portfolio management's true essence is composed of thousands of seemingly insignificant decisions that move names into and out of the portfolio and resize them almost daily. These decisions are the familiar and minuscule choices that are made automatically, just outside of conscious deliberation. Take researching a new stock, for example. How is the sector chosen? What names do you start with? Which information sources do you consider? Which do you look at first? Which are given the most weight? We like to think that the decisions we make along this process are deliberate, conscious, objective choices, but mostly they are not. Instead, they are decisions driven by intuition, heuristics, and emotional desires. And here is the money point: When these unconscious drives are strongly aligned with your intentions, you do your best. When the alignment is poor, you make decisions that feel right but drive you toward unintended consequences. This is why process is so darn important.

Portfolio managers, for the most part, want a helpful investment process but don't want to feel as if their investing is overly mechanical or unnecessarily constrained. The tension between wanting a process without feeling handcuffed to it makes formulating and implementing a meaningful process challenging. Analytics based on the new framework rigorously describe key decision points within investment processes and support their improvement, while respecting the fact that managers must also exercise judgment in order to realize their full potential.

Context Analysis

Context analysis uses a manager's actual decisions both to describe how he is making decisions and to identify clear opportunities for improving. Figure 4.1 shows a buy context analysis for an equity portfolio. This visualization depicts in vivid form several key elements of the portfolio manager's buy process. The visualization is novel and requires a bit of explanation.

A buy context plots how typical new buys look at the time they initially enter the portfolio (i.e., the day of the first buy for each position). For each such buy, a small number of that stock's attribute values are observed at the time of the market close on the day before the initial purchase (for many data items, that will be the most recent information available to the decision maker). Any number of attributes can be used, and they can comprise any information for which there is sufficient market coverage and history. Common choices of attributes include fundamental factors (e.g., ROE, price momentum, book to value, etc.), proprietary research results (e.g., intrinsic value, fair market value, or upside/downside prices, etc.), and custom-built factors (e.g., alpha ranks, super factors, etc.). The five attributes shown in figure 4.1 are common choices for traditional bottom-up strategies. In practice, the visualization works best when between four and six attributes are

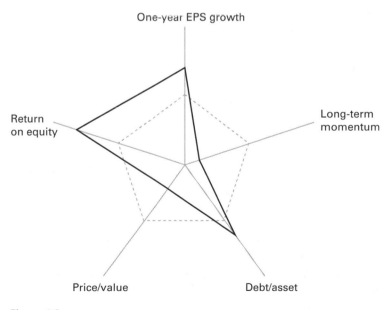

Figure 4.1
Context analysis.

utilized. More than six makes the diagram too busy and weakens its value as a quick, high-impact visual reference.

For each stock purchased, the values of its attributes are compared to the sector median values of the same attributes on the same day. Using ROE, for example, the ROE of a stock entering the portfolio is compared to those of its sector peers on the same day. This is done by ordering all stocks from lowest to highest ROE, and then assigning to each a percentile rank based on the cumulative market capitalization of all stocks thus ranked. Consider a three-stock example. Stocks A, B, and C have ROE values of 5%, 10%, and 15%, respectively. If stock A has a market capitalization of $300, stock B a market capitalization of $250, and stock C a market capitalization of $450, then the median attribute value is 10% (where 50% of the sector market cap is achieved), and stock A would have a rank of 30%, stock B a rank of 55%, and stock C a rank of 100%. The same type of relative comparison is performed for each of the attributes. When completed, this buy can be described as a set of percentiles, one for each attribute. Since the percentiles are sector relative, they can be combined across sectors and over time into typical or average values.

Each of the five axes in figure 4.1 represents one attribute. The origin (where they all meet) corresponds to the lowest percentile values. The farther away from the origin, the higher the percentile values. There is a thin dotted line connecting the midpoint of each axis. This denotes the attributes' median values (50th percentile) over the analysis period. The bold, irregularly shaped polygon represents the portfolio manager's typical buy at the time of initial purchase. When the bold line is outside or above the median value, this indicates that, on average, the new buys contain relatively high amounts of this attribute. Likewise, when the bold line is inside or below the median value, this indicates that, on average, the new buys contain relatively low amounts of the attribute. In the example shown, the portfolio manager's typical new buy tends to possess very low long-term momentum and low price to intrinsic value. The new buys also reflect relatively high levels of ROE and trailing earnings growth, with above average leverage. When I first presented this visualization to the value manager whose portfolio history it reflects, he said, "Yep, that's me. I like to buy high-quality companies that have been beaten up recently. And I don't mind a little hair on the balance sheet."

The clearer the portfolio manager's buy process and the stronger it is adhered to, the more likely it is that the context diagram will confirm the manager's expectations. Occasionally, there are surprises, where the information reflected in the diagram is not precisely what the portfolio manager intended or believed was happening. Naturally, when the story presented in the context diagram departs from the portfolio manager's expectations, this suggests a lapse in the process or its use.

Finding the Sweet Spot

Context analysis is also used to help portfolio managers understand where their process is working well and where it needs improvement. An example of how context analysis may uncover these more granular insights is presented in figure 4.2. This graph is identical to figure 4.1, with the addition of the light and dark shaded areas. Since many of the buys in the portfolio history have had time to perform, it is possible to separate them into two groups: buys that went on to outperform (i.e., winners) and those that went on to underperform (i.e., losers). The attribute levels of the typical buy that goes on to become a winner or loser is computed using the same analytic process described above for determining the average attribute values for all buys.

For any attribute, the outer edge of where the light shaded area intersects its axis is the average amount of that attribute present in buys that tend to go on to become winners. Likewise, the outer edge of the dark shaded area's intersection with the axis represents the average amount of that attribute

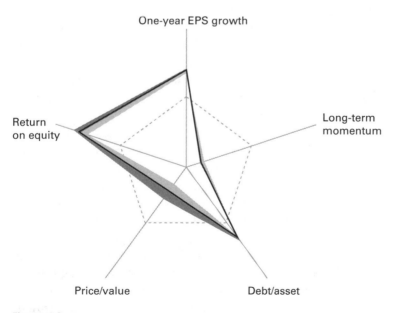

Figure 4.2
Winners and losers.

present in buys that tend to become losers. In figure 4.2, the differences in attribute levels between winners and losers are most pronounced with regard to the price-to-intrinsic-value attribute. The buys for this specific portfolio that tend to outperform are those that are cheap but not heavily discounted. While this value strategy does well with cheap stocks, it doesn't do as well when bottom fishing. Whether the shortcoming in buying heavily discounted stocks rests primarily in research, process, or judgment cannot be ascertained from this visualization. But the context diagram clearly shows that cheap stocks are effective for this portfolio manager's process up to a point, while heavily discounted ones are not.[1]

The amounts and locations of light- and dark-shaded areas vary considerably from portfolio to portfolio, reflecting the facts contained in each history. For portfolios like the one described in figure 4.2, a single attribute highlights the greatest differences between strong and weak buys. In other portfolios, several or all of the attributes may help differentiate buys that go on to become winners or losers. Sometimes the context analysis provides a clear description of the buy process but offers little or no insight about identifying potential future winners. In such situations, substituting different attributes can help better differentiate stronger from weaker buys.

Finding Buy Candidates

Using the information depicted in figure 4.2, it is possible to identify new stocks that are strongly aligned with this manager's buy process. This is accomplished by first identifying those attribute values associated with historic winners (i.e., where the light-shaded areas intersect each axis). We call this group of attribute percentile values the "sweet spot" of the buy process. Once defined, all stocks in the portfolio's universe are then compared to the sweet spot based on their individual group of attribute values. The closer all five of the attribute values for any stock are to those composing the sweet spot, the more the stock fits the manager's buy process. Ultimately, each stock is ranked based on how close its attributes are to the sweet spot. Stocks that are closest are given a fitness rank nearer to 1%, and those that are farthest from the sweet spot receive a fitness rank nearer to 100%. All stocks in the top 20 percentile are referred to as "candidates," in that they most closely fit what works for this manager.

The portfolio manager can quickly assess how well a potential new buy fits her process based on its fitness score. Stocks that have a high fitness score (top 20th percentile) are the type that this portfolio manager generally analyzes well. If, on the other hand, the manager becomes curious about a stock that has a poorer rating (say, 48th percentile), she doesn't need to avoid such a stock. Rather, the portfolio manager can learn which attributes of this potential buy are well matched to her process and where she might be stretching. Then, armed with this feedback, she can pursue her analysis, knowing where extra diligence can pay off.

Context analysis is also applicable to other decision points in the investment process. One such use is to identify the attributes of the typical holding after it has been in the portfolio for a specified period of time (e.g., 6 months, 12 months, etc.). Let's say that the manager's information advantage generally begins to fade after 18 months. If we construct a context analysis based on all positions over the past few years at the moment they have been in the portfolio for 18 months, we can see whether, at that moment, they are generally approaching their thesis or have begun to drift. Again, since the future performance for most of these positions is known, it is straightforward to identify which attributes are associated with holdings that from 18 months forward go on to outperform and which do not. Insights gained from this type of analysis can be used to refine sell processes and position sizing.

Context analysis is also valuable in articulating investment processes to current and prospective clients. Sharing rigorous exhibits like figure 4.2 with those outside of your company helps them to appreciate that you are using scientific methods to become more self-aware about your buy, sell, and sizing processes and that you are improving deliberately.

Summary

Context analysis and buy candidates are just two illustrations of how the new framework enables portfolio managers to understand their process better, to compare what is really happening to what was intended, and to identify where the process works best and where refinements are needed. The results of context analysis can be used to guide decisions deeper into the sweet spot of buying, selling, and sizing decisions. Context analysis can also be used to help identify candidates for new buys that fit the manager's process. These diagrams also support stronger relationships between managers and clients, as flow charts and stories are replaced with fact-based analyses.

Managing Behaviors

Adjusted portfolios allow us to evaluate whether an ineffective behavioral tendency exists, how persistently it is exhibited, and what its year-after-year impact on the performance of the portfolio has been. Conceptually this is done in a manner similar to that described for evaluating skills in chapter 3.

If, for example, we were investigating the propensity to hold on to winners too long, this could be accomplished by constructing a series of adjusted portfolios in which older positions are sold sooner. It would begin by identifying the position with an unrealized gain that was held for the longest period at any time over the analysis period (i.e., the oldest winner over the portfolio history). The first adjusted portfolio would simply shorten or modify the holding period of this position by, say, one month. For example, if the oldest winner had been held for 52 months, then the first adjusted portfolio would shorten its holding period (and any other position with a holding period as long) to 51 months, with no other changes. Each successive adjusted portfolio would sell older winners sooner and sooner (e.g., 50 months, 49 months, etc.). Naturally, as the maximum holding period shortens, the number of older winners sold increases. The result would be a series of adjusted portfolios whose maximum holding period for winners is successively shorter and shorter, reflecting the impact of modifying increasing numbers of older winners.

Computing the performance of these adjusted portfolios and comparing their results to that of the actual portfolio provides initial insight into whether older winners are being held too long. Specifically, if shortening the holding period for older winners increases portfolio performance (at least over some range), this result may point to a behavioral tendency, and further investigation would be warranted.

The next step involves a more granular and exacting analytic method referred to as "out-of-sample simulation." Here the early portion of the portfolio history is studied to determine a rule for selling older winners such that, if it had been applied consistently over this in-sample time period, the rule would have most benefited portfolio performance. Once this in-sample rule is identified, it is then applied in subsequent time periods to ascertain whether the rule is helpful in guiding future investment decisions. When the in-sample rule is applied in the subsequent time period, the output is referred to as the "out-of-sample results." If the out-of-sample results are favorable, they confirm that a persistent behavioral tendency exists.

The persistence of the behavioral tendency may be further confirmed by computing a measure of statistical significance known as a *P*-value. This test essentially explains whether the out-of-sample benefits are produced evenly over time (i.e., suggesting a common occurrence), or whether they occur in a more concentrated, periodic fashion. Strong *P*-values can be used to guide the portfolio manager toward that one behavioral tendency which, if eliminated, would have the most likely benefit on portfolio performance going forward. In addition to using statistical tests, we can interrogate persistence visually. This is accomplished by plotting the out-of-sample results over the complete out-of-sample time period. If there were five years of out-of-sample results, and the quarterly benefits were plotted, then the more quarters in which the impact is positive and the higher the average impact observed, the stronger the consistency of the behavior. Combining this type of visual inspection together with *P*-value analysis provides an intuitive interpretation of the results, backed by a rigorous analytic assessment. Ardent bottom-up investors might also find it useful to look at each individual position impacted by the rule over the entire out-of-sample time period.

Adjusted portfolios that reflect different changes to positions are used to investigate other types of behaviors. Just as older winners can be modulated, so it is possible to advance the sells of older losers, to more rapidly build up young winners or delay the selling of young winners. The new framework supports these and other investigations rigorously and efficiently.

Specific Behaviors

Dozens of behavioral tendencies have been identified in the literature, ranging from overconfidence and self-attribution to anchoring and loss aversion. A number of behaviors are readily analyzed using the new framework; their existence is easily confirmed and their impacts readily quantified. Five such behaviors are described below.

Regret Aversion   Regret aversion is the avoidance of an action today out of fear that you may come to lament its effects tomorrow. You essentially avoid the possibility of regret by not acting at all. Among professional equity investors, regret aversion manifests as the tendency to not feed younger winners sufficiently or in a timely manner. While individual motivations may vary, the underlying unconscious mechanism spurring regret aversion is described in the following example.

A portfolio manager buys a stock for $15 per share with the expectation that it will go up to $50 within an acceptable time period. The amount of the price increase and the time it takes to materialize constitute what might be thought of as the portfolio manager's (hoped for) information advantage for this stock. The portfolio manager intends to buy an initial position (say, 30 basis points) and use this initial investment to become more familiar with the stock and see if her thesis starts to prove itself. Once the price of the stock begins to move and the thesis is confirmed, the portfolio manager intends to buy more and quickly build this position up to full weight, which for her is 150 basis points. Not long after the initial purchase, the price of this stock starts to move. Soon it hits $19 per share, which is her trigger point to move into full position weight. But she doesn't make the move. Instead of going right to 150 basis points, she adds only enough to bring the position up to a total of 50 basis points. What went wrong?

Lacking a strong enough process, she was relying on her own judgment and internal fortitude to build up the position when its price trigger point was reached. Yet at that moment, having to make an important and risky buy decision, her unconscious seems to have dampened her motivation and held her back. It's as if her unconscious were saying, "Wait a minute, hold on here. You could have purchased all of this stock you wanted for $15 per share just a couple of weeks ago. Now you are going to pay $19? What if tomorrow, after buying lots of this stock, you find that the price drops to $18, or $17, or all the way back to $15? Aren't you going to feel foolish? If that happens, you'll really regret it." So, out of fear of possibly regretting moving to full weight today, the manager takes a half-step or less. She slowly adds to the position. But if her original analysis was correct, the stock is continuing to run. As it hits higher and higher prices, her position remains a fraction of what she intended, and the portfolio is losing out on a great opportunity to capture substantial excess return.

Risk Aversion   Risk aversion is the preference for taking small profits, rather than risking unrealized gains in hope of doing even better. Essentially, you cash out quickly to avoid the risk of a price reversal. Such decisions are influenced unconsciously, without regard for the go-forward potential of the asset. This behavior is most commonly seen among professional money managers as the propensity to sell young winners well before they have contributed their full alpha potential to the portfolio. Fear is what underpins this behavior.

Consider a portfolio manager who buys strong stocks that are capable of delivering excess returns for a relatively long time. But once these stocks take off, all the portfolio manager notices is that he has unrealized gains that alternately make him feel great and then feel tremendous angst that the gains might go away.

This sort of emotional tug-of-war can be very stressful. It is one thing to not have made a gain, but something much worse to lose one. His unconscious is putting him on alert: "Even with these modest gains, you are today a winner. But if you lose them tomorrow, then what? The portfolio will have taken a loss and you'll be a loser, too." Lacking sufficient self-awareness about one's typical information advantage and supported by an inadequate process, it is all too easy for the unconscious to make its case and prevail. And so the manager pushes young winners out of the portfolio, and with them goes his fear, along with substantial incremental alpha—alpha that was available from strong buys but not fully captured.

Avoidance of Pain   Avoidance of pain is the tendency to sell off positions whose prices have fallen in order to avoid potential further mental anguish if they fall further. To avoid pain, you sell a short-term loser out of fear that it will become an even larger loser. Professional investors will thus sell stocks that have recently experienced a price drop, regardless of whether the stock's future is bright or questionable. Motivating this behavior is the fear of experiencing deep emotional pain if you hold on to a position whose price continues to erode, particularly knowing that you might have limited your losses if you had sold the stock when it first became a loser. Avoidance of pain is a behavior right out of the teachings of emotional finance, as discussed in chapter 1.

This behavior can sometimes be observed when an uncalibrated stop-loss rule is used to manage losses. Portfolio managers often think, "When a stock is down by 15% or more ... well, life is too short and I just get rid of them." While this approach may work, it is certainly no guarantee. Once the position is gone, the managers might sigh as they think, "I don't have to worry about that stock anymore ... I got rid of that problem. Now with the decks clean, I can refocus on generating excess returns." Unconsciously, of course, fear might have been sending this message: "... when I get rid of this loser, I won't need to think about it any more nor risk that it can pull down performance further." When losers tend to bounce back, more often than not an uncalibrated stop-loss rule can take a heavy toll on portfolio performance.

Loss Aversion   Loss aversion is the tendency to hold onto assets whose prices are down, in order to avoid realizing the loss. You postpone selling the asset with the hope that it will rebound, or (unconsciously) to avoid recognizing that your initial decision to purchase it was incorrect. Loss aversion can be observed within an equity portfolio as a much lower turnover rate for substantial losers relative to other positions held. The underlying motivation—reflective of prospect theory—is that losses loom large in the psyche, and not selling these positions is a way to avoid the pain or discomfort associated with losses. It is as if at some unconscious level the mind is struggling to deal with the conflict between feeling good and doing what's right. Owning a stock that has gone down in price means that you own a loser, but it could come back. Selling that stock and realizing the loss means that at an important emotional level, the stock will then become a loser forever in the mind of the portfolio manager. As a byproduct, the portfolio manager may cringe at being just a little bit of a loser himself, a feeling anyone would want to avoid. Long-term losers cause damage in two ways: They erode capital due to their price drop, and they hurt ongoing performance by locking up capital in unproductive positions.

Endowment Effect   The endowment effect is the tendency to overvalue items in one's ownership, or endowment. Mere possession makes the item seem more valuable than it was before we owned it. Professional money managers with this tendency will hold on to some positions, especially winners, far beyond their productive lives. The unconscious motivation is fear, especially the fear that if you sell at today's price, you'll miss out on the potentially better price that may be offered tomorrow. In other words, the endowment effect is a form of loss aversion where the fear of a loss stems from anxiety about missing a better price that might be offered tomorrow, as opposed to the dread of realizing a current loss which is the more common interpretation of loss aversion. The cost to portfolio performance of engaging in the endowment effect increases rapidly when the manager's information is strong and somewhat short-lived.

Eliminating Behaviors   Once a behavior has been identified objectively and its impact rigorously quantified, it is then possible to eliminate it from your investing repertoire. The process involves replacing the unproductive behavior with choices that reflect intention and that help the portfolio to achieve stronger and more consistent performance. This is how deliberate improvement is used to manage behavioral tendencies.

This type of deliberate improvement builds upon three levels of feedback. The first is the thorough analysis of the portfolio history using the new analytic framework. This uncovers behaviors, their persistency, and their impact on performance. These facts are essential in order to fuel the motivation required to initiate a change and follow through until you're successful. Change is hard, and you need a strong reason to engage in change for success to even be a possibility. Therefore, feedback about your propensities sets the stage for improvement. The second level of feedback involves receiving reminders or nudges when you are about to make a decision that is similar to those where your unproductive behavior tends to appear. If the behavior you are working on is, for example, eliminating the endowment effect, then you will need to be signaled about older winners in the portfolio that reflect characteristics consistent with positions that have hurt the portfolio in the past. This is feedback about specific moments where you need to be at your most attentive, make very deliberate choices, and overcome old, ineffective habits. Just because you know you engage in a behavior doesn't guarantee you won't repeat it. Being mindful when the urge to misbehave is upon you is the next, sometimes difficult step. The third and final level of feedback measures how well you are doing at implementing your change and eliminating the unproductive behavior. This feedback can come in the form of data about how many nudges or signals you received over a period of time (say a quarter), how many of these you acted upon and how many you didn't, plus granular analytic results about which decisions helped the portfolio and which did not.

The assessment of behavioral tendencies is probabilistic, much like the determination of intrinsic value for a stock. Although the overall effect of a behavioral tendency may be negative, and that tendency may be persistent, not every choice consistent with the observed behavior will produce a negative result. Consider, for example, risk aversion. If identified within your portfolio, it means that on average you tend to sell young winners prematurely. In other words, the majority of the younger winners that you kick out of the portfolio go on to generate additional alpha that your portfolio misses. But, even though this finding is true for the majority of young winners sold, it may not be true for *every* young winner you've sold. It is, however, true for the *majority* of young winners sold. Going forward, sorting out which young winners to keep and which to let go requires improvements at both skill and process.

This means you need a nudge about those younger winners in the portfolio today that possess the characteristics that tend to make your trigger finger itch. Once informed, you should neither ignore the signal and continue with the old habit of selling too quickly, nor use the signal as a hard and fast rule not to sell. Instead, at this moment you might extend your process by inserting a minor speed bump, building in a pause that causes you to reconfirm the thesis of positions that receive this signal. If their thesis is still intact, then hang on to them. If the thesis has changed or been realized, then it might be time to sell. One additional idea is to use the concept of framing to help push your process further toward success. Since, in the past, your tendency has been to sell first and ask questions afterward (or not at all), you can try to retrain this tendency with an explicit opposing rule. In this case, you could include in your process the intention to hold any position that receives a signal for another quarter or two, unless the thesis confirmation produces a poor result. This basic reframing places a higher hurdle between the young winner and its sale. Reviewing thesis confirmations with colleagues or the investment committee can help, as can assigning these positions to someone else to manage. Then you need to study the data about your judgments regarding these positions. Are your judgments getting better? Are there pockets where you are doing better and where you're not? What else might you add to your process to squeeze even more alpha from these young winners?

Such efforts toward deliberate improvement enable you to reach expert status at granular skills. Using the three levels of feedback described, you learn about your propensities, implement an improvement plan to eliminate a negative behavioral tendency, and measure how well implementation is going. As part of your implementation, you improve your process for confirming the thesis of these stocks, you improve your skill at judging which to keep and which to sell, and you eliminate an unproductive behavioral tendency.

General Observations

Professional equity managers have their share of behavioral tendencies. Here are a few observations from my nine years of field experience:

• Ineffective behaviors tend to arise where either skills are weak or process is incomplete.
• The vast majority of equity managers engage in one or more behavioral tendencies. These ineffective habits tend to be very persistent and erode substantial alpha and return annually.
• The two most common behaviors observed among equity managers relate to the management of winners. The endowment effect (holding winners too long) is the most frequent, and regret aversion (not feeding young winners sufficiently) is the second most common.

Summary

The new framework is used to identify and quantify behavioral tendencies. The analytic process involves the comparison of the actual portfolio and one or more adjusted portfolios. This analytic approach is helpful in assessing any of the five most common behaviors described.

The new framework also includes the delivery of signals that warn the manager about the potential for engaging in an old, unproductive habit. The signals are used to refine investment processes and to sharpen judgment and skills. The new framework enables managers to become more self-aware and improve deliberately.

Conclusion

Skills, processes, and behaviors are deeply intertwined. Efforts to improve one demand a thorough understanding of the others. The stronger a portfolio manager's skills and processes, the less opportunity for behavioral influences. Keeping investment actions aligned with intention requires rigorous feedback about the choices a manager is making and when they tend to work and when they don't. Pockets of ineffective decisions tend to be coincident with weak skills, incomplete processes, and the influence of behavioral tendencies.

Similar to the way the new analytic framework was shown to help improve skills in chapter 3, it can also be used to refine processes and eliminate unproductive behaviors, as described above. Context analysis is just one way that the new framework is used to help codify and refine investment processes. Context analysis helps to identify sweet spots within existing processes and then supports more effective decision-making going forward. The use of adjusted portfolios is the primary means for isolating and quantifying behavioral tendencies. Once verified, the new framework provides signals that remind managers to be more mindful and evaluates success in implementing improvement plans.

Unambiguous feedback is essential to support improving. It is needed in a robust form across skills, processes, and behaviors, at the right granular levels, and it must be updated regularly. The new analytic framework provides the type of feedback critical to improving. And the time to begin improving deliberately is right now.

Notes

1. A cautionary note: This is not a quantitative result. The analysis is not suggesting that highly discounted stocks are universally bad stocks, or that they always underperform. The analysis instead confirms that for this specific portfolio manager, her buy process does not do well with such stocks. And that's it. These same stocks may, in fact, show up in the sweet spot of another portfolio manager whose skill and process result in a different information advantage and buy context.

5   Feedback in Action

To improve is to change; to be perfect is to change often.
Winston Churchill, *His Complete Speeches*

This chapter describes how some equity portfolio managers today are learning and improving with better feedback. Armed with clear insights into their personal strengths and shortcomings and supported with up-to-the-moment decision-making information, these professionals are building stronger skills, refining their investment processes, and eliminating unproductive behavioral tendencies. While their specific circumstances may be unique, the underlying issues and opportunities discussed here are prevalent throughout the industry.

The managers discussed in this chapter represent a cross-section of strategies and styles. All of them are fundamentally bottom-up investors, although some rely upon straightforward factor screens or alpha models to support their process. All have worked at becoming better throughout their careers and now have found a means of improving deliberately. Highlights from their stories are presented below in hopes of encouraging you to challenge old habits and begin your own deliberate improvement.

Selling Can Make the Difference

Sam is the manager of a highly successful small-cap value strategy. His portfolio has low turnover and is fairly concentrated, holding a maximum of 35 positions, which he identifies using a bottom-up, fundamental approach. The portfolio has beaten its benchmark consistently for over a decade. Like many top-performing managers, Sam believed that his success was, in good part, due to his superior buying prowess.

We analyzed Sam's portfolio using the new framework. The results of the analysis provided many valuable insights, including one that was particularly surprising: Virtually all of his portfolio's alpha was coming from selling, not buying. Specifically, Sam's selling was adding approximately 220 basis points annually, while his buying and sizing were neutral or supplying close to zero alpha. It then became essential to understand how Sam was generating top performance without being a great buyer.

Over the course of several conversations and further analytic investigations, more about Sam's investment process became clear. The portfolio's average holding period for all new buys is about 24 months, with a number of names remaining in the portfolio for upward of five years. Some of Sam's buys never work out. Their hoped-for excess performance never materializes, and he sells them relatively quickly. It turns out that Sam and his analyst team are extremely effective at weeding out these lackluster positions within six to twelve months of purchase. In contrast, stocks that do survive this intense post-acquisition review tend to go on to outperform for several years. So, even though Sam's buying is just average—essentially producing benchmark level results overall—his ability to cull out the underperformers while holding on to the stronger stocks enables the portfolio to generate very positive results. His keen assessment of which stocks to kick out and which to let run has the result of placing, at any moment in time, most of the portfolio's capital in stocks that are outperforming.

Improvement
Being much more self-aware, Sam is choosing to transfer some of his skill at selling underperforming stocks to aid in his buying. Using context analysis and other rigorous feedback, Sam is deliberately modifying his buy process to incorporate as many of the skills and process elements from his successful culling-out efforts as he can. Over time Sam is benefiting from both reinforcing his sell process and upgrading his name identification, with specific goals of better initial screening of buy candidates, increasing his hit rate, and strengthening portfolio performance.

Losing Alpha While Avoiding Pain

Tom manages a large-cap growth portfolio that consistently performs in the top quintile of its peer group. His portfolio typically holds 90 or more positions and has turnover of roughly 120% annually. Tom's buy process is heavily tilted toward stocks that exhibit momentum across the board, since for him this is a key indicator of potential alpha.

While all three of Tom's skills were positive (buying, selling, and sizing), he did uncover an important opportunity for improvement. The portfolio had in place a top-down rule to sell off positions when early indications of waning momentum were detected. The belief at Tom's management company was that such positions were highly susceptible to price reversals, and kicking them out quickly could avoid a loss, thereby boosting performance. This view was deeply entrenched throughout the company. The internal shorthand for explaining this quick sell rule was, "When we find a potential problem, we want to panic ahead of the market."

In effect, it was a stop-loss rule premised on the idea that declining momentum signals strongly that a growth stock is likely to experience a price reversal. The problem was that the rule had never been rigorously calibrated. Our careful analysis of the portfolio's history revealed that this stop-loss rule actually hurt performance when Tom applied it to his younger positions. Specifically, selling positions that were held less than six months was costing the portfolio in excess of 160 basis points annually. This finding was very persistent over the analysis time frame, mirroring the rule's diligent implementation.

The negative effect of the rule was also consistent with the fact that the buy skill was strong and that the portfolio's information advantage typically lasted well past six months. By implementing an uncalibrated stop-loss rule, Tom and his colleagues may have been unconsciously trying to avoid the psychic pain of holding positions that could quickly become substantial losers. Through their efforts to avoid pain, they were overreacting to early indications of slowing momentum, often tossing out perfectly good stocks that had more alpha to deliver.

Improvement

Tom has refined his process by changing his old stop-loss sell rule to his new thesis confirmation rule. Now when he or his analysts suspect that a younger position might be going sideways, they reassess its thesis. More often than not, these stocks stand up to the additional scrutiny and are kept much longer than before. Tom's portfolio is capturing the benefits of his strong buys that he had previously been selling too quickly. Tom's sell discipline is now refined and avoids everyone's panic, both the market's and his.

Hidden Growth Pains

Kathy is the manager of a mid-cap growth strategy whose returns had begun to suffer in recent years. Her portfolio holds between 50 and 60 positions and has a current turnover rate of 40%. Assets under management (AUM) had grown dramatically for a decade, as the portfolio beat its benchmark year after year. Then performance began to slump, with total return below the benchmark for the three years up to the time that Kathy engaged in deliberate improvement.

The portfolio analyses showed that Kathy's buy skill remained strongly positive throughout, but her sell skill had deteriorated and now was nega-tive. This relatively new skill asymmetry was the source of the portfolio's underperformance. The analysis indicated that the poor selling was primar-ily due to the endowment effect, or holding on to winners well past their ability to generate excess returns. Portfolio turnover had declined over time and, as a consequence, the average holding period of positions was stretch-ing out. During a collaboration session with Kathy, she realized that she had felt under increasing pressure from consultants and others to justify what they perceived as initially high turnover. This pressure increased as her portfolio's AUM grew.

Armed with rigorous and granular feedback, Kathy came to see that she had unintentionally been slowing down her selling of older winners in response to the steady questioning of her earlier turnover rate. This change in selling had the short-term benefit of quelling some of her critics, but at considerable cost to performance. In examining the information advan-tage for this portfolio, we observed that younger positions (those held less than two years) generated approximately 250 basis points of alpha annu-ally, while older positions (those held over 24 months) were costing the portfolio nearly 400 basis points of alpha per year.

Improvement
Earlier selling of older winners was identified as the greatest source of incre-mental improvement for the portfolio. However, Kathy and her analyst team were slow to implement this needed change. During the first year of implementing her improvement plan, she followed few behavioral signals, and the portfolio missed out on capturing 190 basis points of incremental alpha. In year two of implementation, the company's CIO got involved and initiated a process refinement that required each analyst to confirm the theses of older winners on a quarterly basis. By reversing the status quo from "sell an older winner when it starts to crumble" to "assume we're sell-ing older winners unless they have extraordinary potential," this portfolio began to manage its endowment-effect behavior. They became so good at it that in year three of implementation, the endowment effect was gone and the sell skill was positive again. Kathy's portfolio is now benefiting from stronger selling. It is back above the benchmark, and her clients are delighted. She is now working to implement the next most helpful change to strengthen performance further.

Harnessing an Alpha Signal

Sally and Ed co-manage a small-cap core strategy. They use a hybrid process that combines a multifactor quantitative model to identify potentially
interesting stocks and then confirm which they want to own through fundamental research. Their process restricts purchasing to only those names
that have a model rank in the top two quintiles and that also receive a
strong analyst recommendation. Their model had less influence on sizing
and selling, which reflected more the judgment of the co-managers and
analysts. The once top-performing strategy was significantly underperforming, and Sally and Ed wanted to get to the bottom of the problem and turn
things around.

The portfolio analysis indicated a striking change in the alpha signal
of their quantitative model. Until recently, the model's top-ranked stocks
were able to generate alpha for as long as 18 months. Consequently, the
company's investment process involved analysts covering stocks once they
became top quintile but usually not before. If the analyst then took two
weeks or more to provide a recommendation, this delay was acceptable.
The co-managers could then buy the stock, which might go on to generate excess returns for well over a year. More recently, however, the model's
signal was generating alpha for between four and six months, significantly
less than the team was prepared for. Under this shorter alpha signal, whenever the analysts took a few weeks to provide recommendations on new
top-ranked names, it was costing a huge amount of the stock's total alpha
potential.

Improvement

Armed with a better understanding of the model's current alpha signal and
the poor alpha capture provided by the analyst regime, Sally and Ed implemented critical changes to their process. Now analysts were to commence
analyzing stocks as soon as their model ranks passed from third quintile
up to second quintile, with the goal of completing recommendations on
or before a stock reached a model rank of first quintile. By shifting their
buy decision time frame from several weeks after achieving the top rank to
the same day it occurs, the team was able to move into first quintile stocks
more quickly and capture 115 basis points of incremental alpha that previously was leaking from their process.

Further analyses using the new framework enabled Sally and Ed to utilize
the model ranks more effectively to guide their sizing and selling decisions.
The ability to extend the value of alpha-sourcing models further into the

full range of portfolio management activities is yet another benefit of the new analytic framework. Because the new framework analyzes actions, not just position weights, its results tend to be complementary, or "orthogonal," to those resulting from alpha-sourcing models. This independent and additive assessment enables managers to experience an outside view of their combined model and process (see chapter 21, "Inside-Out Investing," in Part Two). One general observation along this line is that the ranks that alpha models produce by themselves are rarely effective at guiding sell decisions. As intuitive as it seems simply to sell stocks whenever their ranks drop below the ranks used to signal buys, this approach is often flawed. One reason is that the factors that identify stocks about to take off (alpha-sourcing) may not be best in identifying when a stock is beginning to get tired (a sell). Consequently, combining the alpha ranks with factors or attributes used in its computation and other information into the new framework frequently leads to stronger signals for selling and sizing decisions.

Relationship Metrics

Dan is the manager of an emerging markets core strategy. His portfolio typically holds around 130 positions with a turnover rate of 80%. Performance for the portfolio has been top quartile year after year. Dan is working hard to build assets under management for this relatively young product. Dan and his portfolio were in the midst of competing for a new pension fund allocation during 2011. He made the short list, but the consultant managing the process, still smarting from client relationship issues during the market crash, voiced serious concerns that Dan did not have in place a clear stop-loss rule. The consultant believed that prudent risk-management dictated that all equity managers have and use a stop-loss rule. Dan believed that he was handling losers appropriately but did not have a way of explaining or defending the judgments used in his sell process. He needed help in finding out whether he was in fact managing losers well and, if so, how to present his process to a cautious if not skeptical audience.

A rigorous analysis was performed on Dan's portfolio history. The focus was, of course, to ascertain whether Dan was managing losers appropriately or whether he would benefit from an explicit stop-loss rule. A series of adjusted portfolios were constructed, each selling off losers at increasing levels of unrealized loss. The results were used to plot a graph whose x-axis indicated levels of loss used to trigger a sell (i.e., the stop-loss thresholds) and whose y-axis plotted the annualized benefits (alpha) of implementing such rules over a six-year history. The analyses showed very clearly that at every level of stop-loss threshold (from 10% to 50%), the impact on the portfolio was negative. In other words, if Dan had sold losers automatically based on any rule, the portfolio's performance would have been less than it was in actuality. The reason is that Dan's buys were sufficiently strong that many of his temporary losers bounced back and did so enough to offset those that did not. Consequently, any mechanical sell rule would be discarding more alpha than it protected.

Improvement

Dan presented his results to the consultant. He explained that he now understood more clearly that his judgments about which losers to hold were working, but he also realized that not every loser bounces back or should be held. So Dan decided to implement what he calls a "stop-and-look" rule. This translates into a process refinement that requires him to confirm the thesis of any stock he owns that drops by more than 15%. Dan expects to keep many of his temporary losers but is preparing to be more selective and, in doing so, to refine his sell skills, his judgment, and portfolio performance. The consultant was delighted with the result. His question had obviously been taken seriously, and the information Dan provided resolved his concern. Dan is having no problem making it onto other short lists with his growing track record and his expanded ability to rigorously describe key parts of his investment process.[1]

Conviction That Stifles

Phil is the founder and senior portfolio manager of a successful large-cap value strategy. The portfolio has two additional co-managers and tends to hold between 65 and 75 positions, with a turnover rate of approximately 70% annually. Their approach to stock selection is primarily bottom-up, supported by quantitative screens that are used inconsistently. Phil had previously announced that he would be retiring sometime in the next year or so and wanted to assist the rising team leadership with an objective codification of the portfolio's skills and investment processes.

The analysis of the portfolio indicated that buying and sizing were both adding alpha, but selling was a problem. The endowment effect, or holding on too long to winners, was again the source of poor selling. The results showed that the portfolio had lost alpha in each of the past eight years by not harvesting older winners effectively. This behavior was observed consistently, quarter by quarter and broadly across all sectors. Adjusting the process to push out more of these older winners in a more timely fashion was shown to help improve performance by approximately 170 basis points of alpha per year. The team response to this opportunity varied. Phil said that the results matched his intuition, and he felt that challenging older winners seemed like the right thing to do. As part of his retirement process, however, Phil had handed over all of the day-to-day decision-making for the portfolio to his two co-managers. Neither of these two individuals was as motivated to change as Phil was. Further historical analyses were conducted to address lingering doubts they both held about the predictive ability of the findings. Ultimately, one of the co-managers did agree that they were holding winners too long, but the other never got past his skepticism. That turned out to be an expensive behavior.

Improvement
The custom sell signals developed and delivered for this portfolio were never acted upon. During the initial twelve months of implementation, the team received signals to consider selling a handful of older winners, but all of these stocks remained in the portfolio. Not selling them had a negative impact of over 140 basis points in just a twelve-month period. Even though the endowment effect had been demonstrated persistently throughout their eight-year history, and then showed up repeatedly during twelve months of implementation, the co-managers were not prepared to begin working with the behavioral signals.

Occasionally the implementation of an improvement plan goes awry, as did this one. The reasons for poor implementation are far from obvious, since the potential benefits seem impressive and highly attainable. What would stop individuals from taking a relatively small step in order to become better investors? The exact explanation for why this team did not embrace clear improvement is not known.

What is known is that the team is deeply committed to their nuanced fundamental approach to understanding stocks. As a result, they construct elaborate thesis stories for each position owned, and such rich narratives can easily elevate tenuous judgments to strongly held convictions. This kind of conviction is painful to change, even in the face of mounting evidence that the thesis may be flawed or needs to be reevaluated.

This specific team may prefer to cling to familiar ways of doing things, even when those ways are shown to have significant shortcomings. Change is hard, and it is all too comforting to stay with the status quo, even if you know it is not in your best interest—just ask any dieter or a person trying to stop smoking.

Conclusion

Deliberate improvement is not only possible, it is happening all around you. Equity managers across the globe are using rigorous feedback to gain greater self-awareness and to become better investors. The newfound knowledge they are developing is helping them manage emotional tendencies, correct false self-assessments, and implement successful improvement plans.

Even more exciting is that the means of improvement discussed above are available to you right now. All it takes is stepping up and practicing deliberate improvement, going a little beyond the use of traditional portfolio analytics to capture objective information about skills, process, and behaviors, not simply outcomes. Then you can begin to slowly strengthen and improve your way to your own top performance.

Notes

1. Stop-loss rules are very helpful for some portfolios. The tilt toward helpful or unhelpful depends upon the average information advantage contained in the portfolio's buys. When significant losers (say, down by 20% or more) tend to not bounce back, then a stop-loss rule can have a very positive effect. In such situations, what then becomes important is calibrating the loss threshold, while linking it to other stock attributes that, for each individual portfolio, are most indicative of stocks that are unlikely to rebound.

6   Phantastic Risks

Unexpressed emotions will never die. They are buried alive and will come forth later in uglier ways.

Sigmund Freud

It comes as no surprise that active management necessitates taking on risk. While the financial literature is brimming over with materials about risk measurement, portfolio construction, portfolio optimization, and value at risk (VAR), precious little has been written on the relationship between emotions and risk. Yet emotions find their way into the portfolio through the buy, sell, and sizing decisions that managers make daily. In this chapter we expand the discussion of the unconscious and consider its impact on portfolio risk.

Some managers make their decisions guided primarily by models, while others prefer a bottom-up fundamental approach. And there is a rapidly growing group of hybrid strategies that use quantitative models to filter ideas and then employ fundamental analysis to support their final choices. Common across virtually every approach is the fact that buy and sell decisions reflect at least some discretion or judgment by the manager, and it is in exercising these judgments that the manager's emotional state can introduce significant risk. While it might seem that emotional risks more typically plague traditional investors, emotions also impact their more quantitative brethren, as discussed below.

You're Phantastic

Richard Taffler and David Tuckett, first mentioned in chapter 1, apply psychoanalytic concepts to help understand missteps in investing. They use the term "phantastic object"[1] to describe assets that are acted upon as much to resolve the manager's unconscious emotional needs as to generate alpha.

This dual purposing of an asset, for financial gain and emotional relief, leads to unintentional choices whose outcomes are disappointing. So what is a phantastic object? Here's how Tuckett and Taffler describe it:

This key concept of emotional finance brings together the psychoanalytic concepts of object relationships and unconscious phantasy to describe subjectively very attractive objects that stimulate high excitement and almost automatic idealization and so a powerful wish to possess. We all imagine that on one level they can satisfy our deepest (and earliest infantile) desires to have exactly what we want, and exactly when we want it, the meaning of which we are only partly aware. Phantastic objects, therefore, are powerful psychological attractors acting beneath consciousness that excite phantasies of gratification or frustration. Possession of such phantastic objects allows investors unconsciously to feel omnipotent like Aladdin, whose lamp could summon a genie, or the fictional bond-trader Sherman McCoy who felt himself to be a master of the universe.[2]

According to Tuckett and Taffler, phantastic objects not only reflect the individual's need or desire but also are associated with items or ideas about which the individual is poorly informed. People are thus set up for an intense and volatile experience by being emotionally needy while simultaneously hoping that their need will be fulfilled by something about which they possess insufficient knowledge. Consider this example. A manager is below her benchmark and desperately wants to do better. Her client relationships, bonus, and self-esteem are rapidly approaching zero. She identifies what she believes is a hot stock, company XYZ. She analyzes this company and its prospects, even speaking with internal and Wall Street analysts and checking out company management. The story sounds terrific, and if company XYZ's stock does half of what is projected, it will help her jump-start performance. She loads up on the stock and watches. The price goes up steadily for several weeks, and all is good. This new name is meeting her emotional needs … uh … I mean, her investment expectations. Then, out of the blue, there is troubling news: Company XYZ's sole supplier of a critical manufacturing component has filed for Chapter 11 protection. The supplier's output will be severely reduced until it is reorganized, which is likely to take months. That means either lower production or higher unit costs for company XYZ. The market is running the other way, and company XYZ's stock price fell precipitously in just one morning.

Now, if the manager had really known company XYZ on the way in, including all of its strengths and shortcomings, then this news and market reaction would not be overwhelming. The manager might calmly reconfirm her long-term thesis about company XYZ and choose to stay the course, or even view this as a buying opportunity. If, however, she purchased company XYZ hoping that it would put some spring back into the step of her portfolio immediately, she might not be sufficiently knowledgeable or dispassionate. That is, if she had viewed company XYZ as a phantastic object, her initial desire would have colored her analysis, and in her unconscious attempts to seek pleasure, she would have made a hopeful buy. Then later, when the bad news came out, her weak understanding of the full complexity of company XYZ would have led her to react to the price drop with emotional distress. At this point, hope would have turned to despair, seeking pleasure would have switched to avoiding pain, and a buy would have turned into a sell, all happening, perhaps, while the mid- to long-term prospects for company XYZ remained unchanged.

Scenarios like this one play out each day in professionally managed portfolios. In their book *Fund Management: An Emotional Finance Perspective*, Tuckett and Taffler recount numerous instances of portfolio managers telling stories that they believed underscored their analytic objectivity, only to expose inadvertently the emotions shaping their choices. They suggest, "The industry directly or indirectly sells the idea that its managers are able to earn superior returns on a consistent basis over time, which is what clients thus demand and believe they are signing up for in their mandates. In fact, as our interviews show, fund managers themselves equally believe, at least on some level, that they are able to earn consistently superior returns. We point out, however, that their high levels of anxiety suggest that, on another level, they are not so sure."[3] They observe that these portfolio managers tended to split risk from return, good from bad, and this emotional splitting caused their understanding of the assets to be fragile, resulting in their loving or hating assets depending upon daily performance.

Underlying phantastic objects is the fact that many aspects of assets and markets are unknowable. How much are earnings likely to grow in three years? What is the fair price of an asset today? Has the market topped, or is there further room to run? Using the best information available, supported with world-class analysts and/or top models, portfolio managers are still faced with ambiguity at the end of the day. And the way individuals resolve ambiguity is through their emotions. They go from feeling unsure or indifferent to staunchly decided, not because of more analysis or a deeper understanding, but because a switch is flipped within their unconscious. They have developed conviction, and it is described in their narratives as an objective assessment, even though it invariably is charged by emotional need that is both powerful and undetectable.

A Fundamental Challenge

Phantastic objects certainly can impact traditional bottom-up investors. The weaker their processes and the more they rely on "gut instinct," the easier it is to see how they can start to love and hate assets. These emotions can also erupt more broadly.

A European-based hedge fund adopted the new analytic framework to understand its strengths and shortcomings better. The analysis showed that this portfolio was generating well over 500 basis points of alpha annually from buying, but was giving all this and more back through poor selling. Consequently, although the portfolio manager and his process were effective at finding great stocks, the mismanagement of positions was keeping portfolio performance below the benchmark.

The strong asymmetry between the buy and sell skills, it turned out, was linked to a unique approach to portfolio construction. The head portfolio manager always invested to a top-down theme. Whatever his current theme was, he wanted it reflected by all of the portfolio's current holdings. Consequently, whenever he came upon a new theme, he simply sold everything and rebuilt the portfolio. The resulting periodic massive turnover had the effect of throwing out the baby with the bathwater.

Whenever the manager shifted to a new theme, he was selling many perfectly good stocks that either were in the midst of generating superior performance or were about to do so. This behavior also resulted in less frequent sells between theme changes, thus allowing once alpha-generating stocks to languish in the portfolio well after they became tired. The portfolio was buying strong names but selling them too late or too early. Rather than allowing each position to be harvested relative to its own information advantage, the positions were being pushed out of the portfolio all at once in order to make room for the next crop of stocks.

Relating this behavior to the discussion above, the manager seemed to be full of hope whenever he found a new theme, and this hope drove his desire to find stocks that reflected his optimism. He loved his new theme and wanted to experience it to the fullest. But whenever a new theme emerged, he quickly soured on the old one. At such moments, he felt that stocks purchased under the old set of beliefs were no longer fit to own. What once was hopeful was now worrisome; what was once loved was now hated; what was once a buy became a sell. Lacking the appropriate feedback, all that this portfolio manager could see was that his buys tended to be good. And they were. But his abrupt mass sell-offs were costing him all the alpha generated from his developing a theme and then finding stocks that matched it. His apparent pursuit of phantastic objects was stopping him from delivering fantastic performance.

Anger, Fear, and Risk

Anger promotes risk seeking, while fear motivates risk aversion. The emotional state of anger causes individuals to experience strong feelings of certainty, a tremendous sense that they can control the current situation, and a feeling of responsibility for initiating action or making things happen. Anger also encourages highly optimistic assessments of future outcomes and dampens analytic thinking. Thus, an angry person will possess only minimal anticipation of the risk or effort required to achieve the desired change. Fear, on the other hand, is associated with feelings of low certainty, weak control over outcomes, and little to no feeling of personal responsibility to influence what's happening. It also encourages pessimistic assessments of future outcomes and the belief that efforts to effect change will require tremendous effort and pose significant risk.

While anger and fear affect one's appetite for risk in opposite ways, both feelings can unconsciously bring about risky behaviors that negatively affect portfolio performance. Anger, as mentioned, can lead to overconfidence, which tends to cloud objective assessments and can induce buys and sells that satisfy an emotional need, while wreaking havoc on the portfolio (as in the case of the hedge fund manager above). Alternatively, fear can induce paralysis with regard to making choices, stifling actions that should be taken. A prime example is the endowment effect, or the tendency to hold on to positions well beyond their ability to generate excess returns. This behavior is driven primarily by the fear that tomorrow's price may be above today's; therefore, it is the fear of selling at too low a price that delays action. Self-awareness about such feelings is difficult to attain, in part because once ignited, emotions can linger within the unconscious and affect choices that are unrelated to the original stimuli. For example, if while waiting to cross a busy street, you're splashed with water by a passing automobile, you might become angry at the driver, the puddle, or the rotten start to your day. Your anger might carry over to the investment committee meeting you attend 90 minutes later, and a stock that you might have found a bit too risky on most days suddenly fits the bill.

Separate from the fundamental needs to seek pleasure and avoid pain, the feelings of anger and fear also shape the way we perceive and accept risk. And since emotions once triggered can last well into the future, it is entirely possible that risk assessments regarding current buy and sell choices reflect feelings that are still smoldering from unrelated prior experiences.

Quantifying Emotions

Managers of highly quantitative portfolios tend to have high confidence in their models. Until they don't, that is. In general, these managers follow their models unquestioningly, connecting the alpha generator to the optimizer, and executing the buys and sells that result. This pattern continues until the manager feels that the model is operating in a market regime for which it is not calibrated. This happens periodically, with the crash of 2008–2009 being an extreme example. When these times hit, quantitative managers react in several ways. Some sell out and park in cash until they believe the market is back in tune with what the models can recognize. Some freeze the portfolio, staying with those holdings until the model regains traction. Still others begin second-guessing the model and introduce judgmental overrides at the individual position level.

Back in the winter of 2010, I was asked to participate in a conference whose audience comprised primarily chief investment officers from a variety of asset management companies. The principal topic was risk and how it might be managed after the market meltdown. Most memorable from this conference was hearing chief risk officers from several highly sophisticated global money management companies talk frankly about abandoning their risk models at various times during the credit crisis. They were expressing a failure of confidence in their models to guide them through uncharted waters. These highly educated and skilled quantitative professionals chose to rely on their intuitions at the very time when market riskiness was extreme. What caused them to abandon their models at this critical juncture?

One explanation is what Nassim Nicholas Taleb refers to as a "black swan,"[4] meaning that the market hit an extremely difficult-to-predict, massive adjustment, a once-in-a-great-while event that statistical models don't pick up. The narrative these professionals relied upon, that the models usually work except during 100-year floods, may be correct, or it may perhaps rationalize the use of models to satisfy deep emotional needs. This latter point is consistent with the view that the models themselves represent a form of phantastic object. As David Tuckett comments on this idea: "Certainly one explanation for the attraction of statistically derived risk measures, benchmark tables, and much of the welter of comment, analysis and statistical reporting of all kinds that constitute the financial market industry, as it was when the railway engineers began it, is that it is a way both to manage anxiety and to create the impression risk is being managed. Such stories disguise the fact that in many ways we have not come very far from the casino."[5]

While it may not be practical today to assign causality for the market collapse across a host of possible contributory factors, the emotional management of risk by professionals surely must be in the mix. Interestingly, during the 2011 and 2012 markets, the phrases "risk-on" and "risk-off" came into vogue. These terms are intended to indicate net market optimism or pessimism at any given time but may in fact describe when the preponderance of market participants are seeking pleasure or avoiding pain, respectively.

One final emotional element of quantitative analysis concerns the act of model construction itself. These models are not divined from supernatural insights, nor are they the result of purely analytic processes. Instead, they reflect what the quantitative team believes represents a reasonable fit of their hypothesis, or theory of what is going on, to what the data can support. Quantitative managers and analysts take their business very seriously and try to develop models that are valuable—that is, able to generate alpha, or manage risk, or whatever the goal. But choosing which factors to include, how to weight or load them, and which steps to employ to avoid overfitting are all subjective. These choices place the quantitative analyst in moments of ambiguity, and as we've seen, it is the human tendency to overcome such ambiguity through emotions. Even though these emotions may be experienced on the unconscious level, they nevertheless can have a powerful impact on the analytic choices that quantitative professionals make and the results derived from their models. This insight suggests there may be more meaning than previously inferred from the quotation generally attributed to R. H. Coase: "When threatened sufficiently, data will confess to anything."[6]

Conclusion

Risk is commonly referred to as a set of known outcomes whose likelihood can be statistically estimated, while uncertainty is those potential outcomes that are either unknown or whose likelihood is unknown. Finance professionals tend to focus exclusively on risk, while paying little serious attention to uncertainty. This splitting of future outcomes into what can be managed statistically and what cannot has the familiar feel of a phantastic object. It may be the industry's way of seeking pleasure by focusing on what can be quantified, while avoiding the pain of what cannot.

Portfolio management involves judgment on many levels. Managers commonly use emotions and intuition as tools to resolve the ambiguities encountered when working with incomplete information or attempting to project the future. In addition, brain science informs us that the resolution of ambiguous choices is often achieved through emotional charges that push judgments in one direction or another. Consequently, sorting out when choices result in greater financial success and when they might be helping to manage emotions requires clear, dispassionate feedback. Not only is the current use of statistically based risk models insufficient in helping to manage the risks brought on by emotions, but it may also foster such risk by providing a quantitatively derived balm that soothes our feelings about things that are unknowable. Use of the new analytic framework together with conventional risk analyses offers an advancement over current practices in that it enables the portfolio manager to better understand her idiosyncratic responses to volatility.

Notes

1. "Phantastic" is a term from psychoanalysis suggesting an item that is highly desirable but not obtainable.

2. David Tuckett and Richard J. Taffler, *Fund Management: An Emotional Finance Perspective* (Research Foundation of the CFA Institute, 2012), 85.

3. Ibid., 91.

4. Nassim Nicholas Taleb, *The Black Swan: The Impact of the Highly Improbable* (New York: Random House, 2007).

5. David Tuckett, "Addressing the Psychology of Financial Markets," in *Economics: The Open-Access, Open-Assessment E-Journal* 3, 2009-40, November 20, 2009, at http://www.economics-ejournal.org/economics/journalarticles/2009-40.

6. R. H. Coase, "How Should Economists Choose?," in *Essays on Economics and Economists* (Chicago: University of Chicago Press, 1994), 27.

Part Two: Behavioral Matters

Great men are they who see that spiritual is stronger than any material force, that thoughts rule the world.

Ralph Waldo Emerson, "Progress of Culture"

Facts, illusions, analysis, and emotions equally conspire to shape your worldview and the judgments you make. Consequently, knowing when your thoughts are being driven more by your desires than your intentions is proving to be an important and untapped source of alpha for professional investors. The ability to distinguish financial merit from fantasy while engaging in the exciting and analytically demanding world of investing requires a tremendous level of self-awareness, the kind that is built on more than self-reflection and a glance at one or two recent decisions. It involves developing a working knowledge of the mental pitfalls that are common to professional investors and then modifying your process to steer your decisions more toward intention and away from behavioral urges. This knowledge includes a strong appreciation for the roles that the conscious and unconscious brains play in shaping the thoughts and choices you make.

The fields of psychology, neuroscience, and behavioral finance are as vast as they are interesting. The preponderance of findings from these disciplines, however, tend to be written by and for academics, with only limited amounts of information making its way into business schools and financial practitioner journals. Consequently, investment professionals whose entire careers are built on analysis and judgment know precious little about how the mind really works or how to harness its full potential.

"Behavioral Matters" was originally written as a series of essays exploring the science of thinking and decision-making. The series was written expressly for investment professionals and was distributed online between 2007 and 2014. The essays cover a wide range of topics from the theories of Sigmund Freud to well-known behavioral tendencies and on through how memory and vision are managed by the brain. Fast-paced discussions of about 1,000 words each, they are intended to assist professional investors in broadening their knowledge of how learning and decision-making really happen. Should you want more, the sources cited in the notes will take you deeper. Each essay discusses a specific topic, and therefore they can be read in any order you choose. All of the essays have been updated since their initial publication.

7 What Drives Selling?

Psychologists have repeatedly demonstrated that recognizing our errors and biases does not lead us to change our behavior automatically. The psychology that underlies errors and biases is remarkably resistant to change.

Hersh Shefrin, *Behavioral Corporate Finance*

Most portfolio managers claim to follow an explicit selling discipline—just look at any pitch book. These statements of sell discipline tend to include phrases such as "sell when full value is recognized"; "sell when fundamentals erode"; or "sell opportunistically when stronger uses for the capital become available." The process of selling is, in practice, much less rigorous—especially in comparison to buying. From the classic bottom-up investor to those supported with quantitative tools, two facts about selling are clear: It's highly judgmental, and its effectiveness is less understood than investment practitioners generally believe. This essay looks at the results of a survey conducted by the CFA Institute and Cabot Research that asked the question, How do you sell?[1]

Judgment, Behaviors, and Measurement

Portfolio managers are hired for their judgment, and it often provides the extra performance that puts a portfolio into the top quintile. But this boost to performance is available only when judgments are effective, a result that necessitates capturing and using appropriate feedback. Absent rigorous calibration, judgment is highly susceptible to many shortcomings, including behavioral influences.

For starters, by its very nature judgment requires tremendous support from our unconscious brain. This is the portion of the brain where heuristics, beliefs, and all rapid decision-making reside. Science makes abundantly clear that individuals are incapable of knowing in the moment when their choices are being unconsciously driven, let alone how well such decisions are playing out. Yet the industry-wide reliance on traditional portfolio measures like return, relative return, hit rates, and attribution offers no hope of providing the clear and granular feedback about selling that is sorely needed.

Studies involving scores of professionally managed equity portfolios conducted by Cabot show that most if not all managers engage in sell decisions that are uncalibrated. This finding is equally observed whether funds are managed by classic "stock pickers" or sell decisions are driven by quantitative signals. Our work also indicates that small shifts in the sell process can result in substantial improvements in portfolio performance—exceeding 100 basis points of incremental alpha annually in 85% of situations.

How Managers See It

We thought it would be useful to compare the results available from the rapidly growing number of portfolios we've analyzed with the perceptions that portfolio managers themselves have about their sell practices. The opportunity to collect such data became available at a CFA-sponsored conference held in Boston during the summer of 2007. Over 100 investment professionals participated in the survey. They answered four questions designed to get at how they make sell decisions and to uncover how well they adhere to their discipline. A summary of their responses is presented below.

Q1. Which best describes your approach to selling?
Slightly more than 81% indicated that judgment plays a substantial role in their sell decisions. In contrast, only 29% said their sell decisions are "Highly disciplined, driven by research and objective criteria." While judgment often plays an integral role in a disciplined and effective process, it is less likely to be the case within selling due to the inadequate feedback available to managers.

Q2. How did your selling discipline develop?
Just 28% of respondents mentioned using research and back-testing to help them learn how best to sell. On the other hand, over 70% indicated that experience, trial and error, and advice from past mentors shaped their sell processes. These responses underscore the absence of rigor that is ubiquitous throughout the sell process. The limited investment made in developing sell disciplines may help explain why managers so often don't use them when actually confronted with the need to sell (see Question 4 below).

Q3. What informs you that your sell discipline is working?

Approximately 60% of survey respondents said that they gauge the success of their selling from portfolio returns. Only 16% indicated that they attempt to quantify selling effectiveness as a specific activity or skill. This limited use of rigor in the assessment of selling is in line with Cabot's experience working with portfolio managers. The suggestion that portfolio performance offers insight into sell effectiveness is hopeful yet misguided. Any form of portfolio performance (e.g., return, relative return, information ratio, hit rate, attribution, etc.) reflects the effects of at least two and often all three of the basic skills of buying, selling, and sizing. This blending of the impacts of multiple skills into composite measures of portfolio outcomes is an inherent limitation of traditional analytics and is at the heart of why they are incapable of providing the feedback needed for improving.

Q4. Which discipline most often results in your selling a stock?

Participants were divided between the answers "knowing the right time to sell" and "selling by the numbers and research." However, the relatively high proportion responding that they sell "by the numbers" does not jibe with the frequent use of judgment observed in the answers to Questions 1, 2, and 3. This apparent inconsistency might be explained behaviorally, in that individuals often intend to do one thing (Explicit Theory) but in the moment do something quite different (Theory in Practice). When presented with Question 4, many were reminded of their explicit intentions, as described in their official sell disciplines, and this recollection may have influenced their answers.

Conclusion

Selling is an essential aspect of portfolio management. It determines, to a large extent, what portion of the alpha generated from strong buys is captured by the portfolio. Selling too quickly or too late can cost the portfolio as much or more alpha than what is generated from buys.

Yet selling is much less analyzed or understood than buying. And since judgment plays such a large role in making sell decisions, the lack of rigor and discipline are all the more worrisome. The survey results suggest that more calibration of sell disciplines and sell effectiveness is in order; this assessment is corroborated by Cabot's experience of working with portfolio managers globally. The time has come to elevate selling from a mere discipline to an important skill on par with buying. Not doing so might be, well, selling your clients short.

Notes

1. The Survey of Professional Investors' Sell Discipline was conducted by the CFA Institute and Cabot Research LLC, at the June 2007 Behavioral Finance Conference, in Boston.

Further Reading

Christophe Faugère, Hany A. Shawky, and David M. Smith, "Sell Discipline and Institutional Money Management," *Journal of Portfolio Management* (Spring 2004).

8   Sell the Way You Buy—Strategically

He who would learn to fly one day must first learn to stand and walk and run and climb and dance; one cannot fly into flying.

Friedrich Nietzsche, *Thus Spoke Zarathustra*

Effective selling is paramount to delivering consistent long-term performance. Good sells, in effect, are how managers capture the performance generated from their buys. Yet little serious attention is given to the practice of selling, as evidenced by the paucity of professional and academic journal articles on this topic. This essay focuses on the inadequate attention given to selling and how this overlooked skill may be undermining the active management industry generally.

Where's the Beef?

Practitioners and academics alike know intuitively that selling is important to portfolio performance. Nevertheless, very little has been studied or written about this skill. In one of the very few serious investigations into this subject, Christophe Faugère, Hany A. Shawky, and David M. Smith write: "The notion of sell discipline has a long history, but the topic has received only occasional mention in the practitioner literature and no attention at all in academic journals."[1] Searching online for studies of selling effectiveness only confirms this assessment.

The asymmetry in attention given to buying and selling can be seen in how each is viewed. Whether it is in requests for proposals (RFP) or manager pitch books, any mention of investment strategy invariably concerns buying, while selling is referred to as a discipline. Innocent as these categorizations seem, they reflect the stature and mind share given to each activity.

Selling the Past

Why is selling relegated to the backwaters of rigorous investigation while massive amounts of research are conducted on buying? Basic emotions may play an important role, according to Terrance Odean. "The act of buying may be more forward looking and the act of selling more backward looking," he suggests. Odean explains the reversal in perspective between buy and sell decisions this way: "Buys have no baggage. A manager picks a buy entirely for what it can deliver to future performance. The entire relationship is prospective. When choosing a sell, however, the manager is likely to consider the past performance of a position. Which positions are winners or losers (unrealized gains or losses)? Am I trying to manage a tax consequence? And of course there are the behavioral forces of feeling good about locking in a gain and avoiding locking in a loss."[2]

Behavioral Influences

If selling is less understood than buying and tends to be backward looking, then just how disciplined is it? In summarizing their research, Faugère, Shawky, and Smith state: "We find evidence that sell discipline variables have a significant explanatory impact on portfolio returns." They conclude, "These findings suggest that in rising markets institutional money managers are likely to benefit from a less restrictive sell discipline criterion, while during declining market periods they might benefit from a more binding sell discipline criterion."[3] The message is simultaneously that discipline is important but, by necessity, must be augmented with judgment. It is precisely in the application of judgment that behavioral influences can have their greatest impact on financial decisions. And the less studied or calibrated those judgments, the stronger the behavioral influence can be.

You Can't Improve What You Don't Measure

So where does that leave managers who want to improve their selling? According to Jason Zweig, financial columnist for the *Wall Street Journal* and author of *Your Money and Your Brain*, "It's important to understand that the brain is designed to ignore [ineffective selling] so if you don't deliberately seek to measure it you will never be aware of the problem at all."[4] Any meaningful measures of sell discipline would include identifying persistent patterns or behaviors within sells, comparing how well sold positions did after sale relative to other positions held, and computing the benefits of shifting a behavior, including measures of statistical significance and predictiveness. But simply knowing the potential benefit from change is not sufficient to assure that change will occur. According to Hersh Shefrin, "Situations where people receive quick, clear feedback about the results of their actions are more conducive to [effective change]."[5]

Thus, while improving is possible, it takes work and deliberate steps. Sorting out when your sells work and when they don't is the first step. The raw information for this type of analysis is there in your portfolio history. Next is reminding yourself when you're about to engage in the type of sell decision that has been challenging in the past. Slowing down and thinking twice at those moments can help you substitute a new habit for an old one. And finally, you should capture timely feedback on how you're doing at making the changes you've decided upon.

Putting It All Together

Scores of equity portfolio managers are improving their selling skills. They are applying the lessons of deliberate improvement and seeing results that are both encouraging and lifting performance. Chief among the sell shortcomings they are working on is the tendency to hold winners long after they have begun to lose their steam. Referred to as the "endowment effect," this behavior is seen in roughly one out of every four portfolios analyzed by Cabot. Impatience with relatively young losers that results in their being pushed out of the portfolio too quickly, or the avoidance of pain, is the second most common sell behavior observed.

Armed with greater self-awareness and the right support in making decisions, managers are systematically eliminating ineffective sell habits. As a result, their portfolios are capturing the full benefit of their buys and not giving alpha back to the market from sells that are too early or too late.

Conclusion

Selling is an important yet highly overlooked skill within equity portfolio management. It continues to be the poor relation to buying in its lack of serious investigation and published research. The virtual absence of intellectual investigation into selling leaves this important skill difficult to appropriately understand and improve.

Nevertheless, managers can initiate their own sell improvement program by studying the decisions affecting their portfolios. Learning where sells are adding alpha and where they're not will highlight how to improve.

Building a few speed bumps into your sell process can allow you to increase attention and focus at critical moments as you shift away from what's not working toward more effective choices.

Notes

1. Christophe Faugère, Hany A. Shawky, and David M. Smith, "Sell Discipline and Institutional Money Management," *Journal of Portfolio Management* (Spring 2004), 96.

2. Terrance Odean is the Rudd Family Foundation Professor of Finance at the Haas School of Business at the University of California, Berkeley. His remarks are taken from an exclusive interview with Cabot Research LLC in December 2007.

3. Faugère, Shawky, and Smith, "Sell Discipline and Institutional Money Management," 104.

4. Jason Zweig's remarks are from the article "Mind Games" in the online research journal *Welling@Weeden*, http://welling.weedenco.com/, no. 9 (May 11, 2007).

5. Hersh Shefrin, *Behavioral Corporate Finance* (Boston: McGraw-Hill/Irwin, 2007).

9 Bearing Up in a Bear Market

The time to buy is when there's blood in the streets.
Baron Rothschild[1]

As Baron Rothschild's maxim suggests, market turmoil can present equity managers with extraordinary buying opportunities. Capitalizing on such opportunities, however, requires that managers create liquidity within their portfolios—and that means knowing the best stocks to sell.

Selling, as has been discussed in previous essays, is prone to behavioral influences. Research suggests that behaviorally motivated sell decisions increase when a manager is facing an underperforming portfolio or riding out a turbulent market. A few ideas to help you check your own behavioral tendencies during these times are presented below.

Buying Yesterday's Answers

No one likes being wrong or the feelings it evokes. The desire to avoid such feelings can influence how information is searched for, perceived, and evaluated. Hesitancy in reassessing weakening stocks is one way that the avoidance of psychic pain can play havoc on a portfolio. Maintaining the original target value for a stock based on old or now faulty information is a common behavioral trap. Anchoring, as this tendency is known, can be motivated by the unconscious desire to avoid feeling bad—which might come about if a write-down on a large position were to occur. Challenging yesterday's assumptions and conclusions can help you to avoid anchoring. Two tools that can help you:

• Compare the trend of your assumptions for current winners versus losers, and you might find a difference that points to anchoring.
• Seek the opinions of trusted and dispassionate experts, including others inside your company.

No Pain, No Gain

Managers sometimes engage in elaborate self-deceptions to maintain losing positions in the portfolio. The most common rationalization for holding on to losers is the expectation of a near-term rebound. Loss aversion, a behavior known to stifle the selling of losers, stems from our desire to avoid locking in a loss and subsequently feeling bad about our decision to own the stock in the first place. This type of self-deception is widespread among retail investors but seems to be less common, although not completely absent, within the ranks of professional money managers.

Tossing the Baby Out with the Bath Water

Managers need to safeguard against the desire to reconstitute the portfolio and hastily place all the bad news behind them. On the surface, this approach can seem entirely motivated by economics. The familiar mantra, "If you wouldn't buy it today at today's price, then you should be a seller," comes to mind as a potential rationalization for clearing the decks in order to start afresh. Overreaction when the portfolio's performance is below its benchmark, however, can be more about selling pain than selling disappointing stocks. It reflects one of the central postulations of prospect theory: Individuals prefer to swallow all their bad news at once, while savoring their good news in little bites—for emotional rather than economic reasons. Maintaining your cool under siege and carefully reevaluating each position in the portfolio can go a long way toward avoiding this type of costly overreaction.

Looking through the Rearview Mirror

Selling is often backward looking in that past performance influences which positions are sold and which are held. This tendency to look back is one reason why current losers with strong go-forward prospects are sold while stocks with unrealized gains that are now exhausted remain in the portfolio. Marketing demands can sometimes affect the choices made. Marketing pressures felt unconsciously can lead to both holding recent winners too long so that they can be presented to clients and prospects as representative holdings and jettisoning recent losers so that they don't have to be discussed at all. Whether they are motivated by emotions just outside of their awareness or engaged in minor window dressing, managers need to stay mindful of their sell choices, especially when the market is in turmoil.

Bad Experiences

We learn our most useful lessons from the careful analysis of our experiences—not merely from having had the experience. In their paper "Once Burned, Twice Shy," Michal Strahilevitz, Terrance Odean, and Brad M. Barber argue that investors may avoid specific stocks now or in the future simply because they previously sold them for a loss.[2] In these instances, the choices investors make are driven more by past experiences than the current alpha potential of the stock. These ineffective lessons, referred to as "counterfactuals," are formulated when the manager's feelings about specific past events overwhelm analytic thinking.

Conclusion

Maintaining your cool in the midst of a market meltdown or when the portfolio is significantly underperforming is hard. Yet staying calm may also be what enables you to work your way back to strong performance rather than getting swamped while flailing around hoping to do better.

Anchoring, loss aversion, avoiding pain, window dressing, and counterfactual thinking are some of the unproductive behaviors that can worm their way into the choices you make during tough times. Staying mindful of your intentions and of how you are feeling are useful strategies across all investing, but they are of particular value when portfolio performance is threatened. Once you've identified the bear, then the question becomes: Who will consume whom?

Notes

1. Quoted in Daniel Myers, "Buy When There's Blood in the Streets," *Forbes*, February 23, 2009.

2. Michal Strahilevitz, Terrance Odean, and Brad M. Barber, "Once Burned, Twice Shy: How Naive Learning and Counterfactuals Affect the Repurchase of Stocks Previously Sold," *Journal of Marketing Research* (2011).

Further Reading

"Getting the Sell Discipline Right," *Citywire*, May 15, 2007, www.citywire.co.uk.

10 Aching Conviction

Doubt is not a pleasant condition, but certainty is absurd.
Voltaire, letter to Frederick II of Prussia, April 6, 1767

The term "conviction" is used universally among professional investors to suggest that rigorous thinking has preceded a buy or sell decision. What is really backing up conviction? Does conviction reflect knowledge and wisdom accumulated over years, or is it merely bluster? Understanding the nature of conviction, and how this can help portfolio performance, are the subject of this essay.

Believe It or Not

The dictionary defines "conviction" as a "fixed or firm belief." How are beliefs formed? Are people aware of their complete set of beliefs? Can we consciously edit or manage beliefs? The answer to the last two questions is a resounding no. Beliefs are created, stored, and managed almost entirely within the unconscious part of the brain, according to modern cognitive science. Commenting on the veracity of beliefs, Harvard psychologist Daniel Gilbert points out, "research suggests that people are typically unaware of the reasons why they are doing what they are doing, but when asked for a reason, they readily supply one."[1] Further complicating things is the fact that a great many choices are the result of emotions and not analytic thinking. Hersh Shefrin, the noted behavioral economist, puts it this way: "We like to think that we are thinking, when often we are just really feeling. That goes on all of the time in the investment business."[2]

Putting this into perspective, the unconscious and the beliefs residing there are credited for roughly 95% of all our daily decisions. These unconsciously driven decisions occur and are implemented well before we are even consciously aware that a decision is required. The lightning-fast processing of the unconscious, together with the fact that its content is obscured from ready analysis, suggest that the use of conviction should be the exception rather than the rule.

Twice the Conviction

Doubling down on a stock that has experienced a downward price movement is a practice observed in many investment processes. The common wisdom about this activity is the thought, "If I like the stock at $30 per share, I should definitely be a buyer at $25." This piling deeper into a current loser implies that the conviction that initially caused it to be a buy is now just as strong or even stronger.

It is equally possible that fear or overconfidence is motivating the additional stock purchase instead of thoughtfully conceived conviction. Since most of us are predisposed to feel horribly when faced with a mistake—and the bigger the mistake, the worse the feelings—adding to a down position could be the financial equivalent of whistling past a cemetery. And while this behavior might get you past an inconsequential fear, it can bury portfolio performance.

Knowledgeable Sells

Selling is a relatively unstudied aspect of investing. Few managers, if any, know how well their selling works, yet sell they must. Some selling is pragmatic—initiated to satisfy outflows. In fact, creating liquidity to fund new buys is among the most commonly cited motivations for selling. Others include invoking a stop-loss, the need for portfolio rebalancing, and reacting to unfavorable company news.

But what about strategic selling? You know, those times when a stock is pushed out of the portfolio because buying the stock was a mistake or the stock has delivered all the alpha it can and is now getting tired. There is no precipitating event, just objective analysis that points to the benefits from selling rather than holding. As desirable as such choices are, there is little evidence that they happen frequently. In discussing the shortcomings of sell processes, author and *Wall Street Journal* columnist Jason Zweig says, "I've yet to have anyone provide evidence that their sell discipline works. Performance, even above the benchmark, is not proof that your selling is good."[3]

Well, this is exactly the dilemma that equity managers face regarding all of their skills, but particularly selling. The only feedback most managers receive about their sell decisions comes from total return. And that is all but useless for learning about the strength of a skill. Lacking rigorous and granular feedback, managers must rely on hindsight, intuition, and their memories to help foster greater self-awareness. The risks of depending on one's memories for learning are many, as suggested by the nineteenth-century commentator Josh Billings: "There are lots of people who mistake their imagination for their memory."[4] Using gut rather than analytic rigor, these approaches to making sell choices are highly susceptible to the known forces that short-circuit intuitive decision-making, including emotions and biases. In his highly acclaimed book *The Black Swan*, Nassim Nicholas Taleb says about conviction, "we are demonstrably arrogant about what we think we know." One factor undercutting conviction, he writes, is that "much of what we ascribe to skills is an after-the-fact attribution."[5] Managers thus have the dual problem of initially making behaviorally motivated decisions and then rationalizing the decisions afterward. With such an active unconscious protecting us from thinking or feeling badly about ourselves, just how can a manager develop bankable conviction?

Question Your Conviction

Understanding the quality of your conviction requires that you question your choices as they are developing and, perhaps more importantly, measure their effectiveness with simple and clear data. Questioning conviction or judgment on the fly is difficult. It requires that you suspend the urges driving your thoughts at the moment and take stock of what, other than strategy and disciplined process, might be propelling you toward one choice over another. Rigorous measurement, on the other hand, is performed after the fact and is less emotionally laden. Since you can approach measurement with greater dispassion, it can yield elements of self-knowledge that can be internalized and help lead you to higher performance.

Conclusion

Conviction, like intuition, comes to us naturally, but that does not mean it is helpful—especially when applied to investing. To ensure that your most strongly held opinions really are helping the portfolio, it is essential to collect a little data and analyze your hit rate of high conviction to high alpha generation. Without the appropriate feedback, you cannot know whether your positions reflect well-reasoned conviction or bluster.

Overconfidence, anchoring, self-attribution, and fear are just a few of the well-documented behavioral traps that can become pseudo-conviction. All that stands between you and misplaced conviction is your own disbelief.

Notes

1. Daniel Gilbert, *Stumbling on Happiness* (New York: Random House, 2006), 190.

2. Hersh Shefrin, *Behavioral Corporate Finance* (Boston: McGraw-Hill/Irwin, 2007).

3. Comments by Jason Zweig were taken from "Mind Games," in the online research journal *Welling@Weeden* 9, no. 9 (May 11, 2007). See also Jason Zweig, *Your Money and Your Brain* (New York: Simon & Schuster, 2007).

4. Josh Billings, in *BrainyQuote.com*, Xplore Inc, 2014, http://www.brainyquote.com/quotes/quotes/j/joshbillin106716.html, accessed April 21, 2014.

5. Nassim Nicholas Taleb, *The Black Swan: The Impact of the Highly Improbable* (New York: Random House, 2007), 138, 31.

11   Unconscious Deliberation

The idea that conscious deliberation before making a decision is always good is simply one of those illusions consciousness creates for us.

Ap Dijksterhuis, *Wall Street Journal*, June 27, 2008

Conscious thinking plays an important role in many choices and decisions we make—but it is a bit player in comparison to the unconscious brain. Neuroscience makes clear that the vast majority of the thoughts, ideas, and choices that enter our minds and direct our actions are the result of unconscious thinking. This essay looks at the role of the unconscious brain in investment decision-making and how the unconscious can be harnessed for better results.

Split Decision

Strategy, discipline, and process are the means that professional investors use to consciously direct their decisions. And it is through objective research, analytic stock scoring, and back-testing of ideas that they develop and implement their intentions. Notwithstanding investors' substantial efforts to remain deliberate and objective, more is going into these buy and sell decisions than you might think.

A great deal of our thinking happens before it hits our consciousness. Thoughts, choices, and urges bubble up from the unconscious and, more often than not, greatly influence if not completely drive what we do. It is as if the conscious brain is mostly there observing—just along for the ride. Brain researcher George Loewenstein describes it this way: "Rather than actually guiding or controlling behavior, consciousness seems mainly to make sense of behavior after it is executed."[1] And while we may not care for the idea that most thoughts erupt from the unconscious, dismissing it will not help us generate the desired levels of performance going forward.

Jurassic Market

Cognitive science tells us that 95% of all decisions are made automatically—by our unconscious brain.[2] The consensus view among scientists is that the unconscious evolved to its current dominant powers in response to survival needs. Consider this story about early man. Here is this fellow foraging for food in the forest when unexpectedly he hears the rustling of leaves. It could be merely the wind hitting a few trees and bushes or it might be a predator about to pounce. So what should he do? One option is to look around and try to determine if he is in danger or if the coast is clear. More than likely, however, when his unconscious brain registered the noise, it assumed danger and pushed him into survival mode. So he ran! And those that ran the fastest went on to become our ancestors while the others became lunch. The point is that survival was rewarded by correct and instantaneous actions. And, over time, numerous challenges like this one promoted to the front of the evolutionary line those with the largest, fastest, and smartest unconscious brains. And here we are today, the beneficiaries of this honing process, with brains that not only can compel us to do things we're unaware of but too often make choices that are in conflict with our conscious intentions. The downside of this unconscious prowess is the accumulation of behavioral tendencies such as heuristics, biases, regret aversion, the endowment effect, overconfidence, and premature dismissal. When these normal but counterproductive behaviors continue undetected and unmanaged, they can lead to our being eaten alive by the market.

Nonintuitive Intuitions

Not only is the unconscious brain super powerful, it is also lightning-fast. A study led by Professor John-Dylan Haynes at the Max Planck Institute for Human Cognitive and Brain Sciences (Leipzig, Germany) using functional magnetic resonance imaging (FMRI) found that the unconscious brain arrives at decisions 7 to 10 seconds before we are consciously aware that a decision is even needed. Even more striking, the study showed that participants' conscious decisions could be predicted with 70% accuracy by studying their unconscious brain activity. Together these results underscore that unconscious processing is both much faster than conscious deliberation and also highly persistent or patterned.[3]

The notion that most decisions are made or influenced by the unconscious is relatively new to professional investing. The industry's traditional dogma includes belief statements such as, "We're totally objective here," "We do things completely by the numbers," and "Facts, not emotions, are how we make decisions." Nonetheless, companies such as Goldman Sachs, Morgan Stanley, and Fidelity Management & Research now have behavioral economists on staff to help their investment teams. These leading money management companies are making conscious choices to help their professionals manage their unconscious decisions.

Active and Passive Thinking

Individuals intuitively believe that automatic or unconscious thinking is fine for simple choices but that conscious deliberation needs to be used when confronted with a critical choice. Not so, says recent research into brain functioning and choice satisfaction; in fact, the data point to the opposite conclusion. Scientists in the Netherlands have shown that we are generally satisfied with consciously deliberated decisions about simple or very familiar choices. But when it comes to complicated decisions—those with many criteria or that we make infrequently—we are better off following our intuitions.

Consider purchasing a house. This is, for the vast majority of people, a decision that is both important and encountered infrequently. Lacking a well-tested formal process for assessing tradeoffs among house options, buyers commonly elevate living space or square footage to a top criterion. Yet research shows that our lives are rarely affected by a few square feet one way or the other. A terrible commute, on the other hand, can make life hell—and yet we often do not even consider this factor carefully when purchasing a house. Researchers believe that through naive efforts to impose some structure on a complex decision process, our conscious efforts nudge us toward emphasizing square footage because it is familiar and easily measured. Commuting difficulty is, by comparison, less accessible to our conscious deliberation and also harder to quantify. Proximity to work may, in fact, be reflected strongly in our initial impressions and then dampened in importance as we move toward consciously analyzing the house itself. The researchers suggest we might ultimately be happier buying the house that just feels right over the one that scores highest in our decision matrix. Although decision satisfaction is not the same as portfolio performance, this research does point out that our unconscious brain can be a powerful ally in helping us arrive at our best decisions.

Conclusion

The idea that most choices are the result of conscious deliberation is conventional and comforting but incorrect. Mountains of evidence demonstrates that it is our unconscious that drives most of life—from thoughts to feelings, to choices and on through to actions. Understanding the major role that the unconscious brain plays in investing is the initial step toward increasing self-awareness about behavioral tendencies and harnessing the unconscious to propel you toward your intentions.

Evolution has endowed humans with a potent and aggressive unconscious that, like Alexander Haig, asserts: "I'm in charge." Not only will it influence the inconsequential choices you make, but it will do its best to hijack deliberation when you are attempting to be your most deliberate. Continuing to think that your most critical decisions are totally objective and strictly by the numbers is one option, or you can step up to reality and start learning how your unconscious is affecting your investing. The choice is yours—or is it?

Notes

1. George Loewenstein, "The Creative Destruction of Decision Research," *Journal of Consumer Research* 28 (2001), 503.

2. Gerald Zaltman, *How Customers Think: Essential Insights into the Mind of the Market* (Cambridge: Harvard Business School Press, 2003), 40.

3. Joseph Ledoux, *The Emotional Brain: The Mysterious Underpinnings of Emotional Life* (New York: Simon and Schuster, 1996), 163.

Further Reading

Ap Dijksterhuis, Maarten W. Bos, Loran F. Nordgren, and Rick B. van Baaren, "Deliberation without Attention," *Science* 311, no. 5763 (February 17, 2006).

"Get Out of Your Own Way," *Wall Street Journal*, June 27, 2008.

Siong Soon, Marcel Brass, Hans-Jochen Heinze, and John-Dylan Haynes, "Unconscious Determinants of Free Decisions in the Human Brain," *Nature Neuroscience*, April 13, 2008.

Know thyself.

Socrates

Self-awareness is quickly becoming a mainstream concept within money management companies. That is because active management requires judgment and its exercise is most successful when all the facts and influences are known. As discussed in previous essays, selling is less disciplined than buying and, therefore, is far more susceptible to behavioral influences. In this essay we examine the role of self-awareness and its potential for helping you make better sell decisions.

Shooting in the Dark

Self-awareness begins with accurate feedback. Without adequate information about decisions they have made and how they worked out, portfolio managers are severely hampered when trying to improve. Consider the feedback differences available to professional athletes and professional investors. What would happen if a golfer never knew the quality of her individual shots? If she received only the final score after each round, how would she know her strengths, or which part of her game is strongest and which needs improvement? Should she be practicing her drives, fairway shots, or putts?

Well, this is exactly the dilemma that equity managers face regarding all of their skills, but particularly selling. The only feedback most managers receive about their sell decisions comes from total return. And that is all but useless for learning about the strength of a skill. Lacking rigorous and granular feedback, managers must rely on hindsight, intuition, and simplistic measures of skill success to help foster greater self-awareness. Authors Childre and Cryer caution about overvaluing this type of learning: "Remember, the mind likes to assume it 'knows what it knows' but often its perceptions are just not accurate."[1]

Memory Is Fiction

Reflection is essential to self-awareness. But memory alone is inadequate if your goal is to improve. Much of what our memory provides is a narrative that makes sense out of what we seem to remember about events. And such recollections are heavily influenced by our emotions; so much so that what's stored and what's recalled can be shaped as much by how we feel as by the event itself.

Consequently, when we try to dispassionately recall the sells executed over the past year, we can't help but remember best those that had the greatest emotional impact: big winners, big losers, or a string of small gains that kept us pumped up. The feelings that accompany these events help them become vivid memories—even if those memories are inaccurate. No wonder, then, that hindsight often leads us to learn the wrong lessons. We then translate false recollections into unhelpful rules that undermine the ability to sell effectively.

A Rule by Any Other Name

The need to make quick decisions in a highly charged environment barely begins to describe the challenges faced by equity managers. Fortunately, nature has endowed us with a powerful unconscious brain to help cope with such demands. One of the abilities of the unconscious is to let choices reflect stored heuristics or rules of thumb for decision-making. "When faced with a complex problem, people employ a variety of heuristic procedures in order to simplify the representation and the evaluation of prospects (choices)," says Daniel Kahneman.[2] But without clear and quick feedback, we are just as likely to formulate the wrong heuristic as the correct one. The use of such uncalibrated rules of thumb can be dangerous to portfolio performance.

Disciplined investing is, however, not the absence of heuristics. Rather, it is the mindful blending of conscious analytic thinking with intuition or gut feelings in order to make decisions effectively and quickly. This integrated approach requires the use of feedback to understand where decisions tend to work best and where refinement is required. Then working with this feedback you can shift toward doing more of what is working as you retool what's not. The result is a higher level of self-awareness that enables managers to invoke intuition effectively.

Buddha, the Ultimate Alpha Source

An extended stay in the Himalayas might be just the thing to help you develop greater self-awareness. This probably is not a practical option. Yet there are steps managers can take toward financial enlightenment that are simple and effective. Here are two ideas that are receiving positive reviews from practitioners.

First, be the oracle. Write down every sell you make and why you chose it. Do this at the very moment you actually decide to make the sell. Add in some color about the position, such as its unrealized gain or loss (i.e., looking for the disposition effect), recent price movement (i.e., volatility often affects sell decisions), and primary motivation for liquidating the position (i.e., stop loss, target price reached, thesis disproved). Fairly soon you will have data that can help you see patterns in selling that might prompt further investigation or improvements to your discipline.

Second, suspend judgment. Investment committee meetings often begin with an outpouring of opinions, judgments, and aching convictions. Once this highly charged momentum is under way, it is difficult to objectively listen to and examine facts. The self-aware investor guards against these group dynamics and works to capture maximum insight from diverse perspectives. Try starting your next meeting by suspending the judgments and asking that you and your associates focus only on facts for the initial 15 minutes or so. This will enable all participants to engage in the conversation with a common perspective and to question opinions before they are regarded as facts. A big part of developing greater self-awareness is simply making room for it.

Conclusion

Self-awareness is rapidly becoming a best practice among top investment companies. This softer aspect of investing can help you harden your active management processes. Self-awareness is built on three essential elements: (1) the desire to improve, (2) a clear understanding of current circumstances, and (3) unambiguous feedback about how any changes you make are working. As you strive for your own self-awareness, keep in mind this ancient philosophical question: "If selling is ineffective but there is no one there to measure its impact, is the portfolio's performance really suffering?"

Notes

1. Doc Childre and Bruce Cryer, *From Chaos to Coherence: Advancing Individual and Organizational Intelligence through Inner Quality Management* (Boston: Butterworth-Heinemann, 1998).

2. In Daniel Kahneman and Amos Tversky, eds., *Choices, Values and Frames* (Cambridge: Cambridge University Press, 2000), 65.

Further Reading

Cassell Bryan-Low, "Yoga Bears: It's No Stretch to Say Traders Are Taking Deep Breaths," *Wall Street Journal*, July 24, 2008, A1.

13 Stressing Performance

Nothing is more difficult, and therefore more precious, than to be able to decide.

Napoleon Bonaparte

No one has to tell you what stress feels like. It is your job to make the tough decisions about which names stay in the portfolio and which go. This is a burdensome responsibility, even in the best of times. But these are not the best of times. Your normal processes are being wrecked by a market slump well outside your career experience, combined with outflows that can be unnerving. If you are sensing in yourself a few raw nerve endings, that is only natural. It is one thing to survive stressful times and quite another to excel during them—ask any jet fighter pilot. In this essay we examine the nature of stress, its impact on critical thinking, and what top professionals are doing to harness its effects rather than allowing it to overwhelm them.

Feeling Performance

Stress isn't always a bad thing. After all, it is simply a state of heightened emotional and physiological awareness. Athletes, actors, public speakers, and others use positive stress to strengthen their performance. "Eustress," a term coined by researcher Richard Lazarus, is felt when the demands being placed upon us seem within our ability to handle.[1] Coping with these stresses is exciting and actually heightens our abilities. In other words "getting pumped up" to perform involves harnessing positive stress.

Negative stress or distress, on the other hand, is felt when we are overwhelmed. Fears of failure or feeling out of control are powerful stressors that can severely limit our thinking and actions. During such experiences, we are heavily driven by emotions that, while instinctive, are not the instincts that propel us to do our best. Learning what stresses you, and how to better manage these stressors, is all part of professional self-awareness.

Dr. Jekyll, Mr. Hyde

Stress can change who you are—or at least how you think and react. A diminished ability to consciously make good decisions is a common reaction to stress. Stress elicits our brain's primitive protective responses, that old "fight or flight" feeling. These ancient instincts worked well when we needed protection from a marauding predator, but they are much less helpful when managing modern sources of stress like market volatility or unhappy investors. This instinctive override of conscious decision-making limits us to only part of our brain, the part that doesn't want to analyze but prefers to feel its way to answers, referred to as the limbic system. It is triggered by one sensation or other and propels you into action. Although this facility for instant responses was vital to survival over the millennia, it is often poorly adapted to modern stresses. Some of the ways that stress and your unconscious can conspire to push you toward poor choices are described below:

• Narrow framing: Distress causes us to curtail research and investigation prematurely. This rush to be done results in limiting the number of options we consider, causing us to emphasize simplicity and expediency over thoroughness and accuracy.
• Shortened time horizon: Negative stress can push us toward a quick fix, even when that fix may be far from the optimal long-term solution. We just want the pain to stop right now, without regard to how much the relief will cost in the future.
• Heuristics: Stress can result in an overreliance on simple rules of thumb. When succumbing to the desire to "do something," we might repeatedly apply ineffective solutions rather than reassess the options available. Consider the simple case of misplacing your car keys—how many times do you look in the place you always put them before expanding your search to places where they shouldn't be?
• Negativity: Stressors can weaken our self-confidence, lower our creativity, and tilt our viewpoint so that more alternatives appear negative. Similar to narrow framing, this behavior both limits the universe of choices considered and focuses our attention on ones that aren't so appealing. This "glass mostly empty" approach to decision-making often becomes self-fulfilling.

Stress This

So how can you benefit from the current market chaos? One approach is to enhance and rely upon your self-awareness, discipline, and process.

Good coping skills help us negotiate stressful times. They enable us to increase our self-efficacy and perception of control. Dr. Albert Bandura defines self-efficacy as our sense of competence, our belief in our own abilities.[2] The more capable we feel in any given situation, the less distress our minds experience. Our sense of control also helps determine whether we experience eustress or distress. According to Drs. Harry Mills, Natalie Reiss, and Mark Dombeck, "The perception of being in control (rather than the reality of being in or out of control) is an important buffer of negative stress."[3] Our sense of competency and control, therefore, act together in determining our personal reactions to stressors.

Self-awareness, discipline, and process are the tools you possess to strengthen your feelings of self-efficacy and control. The more you understand and believe in what you do at each decision point, the better you can manage stressors. As you learn to harness stress, your portfolio decisions will begin to reflect your strategy and analytic thinking rather than those unexamined rules of thumb hiding in your unconscious.

Conclusion

Stress is part of life. Minimizing negative stress is a skill that can be developed. The further you develop self-awareness, discipline, and process, the better you will handle stress and the better the decisions you will be placing in your portfolio.

Managing stress and thinking clearly as markets gyrate around you can have an obvious impact on return. They can also mean the difference between having your portfolio, strategy, and processes well positioned for the eventual market rebound or being caught flat-footed while others are recapturing assets under management.

Notes

This essay first appeared in the midst of the market crash of 2007–2008. Its central message of understanding and managing stress continues to be relevant today.

1. Richard Lazarus, *Stress and Emotion: A New Synthesis* (New York: Springer, 1999), 32.

2. Albert Bandura, *Self-Efficacy: The Exercise of Control* (New York: W. H. Freeman, 1997), 36.

3. Harry Mills, Ph.D., Natalie Reiss, Ph.D., and Mark Dombeck, Ph.D., "Self-Efficacy and the Perception of Control in Stress Reduction," updated June 30, 2008, *Stress Reduction and Management*, http://www.mentalhelp.net/poc/view_doc.php?type=doc&id=15646.

Further Reading

Rhona Flin, *Sitting in the Hot Seat: Leaders and Teams for Critical Incident Management* (New York: John Wiley & Sons, 1997).

Gary Klein, *Sources of Power: How People Make Decisions* (Cambridge, MA: MIT Press, 1998).

Kathleen M. Kowalski-Trakofler, "Judgment and Decision Making under Stress: An Overview for Emergency Managers," *Journal of Emergency Management*, 2008.

14   Thesis, Narrative, or Just Another Disappointing Story

What is most important, then, is not dispelling particular erroneous beliefs (although there is surely some merit in that), but creating an understanding of how we form erroneous beliefs.

Thomas Gilovich, *How We Know What Isn't So: The Fallibility of Human Reason in Everyday Life*

Stocks are often managed on the basis of a thesis. This has come to mean that the manager has a clear expectation of how a stock will add alpha to the portfolio and she can express it in a tight sentence or two. The mere existence of a thesis is intended to suggest thoughtfulness, conviction, and discipline. However, the dictionary defines "thesis" as "an unproved statement or argument put forward as a premise." Too often the tentative nature of a stock's thesis is lost, inviting behaviorally motivated decisions that undermine performance. In this essay, we examine the nature of the investment thesis and how, without sufficient self-awareness, we can create just another disappointing story.

Mind Your Thesis

Science has made clear that the unconscious brain plays a significant role in the decisions we make. An essential role of the conscious brain, on the other hand, is thought to be the creation of narratives so that we can understand what our unconscious brain has already decided or done.

A stock thesis, therefore, can be either the result of intense research, process, and conscious deliberation or merely a story that connects unconscious desires, impulses, and choices into an account that sounds reasonable. In other words, the thesis you generate for stock ABC may be fact-based and built entirely from your analytic process, while the thesis you've constructed for stock XYZ might feel comparably formulated but might actually reflect much less discipline. Learning how to test the veracity of each thesis in your portfolio can help you to feed the strong positions as you weed out the weaker ones.

Selling Your Thesis

In comparison to buying, selling tends to receive short shrift in terms of research, back-testing, journal articles, and other measures of attention. The limited investment in selling is underscored when managers explain somewhat uneasily that their sells are not as disciplined or process-driven as are their buys.

Selling is, therefore, more judgmental and prone to behavioral influences. One manifestation of this lack of discipline is thesis drift. For example, a stock might initially be purchased based upon growth at a reasonable price (GARP), but as the price continues to fall it is reclassified and held as a value stock. This change in thesis might in fact be a case of nimble and responsive portfolio management, but it could also be just another instance of loss aversion. One of the two primary behaviors that make up the disposition effect, loss aversion is the persistent inability to push losers (positions with unrealized losses) out of the portfolio. Motivating this behavior is our need to avoid recognizing the loss and having to accept that our decision to own it was a mistake. We might also hold the unfounded hope that the stock will rebound. Loss aversion is typically indicated by a significantly lower turnover rate for substantial losers than for the balance of the portfolio. Redefining the thesis for a stock, as in the example above, can reflect the unconscious desire to avoid realizing a loss and formulating a narrative to help make that happen.

Painful Avoidance

Thesis drift can also result from cognitive dissonance. A term coined by the social psychologist Leon Festinger in the 1950s, "cognitive dissonance" refers to the discomfort we feel when holding on to mutually inconsistent beliefs.[1]

In finance, cognitive dissonance commonly involves our sense of self-efficacy. We are, after all, smart, trained, and capable investors, yet we often find ourselves owning a notorious loser. Our unconscious wants desperately for us to feel capable, but there is the not-so-small matter of this unfortunate position stinking up the portfolio. How we manage this dilemma can impact performance both today and tomorrow.

The self-aware professional confronts such situations by examining his process. His goal is to learn and improve so as to reduce the chance that the same misadventure will occur again. More emotionally motivated investors might formulate a narrative explaining why riding this stock down to the bottom was a reasonable decision. In such instances, the self-protective mandate of our brain may be initiated before we have even had a moment to think about what happened consciously. Realizing that our unconscious can override analytical thinking can help us learn from the decisions made in 2008 rather than put them behind us too quickly.

Conclusion

The thesis under which you hold a stock is only as good as the process under which it was developed. Self-aware investors with rigorous processes can rely on a stock's thesis to guide their decisions as well as to explain why it was purchased. But when it comes to selling, the lack of discipline and process make reliance on a thesis more challenging. Learning to question why a stock is being held with the same rigor used in deciding to purchase it initially is how many managers are preparing for the inevitable market rebound. The alternative may have you generating a narrative that your clients won't be happy with.

Notes

1. See Louisa C. Egan, Laurie R. Santos, and Paul Bloom, "The Origins of Cognitive Dissonance: Evidence from Children and Monkeys," *Psychological Science* 18 (November 2007), 978–983.

15 Dreaming of Alpha

Sleep is the interest we have to pay on the capital which is called in at death; and the higher the rate of interest and the more regularly it is paid, the further the date of redemption is postponed.

Arthur Schopenhauer, *Parerga and Paralipomena*

Investment decisions reflect the strategy, research, process, and discipline consciously developed over many years. They also, as we have seen, reflect influences from the unconscious brain—even inadequate sleep. Sleep deprivation is epidemic in America. Among stressed-out portfolio managers, sleep seems to be a rare asset. Beyond making you feel drowsy or in need of caffeine, insufficient sleep heightens behavioral responses, inhibits learning, and weakens decision-making. This essay looks at new research about "running on empty" and how it can undermine your performance.

Huh, Yeah, Right

Everyone knows what it's like to be sleep-deprived. Depending on how many hours are lost, and for how many consecutive nights, symptoms may range from a slightly wandering focus to full stupor. These commonly observed effects are easily reversed with extra sleep.

Yet even these transient effects can negatively impact investment decisions. Sleep deprivation can lead to stress, a subject we examined in chapter 13. Stress shifts the thought process, weakening analytic thinking and promoting emotional reactions. Higher emotional states enable behavioral forces to influence investment decisions more powerfully. Behavioral motivations, in turn, push decisions outside of your strategy and process, often negatively impacting return and alpha.

I Must Have Missed That

Inadequate sleep hampers learning—not just memory, but the ability to extract explicit knowledge and insights from new information. Our short-term memory loses its current content before the information is integrated with what we already know.

New research from Harvard Medical School further explains this process. The Harvard study shows that a loss of sleep adversely affects the functioning of the hippocampus, which plays a central role in the sorting and storing of information in the brain. In describing the effect of sleep deprivation on learning, based on research conducted using functional magnetic resonance imaging (FMRI), Harvard's Seung-Schik Yoo et al. write: "the impairment comes from impaired brain functioning—almost as if a temporary lesion had formed on the hippocampus—rather than reduced alertness and an inability to take in the images."[1] In other words, learning is reduced not merely because we have less energy or focus, but largely because our brain is unable to process and store what we think we learned.

It Felt Right at the Time

The amygdala is the part of the brain that helps manage emotions. It is particularly important in providing context and enabling us to effectively deal with negative or adverse stimuli. The prefrontal cortex controls logical or analytic thinking and helps to suppress inappropriate urges from the amygdala. Brain research informs us that sleep deprivation can deliver a powerful one-two punch that undermines our ability to make disciplined decisions. Inadequate sleep causes the prefrontal cortex to shut down, leaving only the emotional portion of the brain available for decision-making.

Compounding this situation is the fact sleep deprivation also leads to hyperactivity within the amygdala. While investigating the effect of inadequate sleep on the emotional centers of the brain, Dr. Yoo and colleagues reveal that the emotional centers of people sleep deprived were 60% more active than those with normal sleep.[2] Combining the reduced capacity of the prefrontal cortex with the higher excitement of the amygdala, the result is a brain that is incapable of logical or analytic thinking and that is likely to overreact to emotional stimuli—particularly of the negative variety.

Before You Doze Off

Being your best means you can attend to the small as well as large challenges you face. As we've seen, lack of sleep impairs decision-making by curtailing analytic thinking, heightening emotional reactions, and diminishing the ability to learn. This is not the sort of mental prowess showcased in the average "pitch book."

So how much sleep do we need? According to Dr. Christopher Drake, a senior scientist with the Henry Ford Sleep Disorders and Research Center, "The human body needs approximately seven to eight hours of sleep a night to maintain optimal alert levels during the day. The idea that many people need just four or five hours of sleep a night is a myth."[3]

Conclusion

A small and seemingly benign aspect of modern life, sleep deprivation can steal alpha from your portfolio. One of its effects is to substantially increase the likelihood of behavioral impulses affecting your buy and sell decisions. This risk is greatest where process and discipline are less developed—and that typically means selling.

Excess tiredness also robs you of focus and the ability to learn from new information. Since it heightens emotional responses, it can nudge you faster toward frustration or a regrettable outburst. All in all, sleep deprivation is not recommended for either your health or the health of your portfolio. Perhaps this information will motivate the addition of a new concept to your investment process—the alpha nap.

Notes

1. Seung-Schik Yoo, Peter T. Hu, Ninad Gujar, Ferenc A. Jolesz, and Matthew P. Walker, "A Deficit in the Ability to Form New Human Memories without Sleep," *Nature Neuroscience* 10 (February 11, 2007).

2. S. S. Yoo, N. Gujar, P. Hu, F. A. Jolesz, and M. P. Walker, "The Human Emotional Brain without Sleep: A Prefrontal Amygdala Disconnect," *Current Biology* 17, R877–R878.

3. See Melinda Beck, "Learning to Live Like an Early Bird," *Wall Street Journal*, updated March 4, 2008, http://online.wsj.com/news/articles/SB120457323625608259.

Further Reading

Ullrich Wagner, Steffen Gais, Hilde Haider, Rolf Verleger, and Jan Born, "Sleep Inspires Insight," *Nature*, January 22, 2004.

16 Motivated Reasoning

Whenever a new observation or thought came across me, which was opposed to my general results, [I tried] to make a memorandum of it without fail and at once; for I had found by experience that such facts and thoughts were far more apt to escape from the memory than favorable ones.

The Autobiography of Charles Darwin

Confronting our own mistakes in judgment is painful. It is one reason we rationalize. Rationalization can alter our interpretation of facts and lead to ineffective decisions. It is, therefore, one of the powerful unconscious forces that will drive you toward behavioral investing. In this essay we discuss rationalization, motivated reasoning, and five simple ideas for greater self-awareness.

Wishful Thinking

Rationalization is something we all do. You might even think of it as wishful thinking. By either name, it's the tendency individuals have to fit perceptions of reality into a mold that is heavily influenced by desire. It underlies why we are highly selective in the information we choose to process or how we choose to process it—for emotional rather than analytic reasons.

When it comes to equity investing, wishful thinking can be devastating. It can blind us to undesirable facts without which we are likely to make poor choices. Rationalizing pushes us toward overreliance on confirming information as we minimize the significance of information that conflicts with our desire. Since rationalizations come about comfortably and naturally, they often hide from our conscious ability to detect, let alone manage them.

Motivation Matters

One model for understanding how and why we rationalize is motivated reasoning, which suggests that the brain works to satisfy two distinct functions simultaneously—analytic thinking and emotional thinking. While analytic thinking strives to achieve the best fit for the data at hand (accuracy goals), emotional thinking tries to reinforce existing beliefs and diminish conflicting data (directional goals). The directional goals reflect our beliefs, biases, and desires—a great deal of which are acquired and recalled unconsciously. Interplay between accuracy and directional goals can result in radically different choices when we are given the same information at different times, depending upon our mood or feelings. Or as Professor Ziva Kunda puts it: "People rely on cognitive processes and representations to arrive at their desired conclusions, but motivation plays a role in determining which of these will be used on a given occasion."[1]

Nobody's Fool

Rationalization is often misconstrued as an intentional effort to fool ourselves. To the contrary, while rationalizing, we are often very sincere in our assessment of our reasons. Consider the commonly observed behavior from prospect theory involving "risk seeking with losses." A new position is down by 30% a short time after purchase. The manager decides to buy more, believing that it is at a bargain price and sure to bounce back. Objectively, this may represent a shrewd purchase of an overbeaten stock. On the other hand, it might simply be a case of taking on greater risk in the hope of ultimately breaking even.

Should the latter motivation be correct, it is likely that the investor truly believes there is good reason to buy more. This choice is not simply fabricated entirely from whole cloth, or as Kunda suggests: "People do not seem to be at liberty to conclude whatever they want to conclude merely because they want to. ... They draw the desired conclusion only if they can muster up the evidence necessary to support it."[2]

We construct narratives because we have a strong need to explain to ourselves and others why we make the choices and take the actions we do. The constructed story resolves the uneasiness that accompanies choices we have to make based on incomplete information and simultaneously enhances our self-esteem and sense of self-efficacy.

Rationalizing Behavior

Rationalization underpins many well-known behavioral tendencies: self-attribution, anchoring, hindsight bias, optimism bias, and overconfidence, to name a few. The emotional demands of investing can lead us to use motivated reasoning, which subtly pushes our information search and analysis toward answers that satisfy our inner needs rather than being the optimal analytic solution.

Moreover, the need to explain why we're doing what we're doing can lead to fanciful narratives that are completely believable. These pseudo-truths can then become part of our learning and knowledge base, resurfacing repeatedly from the unconscious as beliefs, biases, and heuristics. Once integrated into our unconscious brains, falsehoods are not easily dismissed or overwritten, because they possess an emotional charge from once having saved us from feeling bad. Identifying and confronting such inaccuracies among our beliefs is very difficult—or as Artemus Ward once said: "It ain't so much the things we don't know that get us in trouble. It's the things we know that just ain't so."

Conclusion

Rationalization reflects an internal struggle between analytic objectivity and wanting an outcome that coincides with a belief or desire. To satisfy both accuracy and directional goals, the brain converges on a solution that incorporates available information while minimizing negative and maximizing positive feelings.

The process of rationalization positions us to readily accept facts that support our desire or belief while urging us to hold unfamiliar or unpleasant facts to a higher standard. Unconscious filtering results in a narrative that passes both our conscious scrutiny and that of others whose respect we desire. Ironically, scrutinizing why we made certain decisions or took certain actions can provide the illusion of objectivity while serving our emotional needs. To make matters even more difficult, the more intelligent the person is, the better they will be at constructing and presenting a believable narrative.

Tough-minded investment management requires strong doses of introspection. To help you to implement your heightened self-awareness, here are five reminders to pin up on your office wall:

1. The brain tries to see relationships or stories, even when there are none.
2. The brain forgets and remembers what it wants, in a very biased way.
3. Narratives, even the most earnest of them, reflect motivated reasoning.
4. I will actively search for data that was overlooked or that contradicts my theories or beliefs.
5. How would someone who disagrees with me look at this data?

Notes

1. Ziva Kunda, "The Case for Motivated Reasoning," *Psychological Bulletin* 108, no. 3 (November 1990), 3.

2. Ibid., 6.

Further Reading

Thomas Gilovich, *How We Know What Isn't So: The Fallibility of Human Reason in Everyday Life* (New York: Simon and Schuster, 1993).

Thomas E. Kida, *Don't Believe Everything You Think: The Six Basic Mistakes We Make in Thinking* (Amherst, NY: Prometheus Books, 2006).

Brian P. McLaughlin and Amélie Oksenberg, *Perspectives on Self-Deception* (Berkeley: University of California Press, 1988).

17   Regrettable Choices

It isn't the burdens of today that drive men mad, but rather the regret over yesterday and the fear of tomorrow.
Robert J. Hastings, "The Station," *Baptist Press*, July 5, 1988

Equity investing requires the ability to price uncertainty. But at what emotional costs? Having to live with a poor outcome or the knowledge of a missed opportunity makes even the best of us want to kick ourselves. This essay examines how, if left unchecked, these feelings influence investment decisions in unintended ways.

Coulda, Woulda, Shoulda

Regret is the emotion we experience when confronted by a mistake, especially one for which we feel responsible or can easily imagine better options. Regret springs from poor results and foregone opportunities. The consequences can be severe, as in the case of the man who killed himself when, after years of playing a number in the lottery, he neglected to renew his multi-week ticket and missed the winning draw for 2 million pounds.

Thankfully, regret is not usually fatal. But it does cause pain—the sort of psychic pain that etches vivid memories into our brain. Avoiding such feelings again in the future then becomes a powerful motivator for decisions we make, a process called "regret aversion."

Small Gains and Large Losses

Regret aversion is one of the chief motivations behind the disposition effect. Formulated by Hersh Shefrin and Meir Statman, the disposition effect suggests that, when liquidity is needed, investors are more likely, or "disposed," to sell their winners and hold on to their losers.[1] Since the disposition effect is an extension of prospect theory, the motivations associated with it are commonly attributed to risk aversion with gains (taking profits quickly) and risk seeking with losses (preferring to ride them out in hope of eventually breaking even).

Yet Shefrin and Statman identified regret aversion as a fundamental motivator for the disposition effect. In this view, selling winners quickly reflects the desire to avoid the regret of having a stock run up in price through today only to watch it come all the way back down tomorrow—round-tripping. Similarly, holding on to losing positions can be an aversion to the regret associated with feeling like a loser once a "paper loss" is realized. Avoiding painful or unpleasant feelings is a universal defense mechanism. Understanding one's tendency to experience regret aversion can help in making the right risk/return tradeoffs.

Not Adding Up

Investors are more likely to add to or make incremental investments in portfolio positions that are down rather than up, according to analyses performed by Cabot. This behavior is at odds with the time-honored adage, "Starve your losers and feed your winners." It is, however, consistent with what we know about prospect theory, which suggests investors tend to be more risk seeking with losses and risk averse with gains.

Not adding to winners is also explained by regret aversion. In his paper "Are Investors Reluctant to Sell Their Losses?," Terrance Odean suggests that not buying more of a portfolio winner may reflect the manager's regret over not having purchased more of it initially.[2] Thus, in order to avoid the regret of admitting the mistake of purchasing too little, the manager avoids adding to the position despite the belief that the stock will continue to outperform. When the initial buy is significantly less than the average full position weight, such regret aversion can sacrifice significant alpha if it becomes a persistent tendency.

More Than a Feeling

According to researchers Marcel Zeelenberg and Rik Pieters, "Regret is a negative, cognitively based emotion that we experience when realizing or imagining that our present situation would have been better, had we acted differently." They explain: "The core element of regret is cognitive in the sense that in order to experience regret one needs to compare the current state of affairs with what it would have been had one decided differently."[3]

To better understand the effect of feedback on regret, they examined games of chance, specifically the National Lottery and the Postcode Lottery in the Netherlands.

The National Lottery works like most other lotteries, in that people buy a ticket based on numbers they choose. People who actually buy tickets are most likely to be aware of the winning numbers. Regret over not playing this game is therefore experienced by relatively few people. The Postcode Lottery is different. The number you bet is restricted to your postal code—similar to a U.S. Zip Code except that it serves no more than 30 addresses. Your choice is to buy a ticket or not. If your postal code is the winning number, then you very likely will learn both the winning number and who the winners are—one or more of your closest neighbors. This additional feedback about the forgone opportunity provided by the Postcode Lottery makes the outcome more available and produces greater levels of regret, because if your neighbor wins, you should have won too—leading you to think, If only I'd have purchased a ticket this one time. Over the years, the experience of having "just missed out" also produced significant regret aversion—as suggested by the relatively large participation rate for this lottery over that seen in the National Lottery.

Regret aversion is thus linked to how vividly an individual can compare the benefits of what might have been to what really occurred. This type of counterfactual thinking can be triggered easily by owning a stock that tanks or owning too small a position of one that has taken off. Sorting out which experiences are important learning experiences and which are random luck (good and bad) requires a careful examination of investment decisions over time, not just the formation of a vivid memory.

Conclusion

Regret aversion is a powerful force. It can shape which positions we purchase and which we sell in ways that override intention. Adds to existing positions are also affected by the desire to avoid regret.

Feedback involving poor outcomes and foregone opportunities pushes our regret buttons. And this is the very type of information managers confront regularly as they watch once-good ideas turn into losers and see the names they should have owned take off without them. Developing regret aversion is natural. Learning to manage it, however, can save you from regrettable performance.

Notes

1. Hersh Shefrin and Meir Statman, "The Disposition to Sell Winners Too Early and Ride Losers Too Long: Theory and Evidence," *Journal of Finance* 40, no. 3 (July 1985), 778.

2. Terrance Odean, "Are Investors Reluctant to Sell Their Losses?," *Journal of Finance* 53, no. 5 (November 1998).

3. Marcel Zeelenberg and Rik Pieters, "Consequences of Regret Aversion in Real Life: The Case of the Dutch Postcode Lottery," *Organizational Behavior and Human Decision Processes* (March 2004), 156.

18   Endowing Success

The salesman knows nothing of what he is selling save that he is charging a great deal too much for it.

Oscar Wilde, "House Decoration," lecture, May 11, 1882

Holding winners well past their alpha generation is a tendency regularly observed among professional investors. These once highly productive buys inevitably devolve toward reversion to the mean, yet they seem to hold a special place in the minds (or is it hearts?) of the managers. One explanation for holding winners too long is the endowment effect—valuing items higher when we possess them, which makes it more difficult to find a clearing price. This essay takes a look at the endowment effect and how it can impact the management of portfolio positions.

Trials of Being Well-Endowed

The endowment effect stifles selling. Richard Thaler first suggested the theory of the endowment effect in 1980, explaining that once a person possesses an item, he values it more than he did before he owned it.[1] The item becomes part of the individual's endowment and grows in value or importance for that reason alone. In other words, you would refuse to pay the same price for an item that you would want to sell it for. At first blush, this might sound like simple horse trading—buy low and sell high. But the roots of the endowment effect go deeper into our psyche.

Motivating this behavior is loss aversion. Taking a loss is an emotionally expensive experience. Studies suggest that the displeasure of losing one dollar is two to three times greater than the pleasure of winning the same dollar. This asymmetry between winning and losing results in our avoiding losses in order to avoid the associated pain. Adding to this emotional battle is the fact that selling tends to be perceived as a loss, while buying tends to feel more like a gain—even when there is no price movement. An implication of this asymmetry is that loss aversion will, on average, induce a higher dollar value for owners than for potential buyers, reducing the set of mutually acceptable trades.

No Monkeying Around

The sense of attachment we feel for possessions appears to be primal. Studies conducted by Keith Chen of Yale University involving capuchin monkeys and by Owen Jones at Vanderbilt University involving chimpanzees both support the notion that the endowment effect emanates from deep within our DNA.[2]

The capuchin monkeys were taught to trade coinlike tokens for food. They were offered similar amounts of food simultaneously at two windows in a specially designed pen. In any experiment, choosing one window would yield exactly the food offered, while choosing the other window would yield a 50/50 random chance of receiving the proffered amount or a different amount. In one set of experiments, the surprise amount was always more than what was offered, while in another set of experiments the surprise amount was less. After many trials, the monkeys showed a preference for choices where surprises were presented as bonuses rather than losses. They would choose the certain payout when they concluded the surprise was going to be a loss; and they chose the 50/50 payout when they concluded it provided a random gain. They exhibited classic loss aversion.

In a separate study, chimpanzees were given a choice between peanut butter bars and frozen juice bars. The peanut butter bars were preferred by 60% of chimps when both treats were offered simultaneously. But when offered in sequence, their preferences shifted. Specifically, when all the chimps were first given peanut butter bars, only 20% traded them for the juice bars, even though 40% preferred the juice bars initially. Even more interestingly, when all of the chimps were first presented with frozen juice bars, only 20% traded them for the subsequently proffered peanut butter bars—yet the peanut butter bars were the 60% favorites. Their preferences apparently changed based on which treat they were given first or possessed—a sure indication of the endowment effect.

Thinking Is Endowing

The sense of possession can be stimulated merely by thinking about an item. In a 2008 paper, James Wolf, Hal Arkes, and Waleed Muhanna discuss how exposure to an item (thinking about it and holding it) can increase feelings of ownership: "that is, examining an item for longer periods of time resulted in greater attachment to the item and thus higher valuations."[3] Could the act of reviewing portfolio positions also enhance their endowment?

It certainly is possible. The research suggests that asset-specific analysis can promote enhanced feelings of ownership toward that asset, which then inflates the value assigned to it. Add to this scenario the added stimulus of the asset being a winner (i.e., unrealized gain), and the stage is set for hesitancy in selling. Unfortunately, learning from our mistakes is a poor approach for overcoming the endowment effect. Studies indicate that market exposure—that is, repeated attempts at essentially the same choice—does not result in eliminating the tendency to overvalue possessions. In other words, being a professional is no guaranteed defense against our unconscious motivations.

Conclusion

Managing positions is tough business, and managing winners is no less so. The bias toward selling winners quickly (i.e., risk aversion) has received considerable attention in the academic literature. The tendency to hold winners past their prime, however, is less mentioned, although it is proving to be very common among professional money managers and equally detrimental to portfolio performance.

The endowment effect is one explanation for our holding winners too long. We become fond of what we own—to a level where our selling price floats above what reasonable buyers are willing to pay. And the more we evaluate our winners, the more difficult it may become to sell them without a sense of loss. It turns out that discipline, analysis, and thesis confirmation may excite that monkey inside all of us and we, well, just go bananas.

Notes

1. Richard Thaler, "Toward a Positive Theory of Consumer Choice," *Journal of Economic Behavior and Organization* 1 (1980), 39–60.

2. Keith Chen, Venkat Lakshminarayanan, and Laurie R. Santos, "How Basic Are Behavioral Biases? Evidence from Capuchin Monkey Trading Behavior," *Journal of Political Economy* (2006); Owen D. Jones and Sarah F. Brosnan, "Law, Biology, and Property: A New Theory of the Endowment Effect," *William and Mary Law Review* 49, no. 6 (2008).

3. James R. Wolf, Hal R. Arkes, and Waleed A. Muhanna, "The Power of Touch: An Examination of the Effect of Duration of Physical Contact on the Valuation of Objects," *Judgment and Decision Making* 3, no. 6 (August 2008), 476–482.

Further Reading

Daniel Kahneman, Jack L. Knetsch, and Richard H. Thaler, "Experimental Tests of the Endowment Effect and the Coase Theorem," *Journal of Political Economy* 98, no. 6 (December 1990).

19   Counterfactual Investing

So we have the paradox of a man shamed to death because he is only the second pugilist or the second oarsman in the world. That he is able to beat the whole population of the globe minus one is nothing; he has "pitted" himself to beat that one; and as long as he doesn't do that nothing else counts.

William James, *The Principles of Psychology*

Imagination and creativity, when calibrated, help turn good ideas into winning strategies and great stock picks. Imagination also can push investors toward unproductive decisions—ones that feel right while lowering performance. One form of runaway imagination is known as counterfactual thinking. This type of deliberation can negatively affect your interpretation of information, adversely influencing the buys and sells you make. This essay looks at counterfactuals and how they might affect your performance.

Darn, I Just Missed It

Emotional responses to outcomes often are influenced by what might have been. Counterfactual thinking, as such thoughts are known, often ends in regret. As discussed in chapter 17, the emotional response to an event depends on how easily one can conjure up alternate outcomes that are either better or worse. An often-cited example is missing a flight by 5 minutes or by 45 minutes. People who just barely miss their flight tend to kick themselves more than those who missed their plane by a mile. The closer you were to making the flight, the easier it is to construct an alternative outcome or counterfactual that triggers regret.

When Worse Is Better

Who should be happier, the person who wins the silver medal or the one who wins the bronze? The silver medal winner is objectively better off—he or she is closer to gold than the winner of the bronze medal. Yet that proximity is precisely why a silver medalist enjoys second place far less than the bronze medalist enjoys coming in third.

In analyzing medal winners from both the Olympics and the Empire State Games, researchers Thomas Gilovich, Victoria Husted Medvec, and Scott Madey found that silver medalists were less happy with their accomplishment than bronze winners.[1] The silver medalists created a counterfactual based on not having won gold, focusing upward and ruminating about how close they came to first place. This thinking induced feelings of regret and frustration—thoughts of if-only-I-had. The bronze medalists, in contrast, focused downward and formulated a more positive counterfactual. Rather than being among the others hitting the showers, they were at least up on the awards pedestal and very happy to be there. Counterfactual thinking does more than color how we feel about past events; it can also trigger surprising actions.

Phantom Gains and Losses

Investors sometimes generate counterfactuals when they consider repurchasing previously owned stocks. In their paper "Once Burned, Twice Shy," Michal Strahilevitz et al. state that investors are more likely to repurchase a stock when its current price is below that at which it was sold, and less likely to repurchase it when the current price is higher. The counterfactuals motivating these choices are explained as follows: "Investors who buy a stock at a lower price than they previously sold it experience the pleasure of knowing they are better off than if they had never sold that stock. Investors who buy stock at a higher price than they previously sold it are painfully aware that they are worse off than if they had simply never sold that stock."[2] The terms "knowing" and "being aware" express the feelings investors have about these purchases based on their if-only-I-hads.

The more analytic question for these investors is, Which stocks of those I can purchase today—even those that I previously owned—are likely to outperform going forward? Viewed within this dispassionate framework, repurchasing a stock one had once owned at a price higher than one sold it for might be a good investment decision—presuming it offers a strong likelihood of outperforming going forward. The thought of paying more today than the previous sale price, however, is an emotional obstacle that is often difficult to get around.

The counterfactual thoughts make the investor feel a loss or gain based on price movement over a time period when the stock wasn't even owned.

This distracts from focusing on today's thesis and how the stock will perform going forward. The result can be murky judgment—where emotions emanating from if-onlys override objective analysis.

Can't Win for Losing

Counterfactuals can also shape the choices made when adding to current positions, according to Strahilevitz et al. Investors tend to add less frequently to holdings whose price has gone up since being purchased ("winners") and add more frequently to those whose price has dropped ("losers"). The counterfactual created for winners is, "I should have purchased more when it was cheap." Investors prefer to avoid feeling the regret that this counterfactual brings, so they tend to avoid these buys. The counterfactual for buying losers seems to be associated with avoiding the pain of losing, as in, "If I buy more now and the price moves up, I can regain my current losses." This counterfactual is consistent with prospect theory and resetting one's reference point. The team's research demonstrates, however, that the investors were no better off preferentially adding to losers rather than to winners. Feeding their counterfactuals did not enhance their returns.

Conclusion

Counterfactual thinking can hurt performance. It has the power to make Olympic silver medalists feel worse than those taking bronze. It can drive investors to make decisions based on if-onlys rather than facts. Counterfactuals can cause you to consider repurchasing stocks based more on price movement since you last sold them than on current theses. They can also keep you from adding to current portfolio winners—perhaps missing a huge run-up in the bargain. Self-awareness counters such ineffective thinking—it keeps decisions factual.

Notes

1. Thomas Gilovich, Victoria Husted Medvec, and Scott F. Madey, "When Less Is More: Counterfactual Thinking and Satisfaction among Olympic Medalists," *Journal of Personality and Social Psychology* 69 (1995), 603–610.

2. Michal Strahilevitz, Terrance Odean, and Brad M. Barber, "Once Burned, Twice Shy: How Naive Learning and Counterfactuals Affect the Repurchase of Stocks Previously Sold," *Journal of Marketing Research* 48 (2011), S102–S120.

Be not afraid of greatness: some are born great, some achieve greatness, and some have greatness thrust upon them.

William Shakespeare, *Twelfth Night*

Success in active management demands skill. But where does this skill come from? Some believe it is innate, as Warren Buffett suggested when he said, "I was born at the right time and place, where the ability to allocate capital really counts. ... I won the ovarian lottery. I got the ball that said, 'capital allocator—United States.'"[1] A growing body of evidence, however, points to nurture, not nature, as the source of greatness in all manner of performance. This essay examines the importance of improving deliberately in order to achieve top performance.

The Source of Success

Remarkable talent is no longer attributed solely to inherited special traits. One supporting fact for this turnaround in perspective is that child prodigies very rarely develop their early gifts to become top talents as adults, whereas the elite performers in virtually every field showed no special aptitude for the work as youngsters prior to extensive coaching. Research points to simple hard work as the deciding factor.

Well, maybe it's not that simple. In spite of extensive education, training, and hard work, most professional investors still do not realize top performance. One reason is that all too many investors fall victim to the skill trap. They become experts but have difficulty delivering expert performance. Great professional performance necessitates more than mastery of the field; it requires the right kind of learning.

Learning to Win

Practice does not make perfect—it only makes permanent what you practice. Ironically, the lengthier the career, the more challenging it can be to perform. According to Anders Ericsson, Roy Roring, and Kiruthiga Nandagopal of Florida State University, "three decades of research into expert performance has shown that experience itself—the raw amount of time you spend pursuing any particular activity, from brain surgery to skiing—can actually hinder your ability to deliver reproducibly superior performance."[2]

Ericsson's pioneering work demonstrates that great performance comes about not from innate talents or experience, but only from what he terms "deliberate practice." Deliberateness has been described as "activity that's explicitly intended to improve performance, that reaches for objectives just beyond one's level of competence, provides feedback on results and involves high levels of repetition."[3]

Deliberate practice has two distinct qualities. First is focused execution, where learning and improving are the conscious intent of every decision and action. Focused execution helps reprogram skills and heuristics stored deep in the unconscious, enabling us to hone our skills by purposefully doing better. Second is clear, prompt feedback. It supports mindfulness, or staying consciously focused on the task of improving, and is also used to measure improvement progress and to formulate minor adjustments along the way. Top performers, those that stand apart from their peers, never stop improving. They hone every skill needed within their careers. Even Tiger Woods rebuilt his swing twice—after already having become the world's best golfer.[4]

Being a world-class investor is no less demanding, although the skills you isolate and improve will be different. One example is the use of mental models to help guide fundamental analysis toward sound conclusions. Building and refining mental models of your world and how it works can be a part of your deliberate practice. The more complete the model for types of assets or market conditions, the deeper the skills that can be isolated and improved. Mental models also facilitate broader and faster access to knowledge stored in long-term memory—facilitating instant recall of deep domain expertise.

Practice Schmactice

Can investing be improved with practice? Yes, but such practice is done differently than the way one would practice hitting a baseball. You don't have the opportunity of having practice assets tossed your way, nor is it possible to follow the path of an asset without interruption from the moment it's initially purchased through its final disposition. So you have to find ways to improve that fit the profession of money management. This includes learning to practice "in the moment" of actually performing. Doing this means that you bring a heightened self-awareness to the choices you make throughout the day and work at improving as you manage the portfolio. You'll also need to capture the appropriate information to provide useful feedback about how well you are implementing the desired changes and whether or not you are achieving the desired results.

Consider building position size. Let's say that the analysis of the portfolio's history confirms that you are slow in adding to new positions with early gains. This hesitancy with feeding winners is consistent with regret aversion. Not building up these positions more effectively is costing the portfolio considerable alpha. Your goal for improving is simple—be aware of younger winners, confirm their thesis, and get to full weight as quickly as possible. Remaining mindful of this goal throughout the barely contained chaos of a typical day is the challenge. A simple tool can help.

You receive a report each morning listing the newer positions with unrealized gains (i.e., winners), plus their current and target weights. This information provides that extra nudge required to keep your goal at the top of your mind. The report also provides valuable feedback on how effectively you are implementing the desired change.

Deliberate Success

Deliberateness requires a shift in mindset. Active management must focus carefully on every decision point in the investment process: name selection, sizing, adds, trims, and sells. Deliberate practice is formulated to refine the skills required for each decision type, much as a golfer separately improves driving, the short game, and putting.

The new mindset makes improvement its focal point—not merely doing the job. Conscious attention is used to retrain skills and judgments and realize better outcomes. Targeted mindfulness will help you manage behavioral tendencies until specific skills are enhanced. Armed with better insights, you can make better decisions that can deliver better results.

Conclusion

"Naturals" are people who have invested ten years or more in deliberate practice, channeling their energy into becoming better and better. They accomplished this by isolating specific elements of their domain and improving the corresponding skills.

Equity management involves a series of skills that can be improved. Improving requires a mindset that includes deliberate practice. Clear intent and focus, down to the smallest process elements, and quick feedback are what transform desire into results. Perhaps it's time to become unnaturally talented.

Notes

1. "Homespun Wisdom from the 'Oracle of Omaha'," ed. Amey Stone, *BusinessWeek Online*, July 5, 1999, http://www.businessweek.com/1999/99_27/b3636006.htm.

2. K. Anders Ericsson, Roy W. Roring, and Kiruthiga Nandagopal, "Giftedness and Evidence for Reproducibly Superior Performance: An Account Based on the Expert Performance Framework," *High Ability Studies* 18, no. 1 (June 2007), 3–56.

3. K. Anders Ericsson, Ralf Th. Krampe, and Clemens Tesch-Romer, "The Role of Deliberate Practice in the Acquisition of Expert Performance," *Psychological Review* 100, no. 3 (1993); Michael J. A. Howe, Jane W. Davidson, and John A. Sloboda, "Innate Talents: Reality or Myth," *Behavioural and Brain Sciences* 21 (1998).

4. Geoffrey Colvin, "What It Takes to Be Great," *Fortune Magazine*, October 19, 2006, http://money.cnn.com/magazines/fortune/fortune_archive/2006/10/30/8391 794/index.htm.

21   Inside-Out Investing

It is the optimistic denial of uncontrollable uncertainty that accounts for managers' views of themselves as prudent risk takers, and for their rejection of gambling as a model of what they do.

Daniel Kahneman and Dan Lovallo, "Timid Choices and Bold Forecasts: A Cognitive Perspective on Risk Taking"

Analysis is fundamental to equity investing. Deep dives require that you apply extensive energy and talent into understanding a company and its ability to deliver excess returns. Yet this activity can awaken behavioral tendencies that short-circuit your analytic processes. Consequently, rigorous analysis can heighten the potential for over optimism at exactly the moment when greater objectivity is needed. This essay examines the importance of calibrating judgments as a critical element of self-awareness and honing investment skill.

The Deep Dive

The greater the opportunity or risk associated with a decision, typically the more analysis is performed. Investors commonly employ a process or framework to guide them through the steps of detailed company analyses. Such steps are analogous to what biologists, chemists, physicists, and others refer to as the scientific method.

Presented with a challenging decision, we first reduce the problem to its major components. These, in turn, are further deconstructed to smaller and smaller components that facilitate our clear understanding and confident resolution of these more manageable elements. After gathering and analyzing appropriate data for all subcomponents, we reverse the process, with the goal of understanding the initial or larger question by assembling our understanding of the components and their relationships to each other.

Done well, deep analysis can lead to rich proprietary insights about a company's likely performance or intrinsic value. This is the "information advantage" that skilled professionals bring to portfolio management. Intense rigor can also produce overly optimistic conclusions—reflecting a runaway process that is being powered by emotions rather than analytics.

Motivation, Please

Thinking is more emotional than commonly believed. The cognitive process itself draws upon both the analytic and emotional parts of the brain. Reasoning, therefore, is a blended outcome of the "best fit" for the data being considered plus the automatic filtering and shaping of that data to support beliefs, biases, or desires within the unconscious. This model of thinking, discussed in chapter 16, helps explain why even the most careful experts sometimes engage in overly optimistic assessments when performing rigorous analyses.

According to Shelley Taylor and Jonathon Brown, overly optimistic assessments share certain qualities: "three main forms of a pervasive optimistic bias: (i) unrealistically positive self-evaluations, (ii) unrealistic optimism about future events and plans, and (iii) an illusion of control."[1] Rigorous analysis often ignites these unconscious motivations. The results can include both narrow framing of the possible outcomes (resulting in extreme possibilities being heavily discounted or ignored) and higher certainty or success rates being assigned to each subcomponent evaluated (as if by merely analyzing an uncertain event it has been rendered less risky).

Judgment is further affected when issues are viewed as unique. Uniqueness is a favorite rationalization for why relative comparisons are not applicable or for defending an idea in the face of strong evidence that it is not a particularly good one. Kahneman and Lovallo offer this perspective: "The natural way to think about a problem is to bring to bear all one knows about it, with special attention to its unique features."[2] The tendency to focus on uniqueness is a risk worth avoiding when developing a favorable thesis.

Inside-Out

The deep dive often reflects what Kahneman terms the "inside view." This is the view of a situation that is based on judgments applied to specific facts about that situation, especially when they are not benchmarked to similar experiences. Michael Mauboussin offers a less flattering description: "An inside view considers a problem by focusing on the specific task and by using information that is close at hand, and makes predictions based on that narrow and unique set of inputs. These inputs may include anecdotal evidence and fallacious perceptions."[3] Yet inside views are the very cornerstone of the process used by analysts and managers to shape investment decisions.

One technique recommended by both Kahneman and Mauboussin for managing the perils of inside views is to balance them with "outside views." Outside views are based entirely on facts about comparable alternatives. They ignore the specific attributes of the situation under consideration and instead look at typical outcomes for similar situations.

Consider a company analysis that requires forecasting the expected revenue stream from a drug currently in Phase 3 trials. Formulating such an outcome conventionally involves many steps, including estimating the chances that the trial will be successful, anticipating a likely efficacy for the new drug, and then translating this information into estimates of market size, unit demand, cost, and price. Each of these seemingly objective judgments will reflect selected experiences in your memory and the belief you have in management's ability to think strategically and execute effectively—a classic inside view. Approaching the same task using an outside view, one would begin by identifying like companies that have attempted similar endeavors. Once identified, the results from this group of comparable situations would be analyzed to determine benchmarking information such as percentage of success/fail, mean outcome when successful, and the standard deviation across results.

Avoiding inside views is not realistic for most investors. Seeking assets that can generate excess returns is, by definition, hunting for uniqueness. Highly skilled investors, however, are experts at isolating truly unique characteristics for any opportunity. Then they rigorously analyze these characteristics as appropriate, drawing upon outside views to sharpen judgments and spotlight key risks.

Conclusion

Rigorous analysis is, in large part, what professional investors rely upon to make buy and sell decisions. The risk inherent in such analyses is that they can lead to overly optimistic assessments that reflect the shortcomings of inside views. Outside views can be incorporated into the evaluation process, helping you to calibrate interim steps of your analysis. The take-away for refining your investing is this: Inside views may be essential for identifying opportunities that are well reasoned, while outside views help keep your judgments reasonable.

Notes

1. S. E. Taylor and J. D. Brown, "Illusion and Well-Being: A Social Psychological Perspective on Mental Health," *Psychological Bulletin* 103 (1988), 193–210.

2. Daniel Kahneman and Dan Lovallo, "Timid Choices and Bold Forecasts: A Cognitive Perspective on Risk Taking," *Management Science* 39, no. 1 (January 1993), 26.

3. Michael J. Mauboussin, *Think Twice: Harnessing the Power of Counterintuition* (Boston: Harvard Business School Press, 2009), 3.

22   Beware Phantastic Investments

A great deal of intelligence can be invested in ignorance when the need for illusion is deep.

Saul Bellow, *To Jerusalem and Back: A Personal Account*

By its very nature, investing requires making estimates about future events. These estimates reflect the manager's analysis of facts combined with imagining likely but unsure outcomes. Imagination is what enables skilled investors to see opportunities ahead of the crowd. It can also excite emotions that make it difficult to distinguish real investment opportunities from "phantastic" ones.

Emotional Investing

The theory of emotional finance examines investor tendencies through the lens of Freudian psychoanalysis. Sigmund Freud suggested that thoughts cause people to experience two basic types of feelings, pleasurable or painful. Pleasurable feelings, understandably, are sought out, and painful ones are avoided or repressed. According to Freud, the seeking and avoiding all occurs within the unconscious. In addition, he proposed that the mind often simultaneously holds conflicting emotions about a person, idea, or thing … like/dislike, love/hate, and trust/distrust being common conflicts. Because these conflicting feelings are both strong and unknown to the conscious mind, they affect our beliefs about our relationship with the world. Investing thus involves entering into an emotional and unconscious relationship with the assets you own.

The research team of Richard Taffler, a professor of finance and investment, and David Tuckett, a professor of psychoanalysis, who together developed the theory of emotional finance, extend these Freudian concepts into investing. According to Professor Taffler, "People are prone to unrecognized emotions—fears and fantasies—which Freud described as the main components of unconscious mental life and the deep drivers of human judgment."[1] These unrecognized emotions are often more powerful than either facts or the results of objective analysis, driving investors to oscillate between feelings of hope and fear about their investments.

Taffler and Tuckett are quick to acknowledge the vital contributions that behavioral finance has made to the understanding of decision-making under uncertainty. Their concern with the direction of current behavioral finance inquiry, however, is that it often tends to focus on the cognitive underpinnings of ineffective judgmental tendencies alone. They argue that cognition and emotion need to be studied together to truly explain investor behavior.

Separating Fact from Fantasy

Formulating judgments about information and acting on it before it is fully priced into the market is how managers add value to investing. Typically, they identify promising candidates (either purely bottom-up or supported with systematic screening) and then choose specific names to own. Ultimately, purchasing an asset requires a commitment—capital, ongoing attention, and choosing when to liquidate.

David Tuckett sees the ownership commitment as the formation of an important emotional relationship with the asset—one that can bring happiness or let you down. He suggests, "When they commit to an investment strategy, they commit to an imagined relationship with consequences for reward and loss which induce feelings such as pleasure and pain—not unlike a marriage contract." He goes on to say, "Psychoanalysts postulate three principal kinds of imagined emotional relationships, governed by L (loving), H (hating), and K or –K (knowing or anti-knowing)."[2]

Objective decision-making requires "knowing" the asset—being aware of its potential to please and disappoint and accepting both as a balanced reason for owning it—an integrated view. This reflects the type of unemotional objectivity that is associated with disciplined investing. It grounds manager decisions so that winners are sold as their thesis is achieved and losers are reevaluated and then sold or kept based on their go-forward potential.

Conversely, "anti-knowing" involves splitting potential pain from pleasure. For buys, this amounts to avoiding the unpleasant feelings related to the risk of loss while focusing on the potential pleasure from a gain. This

form of relationship makes assets overly attractive while they are performing and then horribly disappointing when their momentum turns. Such
abrupt and full-throttle reversals between "loving and hating" causes over-
buying and overselling as investors gather up pleasure and disgorge pain.

Emotional Narratives

Assets commonly are chosen because they represent a strong thesis. As discussed in chapter 2, the thesis is a simple narrative description of all the
facts known about the asset plus a judgment of why these facts indicate
likely outperformance. Formulating the thesis involves assessing potential
risks as well as returns. A fundamental aspect of this process requires managers to contemplate future events whose outcomes are highly uncertain.
Contemplating the unknowable produces anxiety for managers, who then
inject emotional content into their analyses. These anxieties push buttons
within the manager's unconscious, having the effect of short-circuiting
their otherwise disciplined approach to decision-making.

There are two types of anxiety produced by investing, according to
Taffler and Tuckett: "One set of uncertainties was caused by unavoidable
information asymmetries as they tried to sort out the mass of ambiguous
information with which they were bombarded at the moment of decision-
making. Another set was determined by the fact that, however well they
know the present, the future is inherently unknowable."[3] Information
asymmetry undermines conviction, niggling away at the manager's resolve,
or as the researchers suggest: "This judgment creates anxiety. First, there is
the fear that the information they have been given by the firm's management is untrustworthy, second there is the fear that even if the information
and their underlying analysis is correct, the rest of the market may never
come to share their view."[4]

While the manager's unconscious is battling information asymmetry, it
is also being harassed by uncertainty about the future. Imagining tomorrow's outcomes is one thing; betting that they will materialize is quite
another. Together, these two sources of uncertainty create anxiety that, as
mentioned, we often deal with by splitting the good feelings (the upside)
from the bad (the downside)—a defense mechanism that calms emotional
stress and bolsters conviction while increasing portfolio risk. Although your
current processes can guide imagination toward a potentially unique idea,
they may offer no protection from the anxieties generated throughout the
analysis and ownership of the asset.

You're Phantastic!

It always pays to be mindful that an asset is a probabilistic mix of risk and return, with the potential to deliver both pain and pleasure. This integrated perspective can enable investors to manage a thesis more effectively— objectively knowing when to hold their conviction and when to change. When assets are held for reasons rooted more in emotion than reasoned expectation, the unconscious has more control over investment decisions. As positions migrate from gain to loss and back again, these shifts in performance trigger emotions that invoke thoughts about your relationship with the asset, and these thoughts foster further emotions, and so on. The cycle repeats until the unconscious has you cornered—you either love or hate the investment.

When you are overexcited, you tend to act emotionally, often running roughshod over any remnants of analytic thinking. This behavior relates to what Taffler and Tuckett have termed a "phantastic object," which is derived "from two psychoanalytic concepts. The term object is used in the same sense as it is in philosophy, as a mental representation; in other words as a symbol of something but not the thing in itself. The term phantasy (which gives rise to the term phantastic), as mentioned in Freud's (1908) view ... refers to an imaginary scene in which the inventor of the phantasy is a protagonist in the process of having his or her latent (unconscious) wishes fulfilled (Laplanche and Pontalis, 1973, p. 314). Thus, a 'phantastic object' is a mental representation of something (or someone) which in an imagined scene fulfils the protagonist's deepest desires to have exactly what she wants exactly when she wants it."[5] Relating this concept to investing, managers initially see the phantastic object as possessing superior qualities, well above the usual investment opportunity, allowing them to achieve their emotional goal of delivering exceptional returns with no downside risk. In other words, this opportunity is simply phantastic. But because this impression of the asset is created in part by suppressing thoughts and feelings about its limitations and risks—what Tuckett and Taffler describe as "splitting"—its inevitable disappointment gives credence to the lingering doubts stored in the unconscious. What once was loved becomes hated and a hold quickly turns into a sell.

The Emotional Factor

In their monograph *Fund Management: An Emotional Finance Perspective* (CFA Institute, 2012), the research team discussed findings from in-depth interviews conducted by Professor Tuckett with over 50 fund managers from around the globe. One of the many insights from these interviews was the nature of risk, specifically risk felt by managers. When talking about their greatest exposures, this group of managers tended to discuss information risk, the unpredictable nature of the future, business risk, and career risk. Professor Taffler explained, "These are very different to conventional measures of risk. Yet these are the real risks managers worry about. So the concept of risk also has a key emotional dimension."[6]

Taffler and Tuckett see conventional risk models as providing pseudo-defenses against uncertainty. They suggest that the practice of performing regressions against historical relationships can lull individuals into believing that they know more about the future than is possible. This overoptimism about the future or, conversely, overconfidence about the ability to control uncertainty facilitates managers in splitting—enabling them to focus on potential gains, since they feel as if they have already managed the risks. This interpretation of unconscious processing is consistent with Kahneman and Lovallo's finding that the mere investigation of uncertainty can lead to an illusion of control and underappreciation of actual risk.[7] One likely example of this behavior is when managers override portfolio optimizers to retain or pump up the size of favorite positions. These decisions to "go against the science" of the risk models are commonly defended as the manager's having a strong intuition about an asset: An alternative explanation is that she is reaching for a phantastic object.

Conclusion

Reasoning involves telling stories to yourself. The more objective the stories are, the more sound is each thesis and investment decision. Thesis formulation relies on making judgments about events whose outcomes are inherently uncertain. These judgments produce anxiety that often has an adverse impact on the assessment of risks as assets are being evaluated.

The new theory of emotional finance examines how the unconscious management of anxiety affects investment decisions. It offers additional insights into how unconscious motivations easily erupt into buy and sell decisions. The brain is terribly adept at substituting emotions for facts in order to make a financial decision that feels right. This unconscious means of decision-making represents a constant counterforce to your intended discipline and process. Heightened self-awareness is one way to combat the unconscious forces that drive unintended decisions. You just can't build fantastic performance by owning phantastic objects.

Notes

1. Richard J. Taffler, Martin Currie Professor of Finance and Investment, University of Edinburgh, exclusive interview with Cabot Research LLC, December 23, 2009.

2. David Tuckett, "Addressing the Psychology of Financial Markets," *Economics: The Open-Access, Open Assessment E-Journal* 3, no. 40 (2009), 5.

3. David Tuckett and Richard Taffler, "Phantastic Objects and the Financial Market's Sense of Reality: A Psychoanalytic Contribution to the Understanding of Stock Market Instability," *International Journal of Psychoanalysis* 89, no. 2 (2008): 407.

4. Richard J. Taffler and David Tuckett, "Emotional Finance: Understanding What Drives Investors," *Professional Investor* (Autumn 2007), 18–20.

5. Tuckett and Taffler, "Phantastic Objects and the Financial Market's Sense of Reality," 395.

6. Taffler, interview with Cabot Research, December 23, 2009.

7. Daniel Kahneman and Dan Lovallo, "Timid Choices and Bold Forecasts: A Cognitive Perspective on Risk Taking," *Management Science* 39, no. 1 (January 1993), 17–31.

Further Reading

Arman Eshraghi and Richard Taffler, "Hedge Funds and Unconscious Fantasy," University of Edinburgh Business School Working Paper, November 26, 2009, http://ssrn.com/abstract=1522486.

Richard J. Taffler and David Tuckett, "How a State of Mind Abets Market Instability," *Financial Times*, September 21, 2007.

23   Thanks for the Memories

Memory itself is an internal rumour.
George Santayana, *Reason in Science*

The bedrocks of professional investing—experience, judgment, intuition, and deliberation—rely heavily on the use of memory. Though it is fundamental to learning and making effective choices, memory is also highly imperfect. While memories are sometimes cherished, they can push you toward investing misadventures. This essay examines how experts look at memory and its potential for generating investing shortfalls.

Motivated Memory

Memory is the result of how information is captured, stored and retrieved. Most of what we remember after an experience (visual, auditory, etc.), happens automatically and pretty much involuntarily. Supporting this process, the brain chooses to capture information it finds interesting, useful or that stimulates strong feelings. It encodes this information into long-term memory that sits in the unconscious brain. Unavailable for conscious or deliberate probing and review, memories are accessed and reconstructed upon demand, through either willful intent or involuntarily. Emotions affect both the encoding and retrieval of memories. Excitement about a series of great buys or pain from liquidation of deep losers can change how information is perceived, making it more vivid and stickier. Incorrect learning results from the deep encoding of such emotionally charged impressions. If such incorrect learning transforms into a strongly held belief, it can lead to repeated ineffective decisions.

Market turmoil and position volatility can cause stress and a high emotional state. When these emotions are present during the retrieval of memories they can limit the brain's searching for information or answers, often pushing it toward simple and emotionally soothing solutions, rather than analyzing a more complete set of options.

Make My Memory

False memories may help explain why ineffective tendencies creep into otherwise sound investment processes. Researchers Brian Gonsalves and colleagues studied the formation of false memories using functional magnetic resonance imaging (fMRI) technology. Participants were shown images of certain objects and accompanying words, with some words matching the objects shown and other words being unrelated. The participants were asked to use their imaginations to visualize the images represented by the words that did not correspond with the objects shown. What they remembered is fascinating. When asked what objects they had been shown, they included in their answer objects that had not been shown but whose images they had imagined. According to Gonsalves et al., many of the visual images that the subjects were asked to imagine were later misremembered as actually having been seen. As their findings indicate, "Object representations produced when an exceptionally vivid visual image of an object is generated are similar to those produced when that object is actually seen." Their findings suggest that a vividly imagined event can leave a memory trace in the brain that's very similar to that of an experienced event. Using fMRI measures, they were able to accurately predict when an imagined image would be remembered as having been seen, because highly vivid imaginings stimulate the same part of the brain as do real experiences. They conclude: "Our findings show that these errors of memory can be produced in a laboratory setting, and that their likelihood is increased when precuneus, right parietal, and anterior cingulate regions are engaged in the service of visual imagery, producing visual representations that may resemble those that would have been produced if the object had actually been perceived."[1]

Memories can also be suggested, even impossible ones. Professor Elizabeth Loftus asked adults if they had met Mickey Mouse when they were children. Some were first shown a video of people having fun at Disney World. Recollection of this experience was significantly higher among those who saw the video. Loftus believes that when in a positive emotional state the participants' old and fragile autobiographical memories were unconsciously rewritten to include a personal experience with Mickey that never happened. To confirm this phenomenon, another group was asked about whether they ever met Bugs Bunny instead of Mickey while at Disneyland. Among those shown the same Disney video, 16% recollected shaking hands with Bugs at Disney land, even though he is not a Disney character, but a Warner Brothers creation. They recalled an event that was not simply unlikely but impossible.

Interestingly, participants in both studies that viewed the video overwhelmingly denied it affected their recollections, suggesting that not only is memory malleable but internal defenses refuse to accept this proven quality. Loftus concludes: "These studies show that with suggestion and imagination, a significant minority of people can be led to believe that they had experiences that were manufactured, and many of them elaborated upon those false experiences with idiosyncratically produced details."[2]

Thesis, Process, and Discipline Remembered

Despite its known flaws, memory remains a primary tool used by managers for learning about their strengths and shortcomings. Other conventional sources of portfolio information like return and attribution help some, but using them to improve is like a golfer playing at night using only the total score for feedback. Whether hitting above or below par, the golfer can't see where performance is strongest or where it needs refinement.

Overrelying on their memories, managers have no choice but to imagine where their alpha comes from. They commonly misidentify which skills are strongest and which need improvement or precisely how to improve. And this leads to missed opportunities regardless of the quintile they are in. Studies of actual portfolios conducted by Cabot repeatedly show that:

• Some strong buyers can and do consistently sell winners prematurely— giving away alpha in the process.
• Managers that pick great names often do not feed them sufficiently— reluctant to pay up for a stock on the run.
• Selling winners tends to be difficult—they are often held well past their ability to generate excess returns and drag down performance.

Ineffective decisions such as these can start with a faulty memory. These memories then go on to produce flawed beliefs and rules of thumb, which then are used to make investment decisions. In addition, critical analysis of skills and process is hampered as recollections reflect motivations as well as facts. You see only what your memories allow and your decisions integrate half-truths as if they were rigorously constructed data.

Conclusion

Memory defines who you are and what you think. It is, however, imperfect, fragile and quite capable of making falsehoods seem like facts. Memory recall can range from consistent and complete, to partial and irregular.

As reliable as memories may seem, their flaws can hurt portfolio performance. This can be the result of false memories that tilt decisions toward ineffective choices. Faulty memories may be the product of weak encoding, retrieval or both. Comparing your treasured recollections to verifiable information is one straightforward antidote to ineffective memories. The alternative may position you as a prisoner of a past that never really happened.

Notes

1. Brian Gonsalves, Paul J. Reber, Darren R. Gitelman, Todd B. Parrish, Marsel Mesulam, and Ken A. Paller, "Neural Evidence That Vivid Imagining Can Lead to False Remembering," *Psychological Science* 15, no. 10 (October 2004), 659.

2. See Kathryn A. Braun, Rhiannon Ellis, and Elizabeth F. Loftus, "Make My Memory: How Advertising Can Change Our Memories of the Past," *Psychology and Marketing* 19, no. 1 (2002), 4.

Further Reading

Tim R. Holcomb, R. Duane Ireland, R. Michael Holmes, Jr., and Michael A. Hitt, "Architecture of Entrepreneurial Learning: Exploring the Link among Heuristics, Knowledge, and Action," *Entrepreneurship Theory and Practice* 33, no. 1 (January 2009).

24 Skills, Process, and Behaviors

Discovery consists of seeing what everybody has seen and thinking what nobody has thought.

Albert von Szent-Györgyi[1]

Skill is what separates top-performing managers from the pack. Ironically, little is known about investment skill, how it is developed, how to measure it, or how to improve it. The inability to isolate and measure, or even knowledgably discuss, specific investment skills has inhibited professional development. A new framework for evaluating investment skills can quantify strengths and weaknesses, calibrate their interaction with management processes, and identify behavioral tendencies. In this essay we discuss the potential of a new framework to help managers achieve their best.

Eagle, Bogey, or Mulligan

Professional performance requires deliberate practice—the kind that identifies and improves specific skills. For instance, in golf, deliberate practice means more than just hitting balls at the driving range. Instead, it takes dedicated time with each club learning to drop the ball within a target range. Skilled golfers who draw crowds at tournaments can consistently hit the right shot in any situation.

Portfolio managers face equally high expectations, and yet their ability to improve is restricted by inadequate feedback. Return, relative return and alpha, performance attribution and factor loading ... that's all there is. These values tell you how you performed overall, but offer little insight for improving. The latter two analytics in particular focus on outcomes of position weights, not the investment decisions themselves. As has been discussed before, this level of feedback is equivalent to a golfer playing with a blindfold and only being told the final score. It's impossible to know what part of the game is working—driving, irons, or putting—and where improvement is needed. Without this insight, a golfer would have no choice but to rely on hindsight and what feels right. Professional investors face exactly this same dilemma.

Oddly, the total absence of useful feedback is so long-standing that neither portfolio managers nor their clients seem to notice. There is considerable consternation and handwringing about underperformance, but it has not resulted in a demand for better feedback. The industry continues to measure outcomes (the golf score) while hoping to see skills improve somehow. Far less than ineffective, the current situation can drive managers deeper into poor performance. The weak feedback they receive together with their highly imaginative memories can lead to completely inaccurate intuitions about what's working and what's not. Incorrect intuitions coupled with the emotional need to "do something" can motivate managers to mistakenly fuss with their one alpha-generating skill while ignoring other skills that are actually hurting performance. What they need is the ability to drill down into a portfolio's history and confirm which skills are strong and which aren't, while also uncovering any process shortcomings and behavioral tendencies.

Your Choice

Investing is built on three basic skills: buying, selling, and position sizing. Familiar as these terms are, few professionals know with any degree of confidence how much of their portfolio alpha comes from just the buying. Not knowing how effective each skill is means that any attempt to improve is, at best, based on a hunch. And that is not how top professionals in other high-performance careers go about improving.

Thinking about performance as a portfolio of decisions, rather than holdings, is at the heart of one new analytical framework that is being developed at Cabot. The goal is to rigorously measure skills, process, and behaviors so that managers can do more of what they do well and have the necessary information to make small refinements that have a high likelihood of helping them improve. They can strengthen their skills and processes as they eliminate behavioral tendencies. This framework sees behavioral tendencies as the manager's being pushed by the unconscious toward poor choices wherever skills and process are underdeveloped.

Examples of the interplay among skills, process, and behaviors are offered below.

• Buying is all about name selection. Skilled buyers choose names that out-perform—more often than not. Their picks tend to lift up portfolio performance. How much buys outperform and how long they do so are measures of the manager's information advantage.

Hindsight bias can dampen buying. For example, a value manager is good at buying beaten-up stocks, yet still has trouble beating the bench-mark. She remembers vividly the great buys she has made over the past couple of years. However, a careful analysis of all of her buys shows that while she is very good at buying cheap, low-momentum stocks, she consis-tently loses when stretching for the super-discounted names. Her strength is identifying value and may not extend to turnarounds.

• Selling is about capturing the alpha from great buys and limiting losses. Selling winners involves pushing them out as they reach exhaustion, not afterward. Selling losers effectively requires knowing when or whether a down position is likely to bounce back.

Risk aversion involves selling winners prematurely, well before they reach their full potential. Typically, it is motivated by a fear that the market will take back any gains. This habit can be very expensive, as great buys are pushed out before they deliver their full alpha to the portfolio.

Loss aversion is holding on to losers far too long. It can reflect the uncon-scious desire to avoid the psychic pain that might accompany selling these positions and realizing the losses. These positions can hurt performance by leading to further declines or by tying up capital in unproductive stocks.

The endowment effect is the tendency to hold on to winners well past their ability to generate alpha. These old favorites have stopped outper-forming but have earned a special place in the manager's heart. They tend to stay at the back of the line when sell candidates are being considered, tying up significant capital that would be more productively allocated to newer names.

• Sizing is a skill evaluated separately from buying or selling in the new framework. Effective sizing means that, on average, most of the portfo-lio's capital is invested in stocks that are outperforming the rest of the portfolio, all other things being equal. Analyzing sizing ability involves looking at initial position build-up as well as the impact of subsequent adds and trims.

Regret aversion is the tendency to hesitate in adding to winning posi-tions. Once the stock begins to take off, the manager mentally kicks himself for not having purchased more when the price was cheaper. The stock then takes off undersized and the portfolio loses.

Conclusion

What distinguishes delivering professional results from merely being a professional is skill. Traditional portfolio analytics have not supported managers well in understanding or honing their skills. Quantifying how well buys, sells, and sizing add to performance is the first step in building self-awareness and improvement.

The rigorous and granular analysis of skills, processes, and behaviors is essential for improving. Lacking this type of fact-based feedback, managers have little option but to continue guessing at their strengths and shortcomings, and how to become better. Incorporating elements of the new analytic framework can help you improve the same way elite golfers do—of course, you could just hope that the rest of the field keeps on hitting mulligans.

Notes

1. See Irving John Good, ed., *The Science Speculates: An Anthology of Partly-Baked Ideas* (New York: Basic Books, 1963), 15.

The ideas expressed in this essay are those of Cabot Research LLC. They reflect the research and pioneering analytics formulated during the development of Cabot Behavioral Analysis® (Patent No. 7,680,717, March 16, 2010; Patent No. 7,756,769, July 13, 2010; Patent No. 7,848,987, December 7, 2010).

25 Processing Success

But over time more thoughtful decision-making will lead to better overall results, and more thoughtful decision-making can be encouraged by evaluating decisions on how well they were made rather than on the outcome.

Robert Rubin, Harvard University commencement address, 2001

Managers should love their process, not the stocks they hold: This is the wisdom handed down by great investors over the ages. The more defined and effective the process, and the more it is adhered to, the better and more repeatable the decisions. Yet evidence suggests that process is not implemented to the same degree that it is talked about. This essay discusses the nature of mistakes and how to avoid them by using a checklist.

Mistakes Happen

The nature of errors in professional decision-making was pondered by philosophers Samuel Gorovitz and Alasdair MacIntyre.[1] Ignorance and ineptitude were the primary reasons for mistakes, according to their theory. Ignorance refers to decisions made without benefit of pertinent knowledge, whereas ineptitude concerns not using all the knowledge available—that is, poor discipline.

It turns out that we are much more tolerant toward mistakes of the first type than the second. In practice, managers are not expected to anticipate every market correction, but they are expected to follow their process when making investment decisions. Perhaps ferreting out ineptitude is an unconscious motivation behind the intense probing by clients and their consultants in the aftermath of poor performance.

It's Complicated

Knowing more makes us smarter and, at the same time, makes managing what we know ever more difficult. Physician and Harvard Professor Atul Gawande, who has studied highly skilled decision-making under stress, points out: "Know-how and sophistication have increased remarkably across almost all our realms of endeavor, and as a result so has our struggle to deliver on them."[2] Expert investment coach Lawrence Evans puts a finer point on this topic: "I have studied experts in a number of areas—race car drivers, surgeons, marketing professionals, portfolio managers, and the like. They are all smart, yet they often succumb to the inexorable infiltration of complexity compounded by innovation."[3]

Evans and his team of coaches work exclusively with portfolio managers, and they regularly see practice fall short of intent. "These often truly brilliant managers know their process and can explain them very articulately, but they don't always follow them as they go about their typical day," Evans explains. A major reason for poor adherence to process, he says, is due to the process itself: "It's often a conceptual model of how decisions should be made rather than simple steps that can be followed."[4] Inconsistent or underwhelming performance is the cost borne when intention and action differ.

Steps to Success

Decision-making processes are being strengthened dramatically in many professions with the help of a simple tool—the checklist. Prosaic as they might seem, these pithy lists are helping professionals improve their performance in all manner of skilled activity from saving lives to protecting fortunes. Pilots have long used checklists. They understand that the complexity associated with flying can lead to mistakes, and even minor errors must be avoided. Surgeons around the world increasingly use checklists to reduce manageable errors. As Dr. Gawande explains, checklists are needed because "[y]ou see increasing mistakes … in almost any endeavor requiring mastery of complexity and of large amounts of knowledge."[5] Simple, well-conceived lists enable top professionals to more consistently deliver their best results, according to a study he and fellow researchers completed for the World Health Organization.

Professional investors are also improving their performance with checklists. Lawrence Evans finds that the majority of his clients embrace checklists as they complete his intense coaching experience. According to Evans,

"Conviction is a powerful reason for buying or owning a share ... but results improve when you know why you have the conviction. It's why I recommend a conviction checklist. The purpose of it is to be consciously aware of why you are making this decision [buy, sell, or hold] and also to consider how you are feeling at the moment it's being made."[6] Evans believes that faithfully jotting down reasons for conviction as decisions are being made is one of the best ways to learn about your real investment process. And this feedback can go right back into strengthening process and decision-making.

Less Downside, More Upside

Avoiding mistakes of ineptitude is just one way process improves performance. Assuring that each decision reflects, or is compared to, the rigor you've set for yourself is the way process enables managers to build a stronger floor to their investing. In explaining how checklists strengthen processes, Atul Gawande suggests: "They provide a kind of cognitive net. They catch mental flaws inherent in all of us, flaws of memory and attention and thoroughness."[7]

Equally important is the fact that process can enable managers to invoke their intuition and creative thinking more powerfully. Extreme situations sometimes require innovative solutions. Piloting through uncharted waters has historically been the exclusive domain of the most senior decision maker—the portfolio manager. Unfortunately, being left to one's own mental abilities at such moments can compound rather than resolve problems. The stress experienced during extreme moments limits creativity or can be just plain debilitating.

A more robust approach for confronting a crisis, while smack in its midst, is to follow your process. That entails developing a crisis management process before it's needed. It involves thinking broadly through what information you'll need, from whom, and what authority each person will have to act; and codifying all this information into a series of steps that can spring into action when needed. It can be your "When the *?#! hits the fan" checklist. The purpose is to cause you to pause, stay objective, and get the facts available to do your best when you might be feeling your worst.

Conclusion

Delivering consistent performance requires more than skill and intuition. Coach Evans offers this keen observation: "Let's not forget that while intellectual superiority can help investing, it's always trumped by superior processes. In fact, behind every legendary investor, you'll find a checklist that is ruthlessly followed."[8]

The challenge is to go beyond believing that process is important and to make it part of your daily reality. Clear and observable process, with or without checklists, enables you to make decisions in line with intentions, guides creative problem solving, and supports more effective learning. The alternative might find you delivering results that are, well, listless.

Notes

1. Samuel Gorovitz and Alasdair MacIntyre, "Toward a Theory of Medical Fallibility," *Journal of Medicine and Philosophy* 1, no. 1 (1976).

2. Atul A. Gawande, *The Checklist Manifesto* (New York: Henry Holt, 2009).

3. Lawrence Evans, Oxygen Coaching, Ltd., exclusive interview with Cabot Research LLC, May 28, 2010. Learn more about Oxygen Coaching at http://investing. businessweek.com/research/stocks/private/snapshot.asp?privcapId=104484229.

4. Ibid.

5. Gawande, *The Checklist Manifesto*.

6. Evans, interview with Cabot Research, May 28, 2010.

7. Gawande, *The Checklist Manifesto*.

8. Evans, interview with Cabot Research, May 28, 2010.

Further Reference

Dr. Sunil Eappen, Chief of Anesthesiology, Massachusetts Eye and Ear Infirmary, exclusive interview with Cabot Research LLC, June 8, 2010. (The MEEI introduced surgical checklists throughout their hospital on June 7, 2010, under the leadership of Dr. Eappen.)

It is nice to know that the unconscious is minding the store when the owner is absent.
John A. Bargh and Ezequiel Morsella, "Mind Wide Open"[1]

All decisions can be explained, but few are motivated for the reasons believed. That's because unconscious forces motivate behavior in ways that are both subtle and stunning. Priming is one mechanism that shapes our thoughts, feelings, and actions. This essay examines the power of priming on financial decision-making and suggests basic steps you can add to your investment process to manage its effects.

Igniting Nondeliberation

Priming is a mechanism that influences decisions unconsciously. As defined by researchers Dalia Gilad and Doron Kliger: "Priming is a process of activating particular connections or associations in memory prior to carrying out an action or task."[2] When activated, these emotional connections and associations make specific knowledge stored in memory more salient and accessible, tilting the way you view and interpret information. The tilting causes you to make different choices than you would have if the priming hadn't occurred.

Priming effects endure well past the moment of exposure, according to Professors John Bargh and Erin Williams. Their work indicates that "most people are aware of the powerful influences that emotions can have over immediate behavior and judgments, but remain unaware that these influences can carry over into unrelated contexts in which decisions and behavioral choices are made."[3] In other words, an update on your fund's peer ranking at the start of the day can affect how you react to new ideas presented in investment committee that afternoon: whetting your appetite for either risk seeking or risk aversion.

Resolutely Malleable

Feelings about others literally run hot and cold. Yale researchers investigated how temperature priming affects perceptions of emotional warmth attributed to a third party. On the way to their presumed task of interpreting the written profile of a fictitious individual (referred to as the target), subjects were intercepted and asked to help a fumbling research coordinator by briefly holding the coordinator's drink. Hot coffee was handed to half the participants and iced coffee to the others. "As hypothesized, people who had briefly held the hot coffee perceived the target person they subsequently read about as 'being significantly warmer,'" write Lawrence E. Williams and John Bargh.[4] The participants who were handed the cold beverage were less favorable in assessing the emotional warmth of the identical target. According to Williams and Bargh's conclusion, the same part of the brain that registers emotional warmth and personal security is also stimulated by physical warmth. The priming tricked the brain, causing the experience of physical temperature to be carried forward and make more available associations that led to inferring either emotional warmth or coolness about the target.

In a separate study, participants who had been exposed to the idea of rudeness were considerably more likely to interrupt a subsequent conversation with a researcher than were those individuals who were primed with the idea of politeness. In yet another experiment, Bargh and Erin Williams found that "subtle priming of the stereotype of the elderly (which includes the notions that the elderly are forgetful, as well as physically slow and weak) caused college students to walk more slowly when leaving an experimental session and to subsequently have poorer memory for the features of a room." In a fourth study, students who said making their mothers proud was one of their goals outperformed others in a verbal test, but only when they were primed about their maternal goal just prior to testing.[5] Central to these and other findings is that priming activates knowledge, beliefs, and emotions that alter decisions and even performance: and it does so completely outside of awareness.

Primed Numbers

Priming also sways financial decisions. A positive mood has been shown to increase the salience of confirming information while making challenging data less vivid. The opposite is true when one feels poorly. How you feel rather than what you know may, therefore, alter the intrinsic value you arrive at for a company under assessment or your willingness to buy or not buy a stock with no change in facts.

In their study "Priming the Risk Attitudes of Professionals in Financial Decision Making," Gilad and Kliger tested the effects of priming on risk taking. First, participants were primed by reading one of two versions of an article about an individual visiting a casino with each version having a different plot and outcome. In one version, the individual gambled heavily and won big; in the second version, the protagonist refrained from gambling and narrowly avoided financial ruin.

Participants then undertook a series of simulated investment decisions. Those primed with the successful gambler story made bigger and riskier choices than their counterparts. In explaining how the priming affected the risk takers, the authors suggest: "They had higher expectations for positive outcomes, and lower expectations for unfavorable ones."[6] The risk seekers appreciated that they were making riskier choices, but believed that the positive outcome was more likely—an acceptable bet.

Priming Is Everywhere

Social primes are one source of priming and can result from a variety of factors. For example, the relative status of investment team members can affect how their input or judgments are perceived. Similarly, the presence or absence of consultants at a client meeting may unintentionally alter the frankness of discussions. Knowing in advance whether investment committee votes are being recorded can unconsciously cause people to filter the ideas discussed toward those that seem reasonable and easily defended, while steering away from ideas that might be valuable but reflect more intuitive connections and lack analytic backup. Priming can also come from environmental cues. Examples of environmental priming include optimistic or pessimistic research consumed prior to a decision, being above or below your benchmark at the close of a quarter, and strong or erratic movement of asset prices. Volatility is a particularly interesting example. It's rarely offered up as an explicit criteria in buy or sell strategies. Nevertheless, it regularly is shown to be highly correlated with the investment behaviors (choices) of some portfolio managers—suggesting that erratic price movement niggles at their unconscious brains in consistent ways.

Prime Ministering

Intentionally priming yourself to make better decisions would be great, but unfortunately does not work. Professor Bargh explains the shortcomings of this approach: "Using subtle cues for self-improvement is something like trying to tickle yourself."[7] In other words, your unconscious is smarter than you are and can't be fooled intentionally. You can, however, build checks into your process to trap or minimize the unintended impacts of priming. In addition to self-reflection, you might consider these simple steps:

• Start meetings with a short discussion of neutral off-topic information. This can help in flushing out emotions and inclinations that were pre-loaded unknowingly.
• Rotate who runs meetings. Formally giving authority to junior team members can help counterbalance the "Big Kahuna" effect.
• Change your environment. Moving to different rooms, reorienting seating, or simply standing for a short meeting can help sidestep habitual behaviors and facilitate conscious deliberation.

Conclusion

Performance is dependent on instinct as well as objective analysis. An idea is often sensed to be good or bad well before it is understood. In support of intuitive judgment, Ap Dijksterhuis suggests that recent theoretical analyses of intuition have emphasized the importance of immediate, automatic influences on choices and decision-making. These have been touted as the mechanisms underlying the "gut feelings" or "hunches" that, far from being random or illusory, do a fairly good job of directing us.[8]

External stimuli, both perceived and outside of awareness, often awaken specific instincts or biased perceptions. Priming can dramatically alter what and how information is perceived: changing like to dislike, openness to dismissal, and risk aversion to risk seeking. Building a few simple precautions into your process can help manage the undesirable effects of priming. Attention to these unintended influences just might help you deliver prime results.

Notes

1. John A. Bargh and Ezequiel Morsella, "Mind Wide Open," *Psychologist* 21 (2008), 297.

2. Dalia Gilad and Doron Kliger, "Priming the Risk Attitudes of Professionals in Financial Decision Making," *Review of Finance* 12, no. 3 (2008).

3. John A. Bargh and Erin L. Williams, "The Automaticity of Social Life," *Current Directions in Psychological Science* 15, no. 1 (2006).

4. Lawrence E. Williams and John A. Bargh, "Experiencing Physical Warmth Promotes Interpersonal Warmth," *Science* 322 (October 24, 2008).

5. Bargh and Williams, "The Automaticity of Social Life," 3.

6. Gilad and Kliger, "Priming the Risk Attitudes of Professionals in Financial Decision Making."

7. John Bargh, interview with Benedict Carey, "Who's Minding the Mind," *New York Times*, July 31, 2007.

8. See A. Dijksterhuis and L. F. Nordgren, "A Theory of Unconscious Thought," *Perspectives on Psychological Science* 1 (2006), 95–109.

Further Reading

John A. Bargh and Ezequiel Morsella, "The Unconscious Mind," *Perspectives in Psychological Science* 3, no. 1 (2008).

27 Fear, Anger, and Risk

Anger rests in the bosom of fools.

Ecclesiastes 7:9

Risk management is as much about emotions as it is about math. Yet emotions are seldom, if ever, discussed at risk conferences or in risk literature. It's a bias, of course, in that the elements of risk are viewed as wholly outside of the decision maker—to be managed analytically like pieces on a chessboard. Decision research says otherwise. Feelings of fear, anger, and sadness can propel you toward risk-seeking or risk-averting behaviors, deftly overriding conscious intent. This essay considers a key element absent from modern risk models—the emotional factor.

Guts and Brains

Risk-adjusted thinking is not natural. Humans are predisposed to focus on gains and losses separately. This bimodal tendency is rooted in the brain's prime motivation to pursue pleasure and avoid pain. Data, news, and environmental cues ignite emotions that cause you to swing from anger to sadness, hope to despair, and optimism to pessimism faster than you can snap your fingers. Emotions can easily affect the way you think and often push you toward unintended choices.

Emotions play many roles in our lives. Scientists believe that emotions initially enhanced our ability to survive—including that old fight or flight sensation. They also help us sense safety and support much-needed connections with others. Emotions also try to help us make financial decisions—a challenge for which they are poorly calibrated. While this ability may improve in another million years or so, managing the impact that emotions have on financial decisions is of critical importance today. Without emotional self-awareness, you are highly susceptible to overruling your well-reasoned intentions—whether stretching beyond established risk guidelines or overriding what the risk model produces. And these urges are more likely to hit when uncertainty peaks and the predetermined path just doesn't feel right anymore—usually the worst time to go with your gut.

Being Driven

Some emotions increase your appetite for risky behavior. For example, anger is known to promote risk seeking, since anger also makes you feel excess certainty about a favorable outcome, greater situational control, and a high amount of responsibility for making things happen. Anger also inspires you because it's accompanied by a weak anticipation of the effort required to do whatever it is you feel compelled to do. It also encourages optimistic expectations about future outcomes and promotes careless thinking.

In contrast, fear is associated with low feelings of certainty, control, and personal responsibility, but high anticipated effort. Fear tilts your brain to more pessimistic interpretations, with risk aversion as the natural byproduct.

Sadness has the peculiar effect of making change preferable, whatever the cost. Jennifer Lerner and Dacher Keltner have found that "sadness has this effect on making people pay more to buy things, and making them impatient and willing to forgo money they could get in the future in order to get something smaller right now. Not only do they want to get more stuff, they want it more immediately."[1] The feelings that Lerner and Keltner describe reflect high risk-taking due to reduced analytic thinking and greatly restricted impulse control.

Pushy and Persistent

Feelings go deep. The forceful influences of emotions on financial decision-making are well documented, exemplified by loss aversion, risk aversion, and the endowment effect. These tendencies prompt investors to make ineffective choices and to do so repeatedly and with a naïve sense of accomplishment.

Feelings also have a long half-life. Once aroused, emotions can linger in the unconscious and impact future decisions that are unrelated to the initial stimuli. Stretching to buy a stock outside of normal parameters may reflect shrewd opportunism or uncharacteristic risk-taking—the latter perhaps due to residual anger from being cut off in traffic on the way to work.

Assessing future events based on emotions that were triggered earlier happens all the time. It's what psychologists refer to as the "appraisal effect."

The impact of an initial emotional experience can dramatically alter how a subsequent emotional event is experienced. One such mechanism, referred to as "emotional blunting," happens when an initial emotion negates the effect of a subsequent and different emotion. For example, if you first experience sadness, it might blunt the onset of anger from a later experience that more typically makes you see red rather than feel blue—whether being cut off in traffic or having to reprimand inappropriate behavior. When individuals each experience the appraisal effect or blunting, it is then possible for generally like-minded team members to find themselves at odds regarding a buy, sell, or hold decision simply because of the way they are feeling on that particular day. In short, the emotions stirring within the unconscious play a significant role in determining how you feel about risk—and that's something they don't teach in finance courses.

Risk Attribution

Emotions sway even the most stoic of risk managers. "Before you can even form a thought, emotions are influencing your judgments," writes Professor Lerner. She adds: "We now know that the model of rational, self-aware decision making fails to accurately describe thought processes in the real world. To begin with, most human cognition is unconscious—that is, we lack awareness of our mental processes."[2] It's this weak awareness coupled with strong emotional drivers that shape many risk decisions well before you're even aware that a decision is needed.

Feelings also shape how we judge the actions and intentions of others. "Individuals induced to feel anger also tend to make more punitive attributions than those induced to be in a neutral state," say Professors Winterich, Han, and Lerner.[3] So when you are angry, it's easier to blame a poor decision on an analyst, a trader, or a research report than to face your own culpability. By placing the source of the problem outside of yourself, you're on the road to making a weaker decision that reflects the misattribution of cause versus analytic judgment.

Conclusion

Emotions drive your decisions when you're not looking. They can substantially and imperceptibly alter the riskiness of choices. You can manage your emotional influences through a combination of self-awareness and process.

Here are three suggestions for managing emotional risks, as discussed in chapter 21:

• Be emotionally self-aware. Emotions from past experiences often carry over. Try to diagnose whether your feelings are integral or incidental to the decision at hand.
• Absorb other perspectives. Use an outside view. This can help you see where your understanding might be affected by your emotions.
• Treat each instance as different. Humans are hard-wired to use past experiences to predict the future. Emotions can push you toward overconfidence, self-attribution, and the availability bias.

Risk management too often is viewed as a model output. While implementing the results of risk models, we introduce a whole set of nonanalytic risk. Being more aware of your feelings and motivations can help you arrive at better risk-adjusted decisions. The alternative may make your clients fearful, angry, and sad.

Notes

1. Jennifer S. Lerner and Dacher Keltner, "Fear, Anger, and Risk," *Journal of Personality and Social Psychology* 81, no. 1 (2001).

2. Jennifer Lerner, "The Emotional Decision Maker," prepared for *Government Executive*, in press.

3. Karen Page Winterich, Seunghee Han, and Jennifer S. Lerner, "Now That I'm Sad, It's Hard to be Mad: The Role of Cognitive Appraisals in Emotional Blunting," *Personality and Social Psychology Bulletin* 36, no. 11 (2010).

You have brains in your head.
You have feet in your shoes.
You can steer yourself
any direction you choose.
Dr. Seuss, *Oh, the Places You'll Go!*

Portfolios are collections of choices. It is through the act of choosing that positions move into and out of the portfolio. Thanks to the unconscious, however, the act of choosing is more fragile than generally thought. It ignites emotions that can push decisions in unexpected directions. This essay looks at choice, its challenges, and what you can do to make more of your best decisions.

Compelling Choices

People are wired to make choices rather than accept someone else's. This desire is more than obstinacy or even the need for freedom; it's rooted in survival. If people did not believe they could think through their options to achieve desired results, they would have little motivation to innovate or to take on challenges. Since the alternative is to follow others like a lemming—and possibly right off the proverbial cliff—it's easy to see why choice has become one of our many adaptive behaviors.

We're hooked on choice to the point that having no choice feels like a loss of control, and that makes us unhappy. Strong as this natural preference is, though, choice does not always make us feel better. Having too many choices increases regret—picking a favorite ice cream from among five choices may be kid's stuff, but having to choose among fifty options can leave us fearful that our choice is suboptimal—erupting into classic regret aversion. Yet picking stocks from a large universe of options is what managers do. The larger the universe and the greater the number of plausible options, however, the bigger the challenge of both sorting to find alpha and of being resolved with the choice once made.

Painful Choices

"Belief in one's ability to exert control over the environment and to produce desired results is essential for an individual's well-being," say choice experts Lauren A. Leotti, Sheena S. Iyengar, and Kevin N. Ochsner.[1] Despite the human desire for control, her research shows that choice among limited options can result in effective decision-making, but too many options can degrade effectiveness. Faced with a small number of options, we tend to sort out the most desirable, or maximizing, choice. As the number of options increases, our ability to assess them is overwhelmed. The task of choosing then turns from one of maximizing to merely coping. One common coping mechanism is to quickly eliminate options, often based on uncalibrated heuristics or rules. This method satisfies the need to choose but not necessarily the goal of choosing wisely. Sidestepping the choice entirely is another mechanism for coping with that overwhelmed feeling. This approach provides stress relief but at the sacrifice of other less emotional goals.

Buying assets involves formulating a short list of likely candidates and then choosing the best from among them. Skilled investors use both process and judgment to find their best buys. Some managers use quantitative screens to winnow down their universe based on back-tested alpha characteristics. This initially top-down approach makes following a process a little easier—at least up to a point. Classic bottom-up investors, on the other hand, use a less defined process for separating the wheat from the chaff. These alpha sourcing efforts are more idiosyncratic from the very beginning. Identifying common fundamental attributes shared by past successes and then using these characteristics to help identify new names that reflect the qualities of previous winners enables bottom-up managers to understand how well a prospective buy fits the sweet spot of their process.

By knowing which combination of attributes describes your winning buys on average (strong earnings growth, low leverage, strong cash flow, low price to value, etc.), you can use that knowledge to identify candidates with similar qualities—the type of stocks you tend to get your arms around the best. You can even use this information to help sort your universe into names that are closest and farthest from your sweet spot—Doesn't that sound like a better choice?

Choosing What to Sell

Choosing can be even harder when we have to say goodbye. Pushing assets out too quickly or keeping them in the portfolio too long are common tendencies observed within professionally managed portfolios. "Selling is basically backwards looking, we tend to decide which stock to sell based on what it has done to the portfolio, and this perspective invokes negative feelings like regret and stress," observes Terrance Odean.[2] And stressful choices appeal to our not so stellar personal qualities, point out Professors Chua and Iyengar: "A large body of research has shown that when confronted with a set of undesirable or stressful choices, people tend to delay choosing, resort to the default, shift the responsibility of making the decision onto others, and often opt not to choose at all."[3] This tendency may shed additional light on two commonly observed difficulties in selling: the endowment effect and loss aversion.

Winners can earn a special place in the hearts of managers, thereby becoming a part of their psychic endowment. This attachment makes pushing them out of the portfolio emotionally straining. Choosing which of these positions to sell can feel like saying goodbye to an old friend. Similarly, selling losers often brings about a loss of self-efficacy. Realizing a so-called paper loss makes that loss permanent and fuels the self-recrimination of having made a poor investment. Aversion to the emotional pain associated with selling losers helps explain why they kick around in some portfolios for years.

As noted earlier, selling has received short shrift in academic research and practitioner focus. In part, this dearth of examination allows sell decisions to be based more on feel and judgment rather than analytics, as uncovered in a CFA Institute/Cabot Research survey on sell practices. The potential for emotionally motivated investing is, not surprisingly, inversely related to the levels of skill, discipline, and process surrounding investment decisions.

Conclusion

Choice is desirable, yet it brings with it emotional challenges. Identifying buy candidates requires sifting through your universe for those worthy of serious consideration. Finding the few among the multitude can seem overwhelming. The more rigorous and disciplined the process for arriving at your short list, the greater your chances of building repeatable performance.

According to Sigmund Freud, individuals tend to avoid pain. Selling assets is stressful and thus painful. Maladaptive behaviors like selling winners prematurely, holding losers too long, and hanging on to winners well past their ability to generate alpha can be signs of avoiding pain.

Learning when you tend to follow your process and make disciplined decisions and when you are likely to drift into behavioral tendencies is a smart first step toward greater self-awareness and improving. In the end, successful choices are those that best reflect your intention rather than your fears.

Notes

1. Lauren A. Leotti, Sheena S. Iyengar, and Kevin N. Ochsner, "Born to Choose: The Origins and Value of the Need for Control," *Trends in Cognitive Science* 14 (2010), 457–463.

2. Terrance Odean, exclusive interview with Cabot Research LLC, November 2010.

3. Roy Yong-Joo Chua and Sheena S. Iyengar, "Empowerment through Choice? A Critical Analysis of the Effects of Choice in Organizations," *Research in Organizational Behavior* 27 (2006), 53–54.

Further Reading

Simona Botti and Sheena S. Iyengar, "The Psychological Pleasure and Pain of Choosing: When People Prefer Choosing at the Cost of Subsequent Outcome Satisfaction," *Journal of Personality and Social Psychology* 87, no. 3 (2004).

Sheena S. Iyengar and Mark R. Lepper, "When Choice Is Demotivating: Can One Desire Too Much of a Good Thing?," *Journal of Personality and Social Psychology* 79, no. 6 (2000).

Barry Schwartz, "The Tyranny of Choice," *Scientific American* (April 2004).

29 Changing for the Better

Intelligence is the ability to adapt to change.
Stephen Hawking[1]

Learning, adapting, and improving are the building blocks of successful investing. And whether you are sharpening skills, adhering more carefully to process, or taming behavioral tendencies, the ability to stay competitive demands change, which is easier said than done. This essay examines changing, its challenges, and how you can go about it more effectively.

I Could If I Had To

Changing behavior is hard, even when it's a matter of life or death. "If you look at people after coronary-artery bypass grafting two years later, 90% of them have not changed their lifestyle," according to Dr. Edward Miller, the dean of the medical school and CEO of the hospital at Johns Hopkins University. This tendency to persist with, or revert back to, unhealthy behaviors is well documented and has been studied extensively. According to Dr. Miller and others, otherwise smart, capable people who know their behavior is both shortening and restricting their lives still find it virtually impossible to change.[2]

What makes change so hard, even when it involves life and death? What is it about how our brains are wired that resists change so tenaciously? Why do we fight even what we know is in our own vital interests? It comes down to how we make most choices. The vast majority of daily decisions are made entirely within the unconscious brain and are strongly influenced by emotions. Consequently, efforts to change fizzle out because they are based on analytic reasons and reflect conscious choices, while deeper motivations that lurk within the unconscious resist such deliberate reasoning and propel us toward emotional desires. "Behavior change happens mostly by speaking to people's feelings." says Harvard University change expert John Kotter. He adds, "In highly successful change efforts, people find ways to help ... see the problems or solutions in ways that influence emotions, not just thought."[3]

Herding Elephants

Why is change so hard? In large part, it is because your brain is of two minds—analytic and emotional. Jonathan Haidt of the University of Virginia has suggested that the relationship of the analytic brain to the emotional brain is akin to a driver sitting atop an elephant. The driver may know where he or she wants to go but getting the cooperation of the elephant is not always possible.[4]

Knowledge and facts inform the driver and help him formulate directions or intent. But when the elephant is stirred—by fear, anger, greed, etc.—then the elephant ignores the driver and does what it feels like. Change is easy when the driver has a plan and the elephant is not riled. But let a mouse run across the road, and the elephant stampedes—rushing right back into old behavior patterns that are familiar and soothing if not actually effective.

Similarly, portfolio managers struggle to overcome behavioral tendencies they've accumulated over the years. When presented with unequivocal evidence that they engage in a persistent behavioral tendency and that it is draining alpha from the portfolio, most managers are willing to consider changing. The majority that work with Cabot are successful at implementing small changes and do improve, while others engage in the change process but don't capture the full opportunity available and a small number never try at all. What is common among those who change and improve the most is this: They believe that the opportunity to improve is in front of them and that they can capture it; they have found a way of aligning their deliberate goals with their emotional ones; and they implement small refinements in their processes to achieve greater mindfulness and to receive quick feedback on how they are implementing their improvement plans. Front-line experience suggests that the identification of behavioral tendencies does help increase self-awareness. How managers internalize this information, however, ranges from the desire for deliberate improvement to feelings of stress and pain—with the former more supportive of change and the latter more likely to result in maintaining the status quo.

You Can Do It

Change is possible, say authors Chip and Dan Heath. In their book *Switch: How to Change When Change Is Hard*, they offer some practical advice for making your changes work:[5]

• Have specific goals. Saying that you want to be a better investor just won't work. It's too vague and you will lapse back into old patterns at the first moment of stress. Instead, pick a change goal that is clear and quantifiable—"I am going to reexamine losing positions every quarter and sell them if the likelihood of rebounding is not exceptionally strong."

• Send yourself a destination postcard. Motivation can be sustained if you see the change you are working on as having already been realized. One idea is to surround yourself with reports, charts, and graphs that show how your portfolio would have performed had your current change been implemented one or two years ago. If holding on to winners too long has been costing you 150 basis points annually, then superimpose a revised performance graph on top of actual history that includes capturing half or all of this potential. Your unconscious brain will begin to anticipate the performance from the adjusted behavior—and then failing to change will feel like a loss, which is a powerful motivation.

• Shrink your change. Make the change as small as possible. If you have been selling young winners much too early, and giving up excellent alpha in the bargain, then your change might read—"Whenever I want to sell a young winner, I will pause and try to hold it at least two weeks more, unless clear erosion of its fundamentals is demonstrated."

• Clear the path. Don't make your elephant jump hurdles to support change; make its path clear and easy. This can be as simple as using a checklist to keep the change behavior front-of-mind. A checklist for feeding young winners: (1) Each week, identify new positions that have unrealized gains. (2) Compare their portfolio weight to my average full position size. (3) Add to these young winners if they are significantly underweight and their thesis continues to be valid.

Conclusion

Efforts to change behavior fail more often than they succeed. Building a reasonable fact-based case for change but overlooking the need for an emotional driver is one reason. Making change too complicated and identifying vague benefits are other contributing factors.

You can make your change a success. It requires no more effort than failure—just a smarter approach. Have clear goals, keep your changes small, send yourself a destination postcard, and clear the path. If you don't learn to harness the power of both the rider and the elephant, you just might find your portfolio among the dinosaurs.

Notes

1. Nola Taylor Redd, "Stephen Hawking Biography," *Space.com*, May 30, 2012, http://www.space.com/15923-stephen-hawking.html.

2. See Alan Deutschman, "Change or Die," *Fast Company*, http://www.fastcompany.com/52717/change-or-die, May 2005.

3. John P. Kotter, *Leading Change* (Cambridge, MA: Harvard University Press, 2005).

4. Jonathan Haidt, *The Happiness Hypothesis: Finding Modern Truth in Ancient Wisdom* (New York: Perseus Books, 2006), 4.

5. Chip Heath and Dan Heath, *Switch: How to Change When Change Is Hard* (New York: Broadway Books, 2010).

When everybody thinks alike, nobody thinks.
John Wooden[1]

Actively managed portfolios are collections of ideas and decisions. New research suggests that teams are better than individuals at generating both ideas and decisions, but only when their behavior enables them to think and act as an integrated alpha source. Ineffective groups, in contrast, may struggle to deliver beta. Attributes of highly effective teams are becoming clear, making it possible for groups to improve deliberately. This essay looks at how small changes to process and behavior might help yield more from your investment team.

Peeling Apart Groups

Anita Williams Woolley and her colleagues investigate what drives group performance. They have conducted extensive research to determine whether "groups, like individuals, do have characteristic levels of intelligence, which can be measured and used to predict the groups' performance on a wide variety of tasks."[2] They sought answers to this question by measuring team outcomes across a range of cognitive challenges.

Investigations began by measuring the IQ and psychometrics of study participants. IQ was measured using one of the standard tests of cognitive ability. Psychometric measures included personality tests (looking for extraversion, agreeableness, conscientiousness, openness to experience, and neuroticism) and social sensitivity. The latter attribute was measured using "The Mind in the Face Test," which measures social awareness based upon the words picked to best match the thoughts or emotions expressed in the eye regions shown in a series of photographs.

Participants randomly assigned to groups of two to five people were given cognitively challenging problems, including visual puzzles, brainstorming, making collective moral judgments, and negotiating over scarce resources. Many tasks required group participation, although participants worked at separate computers. Scores were penalized for poor collaboration such as typing over each other, incorrect answers, and misspellings. "Smart Badges" worn by members tracked and transmitted the percentage of time each member spoke while completing tasks. Group dynamics were examined by asking participants to complete a social cohesiveness test at the end of all tasks.

Sources of Group Alpha

The findings from Woolley's investigations turn commonly held beliefs on their ear. Group performance, the data showed, is only moderately correlated with both group average IQ and the maximum individual member IQ. Interestingly, success was positively correlated with high scores on the psychometric indicators. However, what set highly successful groups apart from the pack was the social sensitivity of members and the extent to which participation in the conversations was equally distributed. Another finding was that group performance increased with the number of female members. This result is believed to reflect the fact that women typically score higher than men in social sensitivity tests. Equally valuable is what did not correlate with group success. Woolley says, "We found that many of the factors one might have expected to predict group performance—such as group cohesion, motivation, and satisfaction—did not."

The collective intelligence of groups, or what Woolley terms the "C Factor," clearly benefits from individual IQ but is more sensitive to how aware each member is to the feelings of others and the equality of talk time. Importantly, group C Factor was not only highly correlated with success, but it proved to be predictive—groups with a higher observable C Factor outperformed in tasks relative to other groups.

Woolley found that dominant personalities often negate the potential benefit of groups; she suggests one reason is that "teams of experts may not listen to each other and forgo the value of diversity." She also points to relative status as inhibiting group performance: "High-status experts may be disinclined to take seriously the views of others, and lower status members may be tempted to give more credence to higher status members than is warranted by their actual expertise."[3]

Developing C Factor

Investment committees and teams are often described as egalitarian in nature. But what really happens when your company meets? Odds are that social sensitivity is not the first trait you'd pick to describe an assemblage of your fellow investment professionals. In fact, sensitivity to anything other than the market may seem barely tolerated, let alone prized. Perhaps the best example is to notice airtime. You can probably anticipate who will be talking the most, who will join in occasionally, and who will be all but silent in your next meeting.

If this seems familiar, then your team may need to change. According to the studies discussed here, the right changes can help you to reach better decisions, and that means giving clients your best—an improvement available for no additional expense.

Here are three ideas that might help generate more C Factor in your company.

• Benchmark talking equality. At your next meeting, collect data on who talks. Create a table with participant names along the far left side. Across the top, add in these column headings: job title, number of minutes speaking, number of minutes actively listening, number of questions asked, number of times interrupted others, and number of times encouraged subordinates to talk. Tally the data at the end of the meeting, share the results, and suggest ways that your meetings might be improved.

• Be the change you want. It's hard to heighten social sensitivity if intensity and abruptness are the conversational norm, so it's your job to lead by example. Ask the quiet attendees to offer up their thoughts. Make it comfortable for change to occur by saying to the group, "I'd really like to hear what Jim has to say on this." And then listen, offer a follow-up question if appropriate, and try asking a big honcho to elaborate on what Jim just said. When you feel the conversational style is reverting to the original pattern, pull out the results of your analysis to remind folks why you initiated the change in the first place.

• Put a face on it. Consider having everyone take a Mind in the Face Test. The results can help team members gain self-awareness about their own social sensitivity and, if you share the results, that of others. (Free Mind in the Face Tests can be found by searching the web.)

Conclusion

The image of a lone portfolio manager driving every decision to rack up return is heroic but far from reality. More and more, top performance comes from groups—and not groups that simply play follow the leader. Today's top-performing groups collaborate to reach decisions that are more effective than even the smartest member would arrive at individually. They use portfolio thinking to drive portfolio results.

The specific means for achieving change need to fit your team and goals. The message is, however, universal: Groups that exhibit greater social sensitivity and equality of speaking make better decisions. To some this might sound like another version of singing "Kumbaya." Yet a deeper look suggests that developing the C Factor is a way of making smarter decisions with covariant thinking.

Notes

1. Michael L. Stallard, *Fired Up or Burned Out: How to Reignite Your Team's Passion, Creativity, and Productivity* (Nashville: Thomas Nelson, 2007), 29.

2. Anita Williams Woolley, Christopher F. Chabris, Alex Pentland, Nada Hashmi, and Thomas W. Malone, "Evidence for a Collective Intelligence Factor in the Performance of Human Groups," *Science*, October 29, 2010, 686.

3. Anita Williams Woolley, Margaret E. Gerbasi, Christopher F. Chabris, Stephen M. Kosslyn, and J. Richard Hackman, "Bringing in the Experts: How Team Composition and Collaborative Planning Jointly Shape Analytic Effectiveness," *Small Group Research* (June 2008), 352–371.

Further Reading

James Surowiecki, *The Wisdom of Crowds* (New York: Doubleday, 2004).

31 Promiscuous Thinking

Self-contemplation is a curse
That makes an old confusion worse.

Theodore Roethke, "Lines upon Leaving a Sanitarium"

Introspection is uniquely human. People are, as far as we know, the only species that thinks about thinking and how we feel. But all reflections may not lead to smarter decisions. When trying to articulate why we like this over that, we are apt to describe what's reasonable rather than what we believe. The results include mislearning and confusion about motivation. This essay looks at issues surrounding introspection and the reasons it is no substitute for rigorous analysis and effective investment processes.

Naive Assessments

Contemplation before making decisions can help managers make smart decisions, but only when emotions and assessment are aligned. When we are caught off guard, our attempts to evaluate options using runaway feelings can throw off our judgment. Psychologist Timothy Wilson, who has conducted extensive research into decision-making, remarks, "There is no reason to assume that introspection is always helpful. Quite the contrary, there is considerable evidence that reflection can readily push people towards poor choices."[1]

Because the vast majority of our thinking is unconscious, when we try to consciously evaluate our thoughts, we naturally tend to focus on reasons that come to mind quickly, seem plausible, and make sense—what psychologists call "high availability." Unfortunately, what's available to conscious recall at any moment is strongly affected by your emotional state—and this can dramatically alter perceptions and assessments. Your emotional state can determine how you interpret, store, and recall facts about a market event, company analysis, or stock trade.

Feelings as Information

When you are analyzing an item, your unconscious brain can include the way you are feeling as one of that item's attributes. In a study, researchers Gerald Clore and Jeffrey Huntsinger asked people to rate their overall life satisfaction—some were asked on warm sunny days when moods were positive and others were asked on cold rainy days when moods tended to be dampened. The researchers found that people's self-assessment changed with the weather: "people reported that their lives as a whole were more satisfactory on warm, sunny spring days. But this effect no longer held true when the interviewer asked 'How's the weather?' before starting the life-satisfaction interview." Switching from unconscious to conscious appreciation of the weather was the trick, according to Clore and Huntsinger: "After people's feelings about the weather were brought into their awareness, the feelings attributable to weather were no longer experienced unconsciously as stemming from life satisfaction."[2] Feelings aroused from independent stimuli were thus disconnected from the life assessment merely by bringing them to mind.

In a different study, Clore and Huntsinger asked mock juries to render their verdicts about the culpability of an audit firm in connection to a corporate bankruptcy case.[3] Different versions of the trial transcript containing varying amounts of detail about the distressing consequences of the bankruptcy were used. Jurors given the most devastating accounts of the bankruptcy were more likely to find the audit firm liable—even though the facts remained identical. The increased distress aroused by the more explicit outcomes affected juror assessments of culpability. This effect was mitigated by first discussing how they felt about being jurors. Once they were aware that the prospect of opining on the case was making them anxious, they no longer attributed their distress to the behavior of the audit firm.

For portfolio managers, assessments about a company, a thesis, or an analyst's report can be influenced by the joy or pain you're experiencing from unrelated stimuli. This is especially true for decisions at the margin, where experience and judgment become the final sources of alpha. To counter any unwanted emotional drives, you might consider reviewing at the outset of team meetings the market performance overall, the performance of your portfolio, or the "batting average" on recent buys. The goal is to get your head into the real topic at hand and to discharge any feelings you may be unconsciously holding that stem from unrelated issues or events.

Sense Making

Individuals feel driven to explain why they make specific choices—especially when they stretch outside of their areas of expertise. Contemplation, however, does not always produce positive results. Consider a study where participants were shown a group of posters—some with impressionistic paintings and others showing photographs of cats with humorous captions. The experimental group was asked to look over the posters and rank their preferences. The control group was asked to think about a neutral subject. At the end of each experiment, all participants were given the opportunity to take home a poster of their choice. The experimental subjects chose cat posters more frequently than the control participants. More interesting, however, is that when contacted three weeks later, the experimental subjects were less satisfied with their choices. Their deliberations over which posters they liked the best drove them to make choices that seemed reasonable at the time but which were not aligned with their emotional desires. Or as Professor Wilson puts it, "Too much analysis can confuse people about how they really feel."[4]

This means there is one more risk that needs to be managed—your feelings when you're engaged in analysis or making a decision. The feelings you bring to a business issue—especially feelings from unrelated situations—can influence how you interpret information and the conclusions you draw. This is another reason for developing and relying on a thorough investment process. Using checklists, requesting peer reviews of conclusions, and just building in speed bumps to slow down and make sure that your deliberations are conscious all help to manage the impact emotions have on your choices.

Conclusion

Analysis involves emotional input as well as objective reasoning. Feeling happy or sad will influence the availability and assessment of information. When you are caught unaware, your mood can become an attribute of what's being evaluated, and the very act of assessing can alter your preferences or judgments.

Faulty cognition can be corralled with self-awareness and discipline. Keying into your mood—or simply the fact that current events may be affecting you—can reduce the amount of emotional loading you bring to decisions. And sticking to your process can keep your thoughts focused on the facts and help rebuff extraneous stimuli. It's one thing when promiscuous thinking leads you to choose a cat poster; it's quite another to find out that your new position is really a fur ball.

Notes

1. Timothy D. Wilson et al., "Introspecting about Reasons Can Reduce Post-Choice Satisfaction," *Personality and Social Psychology Bulletin* 19, no. 3 (1993).

2. Gerald L. Clore and Jeffrey R. Huntsinger, "How Emotions Inform Judgment and Regulate Thought," *Trends in Cognitive Sciences* 11, no. 9 (2007).

3. Ibid.

4. Timothy Wilson, "Don't Think Twice, It's All Right," *New York Times*, December 29, 2005.

32 Getting in the Flow

As Sir Francis Bacon noted almost four hundred years ago, wonder—which is the seed of knowledge—is the reflection of the purest form of pleasure.
Mihaly Csikszentmihalyi, *Flow: The Psychology of Optimal Experience*

Investing combines discipline, process, and rules with the ability to sense the market and the opportunities it offers. Finding and maintaining the balance between the yin and yang of expert decision-making is not easy. Scientists who study these times of peak mental performance refer to them as "flow experiences." This essay considers how flow can help research analysts and portfolio managers improve their focus and make more of their best decisions.

Optimal Performance

Professor Mihaly Csikszentmihalyi, who coined the term "flow," initially observed that elite performers seemed to do their best when they were enjoying what they did. He then studied top performers across a wide variety of activities from mountain climbing to surgery. Thirty years and many research studies later, he has unraveled some of the secrets related to top performance and its connection to a sense of well-being.[1]

What he found is that individuals who regularly achieve flow report feeling energized upon completing a challenging task rather than being tired. They operate in a zone of tremendous self-efficacy—able to tackle increasingly difficult activities with the knowledge that their skills are keeping pace. They often lose their sense of time while absorbed in their work. During execution, they focus on the task immediately at hand, leaving no room to be distracted by thoughts of future steps or ultimate goals. By staying deeply in the moment, practitioners of flow are always improving, doing their personal best, and performing expertly. This same behavior is observed in top equity research analysts as they evaluate markets, sectors, and companies, as reported by renowned research analyst James Valentine in his book *Best Practices for Equity Research Analysts*.[2]

Focusing Deliberately

Mastery and personal improvement are strong motivators even when no score is being kept. These intrinsic drivers propel individuals to do their best—and then a little more. Flow explains the process many use to achieve sustained excellence and endless refinement.

Csikszentmihalyi has identified the process elements that individuals use to achieve and maintain flow: "They have rules that require the learning of skills, they set up goals, they provide feedback, they make control possible. They facilitate concentration and involvement by making the activity as distinct as possible from the so-called 'paramount reality' of everyday existence."[3] This description translates to breaking down complex operations into small and manageable units where skill can be developed and feedback gathered.

Consistent with the notion of deliberate improvement discussed in chapter 15, flow also emphasizes the autotelic experience (or self-directed goal) in pursuit of success. In other words, you achieve flow while striving for and attaining the small goals you create for yourself—whose achievement is in itself rewarding—as you advance toward larger or externally developed goals. Generating a financial statement that more accurately reflects a company's true performance can be a satisfying personal challenge and support you in picking top companies.

Building Order

"Intention is the force that keeps items in consciousness ordered," writes Csikszentmihalyi. It defines needs, desires, and goals, playing a critical role in shaping choices. Intention, he continues, keeps "our mind focused on some stimuli in preference to others." Unfortunately, the brain tends to be promiscuous regarding which intention stays in focus, thus allowing unconscious needs or desires to push aside the job at hand, with the effect of lowering performance. And this is where process can really help.

Here are five essential steps from Csikszentmihalyi's work that can help you build more flow opportunities into your investing:

- Establish clear goals or steps in your process, and as many subgoals as are meaningful;
- Find ways of measuring progress in achieving each subgoal to provide the feedback needed to stay focused and learn;
- Maintain focus and concentration on the particular subgoal at hand, by making the subgoals concise and challenging and providing results that can be benchmarked;
- Hone skills continuously to improve current results and to meet new challenges;
- Keep raising the bar for success at all levels to sidestep the mental entropy that comes with excess familiarity or boredom.

Flowing Cash

One place where flow can enhance results is in constructing company valuations. Whether you are developing single-year multiples or multiyear cash flow projections, the answer relies on both analytic process and judgment. Errors can result from the loss of focus at any of dozens of decision points along the way to establishing the company's relative or intrinsic value.

Using a clear process and checklist with specific subtasks can help. The subtasks need to be important and have measurable outcomes. For example, in estimating a company's revenues, it can help to benchmark growth rates to sector peers, both the average and the top performers. Then you can see how your estimates relate to the broader market. Known as an outside view, this process helps to bring to the surface critical assumptions that may be buried in the analysis.

Conclusion

Applying strategy and process to extract value from the market is at the core of active management. Generating solid performance requires capitalizing on your best decisions while avoiding manageable mistakes. The flow experience is a useful framework for assessing process, maintaining focus, and producing the best inputs to support your ultimate conclusions.

Intention is a powerful motivator that can bring you deeper into or away from the task at hand. By harnessing intention, you can deliver more of your best decisions with the overall goal of greater consistency and stronger performance. Process shortcomings allow distraction and mental entropy to weaken judgment. Managers and analysts will undoubtedly find greater enjoyment getting into flow rather than dealing with outflows.

Notes

1. Mihaly Csikszentmihalyi, *Flow: The Psychology of Optimal Experiences* (New York: Harper Perennial, 1991).

2. James J. Valentine, *Best Practices for Equity Research Analysts: Essentials for Buy-Side and Sell-Side Analysts* (City: McGraw-Hill, 2010).

3. Csikszentmihalyi, *Flow*, 72.

33 Believing Is Seeing

The brain is always constructing things, which is helping you survive. Some of these constructions can be fiction.

Mark Changizi

Facts submitted to a rigorous process are the quintessential definition of disciplined investing. But facts aren't always what they appear. The mere act of looking can alter the fact before you. Visual illusions occur when the brain recognizes something not there, or perhaps it is there but not in the way it is seen. This essay examines vision, how it works, why it's easily distorted, and what impact this can have on investment choices.

The Mind's Eye

Much of what we consciously perceive as seeing actually happens deep inside the brain. Light enters the eyes and is transmitted by the optic nerves to the visual cortex located near the back of the skull. Both hemispheres of the brain are involved in vision. The right hemisphere (commonly referred to as the artistic side) is quick to organize information and might recognize that the image in front of you is a chart. The left hemisphere (or analytic side) discerns details and lets you know that you're looking at a plot of PE ratios across an industry. This sophisticated visual system can, however, fool you.

I Thought I Saw

Visual illusions are commonplace. They're the natural result of your ambitious brain trying to figure out what image is penetrating your eye even before all the information has reached the visual cortex. "When the brain attempts to generate a perception, it basically is taking a guess at the near future by trying to fast-forward a tenth of a second. As a result of this neural delay between what your brain thinks it sees and the receipt of the complete visual data, you might not be perceiving an image as it actually is, but as your unconscious expects it might soon be," says Mark Changizi, a neurobiologist and assistant professor of cognitive science at Rensselaer Polytechnic Institute. "Illusions occur when the brain attempts to perceive the future, and those perceptions don't match reality," he adds.[1]

A well-known example of a visual illusion is the profile-versus-vase illusion (see figure below). When the brain focuses on the black objects, the profiles of two female faces emerge. When the brain latches on to the white column, a vase appears. Staring at the illustration will cause the different images to appear and disappear as they move in and out of mental consciousness. Priming can heighten the illusionary experience. For instance, had you, just prior to looking at the image, been shown a list that included the words "museum," "porcelain," and "urn," you would be much more likely to have first identified the vase. Try showing the image to coworkers,

Visual illusion: Which do you see, the vase or the profiles?

mentioning these words to some and not others, and see if you are able to influence them with subtle priming.

Parallel lines offer another common illusion. The longer they are, the more they seem to bend inward toward each other at the center. Ancient Greeks understood this illusion and purposely made the columns of the Parthenon slightly wider at the middle to counter this visual distortion. Today, visual illusions are being used to slow drivers' speed on a hazardous curve of Lake Shore Drive in Chicago. According to reporter Cari Nierenberg, "Stripes on the road are painted closer together as drivers approach the sharpest part of the curve. The illusion makes drivers think they're speeding up—so they slow down and, it's hoped, have fewer accidents."[2] Might such benign use of intentional illusions someday help investors avoid their unproductive behavioral tendencies?

Facing It

Even your own brain can manipulate your impressions. In daily life, your brain prefers a slightly better-looking you—Can you blame it? Research conducted by the University of Chicago's Nicholas Epley and Erin Whitchurch described experiments in which people were asked to identify pictures of themselves amid a lineup of other faces. "Participants identified their personal portraits significantly quicker when their faces were computer enhanced to be 20 percent more attractive," their research shows. And, they add, "Such internalized photoshoppery is not simply the result of an all-purpose preference for prettiness: when asked to identify images of strangers in subsequent rounds of testing, participants were best at spotting the unenhanced faces."[3] Somewhere in the unconscious lurk desires that choose to see others for who they are while preferring a more attractive version of ourselves.

Recognizing a Feeling

According to research psychologist Eric Anderson, "What we know about someone influences not only how we feel and think about them, but also whether or not we see them in the first place." In a study he and his colleagues conducted, participants were asked to view a neutral face, one expressing no clear emotion. This facial image was also paired with one of three kinds of statements about the behavior of the individual in the photo: negative (e.g., He threw a chair at his classmate), positive (e.g., He helped an elderly lady with her groceries) and neutral (e.g., He walked by a man in the street). Subjects were then placed in front of a stereoscope—an optical system that presents different images to each eye. The original neutral face was then presented to one eye, while a neutral nonfacial image was presented to the other eye.[4]

When presented with two competing images like this, the brain chooses one to focus on at any point in time—termed the "dominant image." The researchers were seeking to learn whether the brain would focus more on the faces than the nonfacial images and, if so, whether the accompanying emotional story played a role. The results showed that faces paired with negative behavioral statements were highly dominant—they were placed into conscious vision more often and for longer periods of time than faces paired with positive or neutral behavioral statements. In other words, emotions can directly influence which neurons are fired in the visual cortex—directing our attention and controlling what we see.

Glimpsing Success

If it weren't already hard enough to deliver strong performance, now you find out that you can't even trust what you see. The uncertainty of visual perception is one more example of how emotions and cognitive mistakes can lead to learning false facts and making poor choices. Quick glances at screens, research reports, and newscasts are commonplace, unconscious activities. And it is precisely at these moments when you are most vulnerable to visual illusions—especially when stress and emotions are high.

Avoiding illusionary investing is one of the many benefits provided from a well-conceived investment process—one that encourages you to stop and confirm facts on the way to forming judgments. Thinking twice, to play off the title of Michael Mauboussin's excellent book, can help you avoid the false impressions that often result from cognitive errors and from being emotionally charged.[5]

Conclusion

Successful investing is built upon objective analysis applied to verifiable facts. The role the unconscious brain plays in both facilitating and muddling judgment is a common topic within these essays. This same ambitious and relentless unconscious can also fog up your vision. Once they are learned, distorted or inaccurate facts can push you toward the wrong decision.

Checklists, outside views, decision diaries, and thinking twice are among the many tools that top managers build into their daily investing to align the workings of the unconscious with conscious intent. An investment process that deliberately supports careful observation can enable you to make top quartile performance a reality, not merely an illusion.

Notes

1. Mark Changizi, quoted in Carl Nierenberg, "Optical Illusions: When Your Brain Can't Believe Your Eyes," abcnews.go.com, October 3, 2009.

2. Nierenberg, "Optical Illusions."

3. Nicholas Epley and Erin Whitchurch, "Mirror, Mirror on the Wall: Enhancement in Self-Recognition," *Personality and Social Psychology Bulletin* 34, no. 9 (2008).

4. Eric Anderson, Erika H. Siegel, Eliza Bliss-Moreau, and Lisa Feldman Barrett, "The Visual Impact of Gossip," *Science* 332, no. 6036 (2011).

5. Michael J. Mauboussin, *Think Twice: Harnessing the Power of Counterintuition* (Boston: Harvard Business School Press, 2009).

It's not clear what the rational thing to do is in most situations.
David Tuckett

Portfolio management is built on intentions—expressed by the theses of positions held over time. Each buy, hold, and sell decision comes with a story describing and defending the position's role in the portfolio. Though research analysts and portfolio managers consider the thesis to be the objective assessment of an asset, the actual arc of these stories over the life of a position often tells a different tale. New research suggests that what goes into a thesis is more emotional than generally acknowledged— reflecting deep desires, not just facts, triggered by the need to resolve unsettling uncertainty. This essay discusses the storytelling that goes into thesis formulation and how professionals can harness the emotional factors within it for stronger and more repeatable results.

Talking to Yourself

Psychiatrist David Tuckett's book *Minding the Markets* examines the role of emotions in shaping our relationships with financial assets. Much of the book reflects in-depth conversations conducted with roughly 60 top portfolio managers around the world from which he learned that even highly experienced managers (over 20 years on average) love and hate their assets, and these feelings often show up in the stories they tell about investments held in their portfolios. In addition, he observed that the emotions they expressed about companies and their managements shifted dramatically as once beloved names in the portfolio began to falter—underscoring the interplay between facts, performance, and emotions throughout the ownership of financial assets.

Building upon his decades of work in psychoanalysis, Tuckett sees a crucial link between risk taking and storytelling. He explains, "Narratives probably developed in humans in order to help make choices. You can imagine early man on the African Plains observing a wild animal; it's either coming towards him and increasing his danger or moving away and reducing it. That's telling himself a story to understand the situation and preparing to act."[1]

Managing the Unknowable

Confronted with an asset's uncertainty, the professional investigates and assesses available information and then arrives at the best understanding possible. Fundamental to arriving at an assessment is a formulation about those things that are unpredictable. Tuckett describes the challenge this way: "while any investor may try more or less to the best of his or her ability independently to calculate the future on the basis of factual premises, the future is inherently uncertain. Future values can only be calculated by making assumptions that we have arrived at through imagination and anticipation. Inevitably those involved having feelings about what they anticipate and imagine, as well as feelings about their observations of others."[2] Consequently, investing is built upon narratives, stories about what might come to pass. These narratives are essential, but they're also emotionally laden and error-prone.

Emotional Factor

Unlike most choices we face, Tuckett believes that investment decisions are uniquely challenging and intrinsically emotional. He identifies three fundamental characteristics of financial assets that make them tricky to cope with:

• Volatility—their price can go up and down, over short or long time periods, and their value can go to zero. Such precariousness can ignite primitive feelings such as fear, greed, hope, and despondency—alternating with each tick. Price, therefore, has the effect of making our emotional commitment to financial assets unstable.
• Abstraction—assets cannot be consumed or enjoyed directly, and thus their value is derived from items for which they can be exchanged. For example, the value of art may go up or down over time, yet it may be enjoyed without regard to its market price. In contrast, financial assets taunt our emotions with their niggling and sometimes seismic price movements—cycling our hearts through elation and regret, love and hate.

• Feedback—information about the effectiveness of financial decisions is irregular and murky at best. A buy initiated today can take weeks, months, or years to play out; meanwhile, the manager is involved in creating new positions and managing others in the portfolio. Traditional measures such as return, relative return, attribution, and even "hit rates" provide weak insight into skill or decision quality—offering the illusion of understanding and the avoidance of uncertainty while facilitating emotional roller-coastering.

Together these characteristics shape the thoughts and feelings we have about financial assets. Investors may possess a relatively small number of theses that reflect their unique skills, experiences, and worldview, according to Tuckett. As a result, the narratives developed for new investments often reflect the fitting of select information into the framework of a favorite thesis. It's not so much forcing a square peg into a round hole as it is mentally squinting to see what story works.

Investment theses based on connecting the dots rather than on objective analysis point to the manager's understanding that the asset is flimsy. This helps explain why individuals may overuse tactics like "stop loss rules" and "averaging down" when their confidence is shaken.

Splitting Ambiguity

Faced with irresolvable uncertainty and the need to act, we rely on one of our greatest powers—emotions. Emotions assist us in deciding which way to turn when confronted with a difficult choice by unconsciously focusing our attention more on either the positive or negative aspects of the idea or item under deliberation. For financial assets, this means fixing more on the return or risk, the upside or downside. In doing so, we construct narratives that enable us to avoid the angst associated with ambivalence and to find the way to answers and choices with incomplete and imperfect knowledge.

This approach to resolving ambiguity results in the thesis splitting the risks from the returns. Tuckett suggests: "Conflicting thoughts and ideas tend to not be available at once; we're either seeking pleasure or avoiding pain."[3] In response to these basic emotional drives, our minds split off the risk to help form a buy decision. Then, should that position underperform, we are reunited with what we had unconsciously denied while being blinded to the potential for further reward. We become flooded with regret over the decision to own the asset at all. Unless our thesis—or more accurately, our understanding of the asset expressed by the thesis—can withstand the emotional assault of the poor performance, a once loved asset is quickly hated, and that buy or hold asset becomes a sell.

Learning and Improving

Rather than merely disparaging emotions as negative factors that push potentially good decisions bad, Tuckett sees them as essential elements of effective decision-making. Rebuffing the claims of experts who suggest investing must be emotion-free, he counters: "they miss the real point, emotion exists to help economic human actors when reason alone is insufficient."[4] And that point is encountered where facts end and judgment takes over—essentially, in every decision you make.

Harnessing emotions for their alpha potential is not easy. It requires tremendous self-awareness and a decision process that both guides and challenges the judgments you make. Tools that help include writing down the thesis of each position, reconfirming or updating it regularly, using checklists to help ensure consistency of process, and using outside views to benchmark assumptions and judgments that go into your thesis. The goal is to harness emotions for their power to inspire creative thinking while avoiding their pernicious tendency to fill factual vacuums with unfounded confidence.

Conclusion

No amount of analysis can rid financial assets of their characteristic uncertainty. Consequently, choices about what to buy, hold, and sell reflect both facts observable today and judgments about what might happen tomorrow. In forming these judgments, we create narratives that reduce ambivalence, enabling us to move ahead. This process often results in splitting risk and return—with the fallout that we unconsciously shift toward loving or hating an asset.

The dual objectives of achieving superior returns with modest risk place an extraordinary psychic burden on professional investors. The thesis can unintentionally be used to relieve the internal turmoil created through the formulation of a narrative that helps position assets as more or less than facts indicate. Understanding when your theses tend to be charged with excessive emotion can help you deliver more asset stories with happy endings.

Notes

1. David Tuckett, exclusive interview with Cabot Research LLC, September 22, 2011.

2. David Tuckett, *Minding the Markets* (London: Palgrave Macmillan, 2011).

3. Tuckett, interview with Cabot Research, September 22, 2011.

4. Tuckett, *Minding the Markets*.

35   The Trouble with Improving

Learning is not compulsory; it's voluntary. Improvement is not compulsory; it's voluntary. But to survive, we must learn.
W. Edwards Deming[1]

Portfolio managers want to improve. The motivation is simple—the market is forever evolving and underperformance is poorly tolerated. Nevertheless, improving is tricky business, as evidenced by the vast amount of time, energy, and capital invested toward this goal year after year with relatively modest results. This essay considers why improving is so elusive and what steps you can take to more confidently become your best.

Trying Is Not Enough

Don't look now, but the portfolio manager next to you is trying to figure out how to be a bit better this year, as are the tens of thousands with whom you compete. Their drive is partly intrinsic (i.e., competitiveness and wanting to excel) and partly pragmatic (i.e., capital flows to strong performance). These professionals utilize a myriad of activities to improve, ranging from third-party process reviews and forensic portfolio investigations to company retreats and skills development workshops. Despite the best intentions, however, they uniformly regard the results of their attempts at improving as disappointing, as revealed by hundreds of interviews conducted by Cabot.

Clear and Granular

Improving requires building on your strengths and retooling shortcomings. It also demands fact-based insight about how you perform at each and every step in your process, down to the smallest detail. Traditional portfolio analytics offer only coarse feedback. Measures such as return, relative return, information ratio, alpha, hit rates, tracking error, and attribution analysis provide useful scorecards but offer little help for improving. The other common source of ready feedback is even worse—it's your memory. Mountains of brain research have confirmed that memory is more likely to teach us what we want to learn rather than what we need to learn.

When contrasted with other high-performance occupations like jet pilot, orchestra violinist, PGA golfer, and neurosurgeon, the investor's paucity of useful feedback is even more apparent. Noninvestment professionals receive clear feedback on each movement they make, each decision they take. Violinists aren't limited to merely weighing the applause from each performance delivered. When it's time to improve, they can dig down into feedback on distinct skills, such as how well they hit specific notes, enter and exit movements, harmonize with other musicians, and produce different tonalities. Doctors, jocks, musicians, and pilots know their strengths and shortcomings at very granular levels. Only with these facts in hand are they able to capitalize on their strengths and confidently set about improving, whether on their own or with the help of a professional coach.

Disentangling Performance

Golfers execute and experience driving a ball off the tee as a distinct event. There is no wondering how that shot might play out—the answer is evident within seconds and is recorded before another shot is attempted. Consequently, these athletes have ready access to hordes of hard facts about discrete choices and actions that enable them to assess and refine their skills. Not so for professional investors. Just ask any portfolio manager how much of their alpha comes from buying versus everything else they do. No one really knows, and ignorance of this sort is hurting active management.

Murky feedback is the principal culprit. A buy initiated today might stay in the portfolio for weeks, months, or years before being sold. And during its stay in the portfolio, it is likely to experience a series of adds and trims while other positions are being initiated, resized, and sold. While the portfolio manager is orchestrating thousands of investment decisions annually, what is being tracked ad infinitum is the monthly portfolio return. This mismatch between what's measured and what can lead to improved performance is stifling the success of tens of thousands of portfolio managers around the world. Or, as James Harrington succinctly put it: "Measurement is the first step that leads to control and eventually to improvement. If you can't measure something, you can't understand it. If you can't understand it, you can't control it. If you can't control it, you can't improve it."[2]

Sourcing Better Ideas

The key to improving is the ability to measure individual skills. Yet this type of measurement has never been done for portfolio managers and is long overdue. The first level of measurement is how much alpha is generated on average from the three basic skills of professional investing, defined below.

• Buying is the skill of name selection. It answers the question: How good are you at identifying stocks that go on to outperform?
• Selling is the skill of unwinding positions. It answers the question: How good are you at maintaining a dominant proportion of holdings that are currently outperforming, versus hanging on to losers or selling winners too early or too late?
• Sizing is the skill of building new positions and managing trims and adds. It answers the question: How good are you at aligning position weight with outperformance?

Without fact-based answers to these basic questions, efforts at improving have about the same chance as tossing darts wearing a blindfold. You might try like heck, but your skill development is unlikely to dazzle or feel satisfying.

Behavioral Traps

The industry's lack of meaningful skill measures may be fostered unintentionally by unconscious drives. The desire to improve can easily be thwarted by deeper, less apparent needs. Here are three behavioral tendencies to watch out for as you formulate and implement your improvement plan.

• Status quo bias. Change may make sense, but it is also scary and requires hard work. How many New Year's resolutions are all but forgotten by March 1? Making small refinements and coupling them with measureable feedback is how top performers stay committed to their change goals.
• Self-attribution. "Success has many fathers while failure is an orphan," says Confucius. The brain is adept at instilling the belief that positive outcomes are the result of your genius while unfavorable outcomes are the result of factors beyond your control. Owning both your individual shortcomings as well as your strengths is essential to becoming a top performer.
• Premature dismissal. If you've ever traveled with someone reluctant to ask directions—especially before GPS—then you know the havoc that closed-mindedness can entail. Heuristics that guide investing are often buried deep in the unconscious and form important emotional protection.

Quickly overriding an analyst's recommendation to hold on to a position that is down 10% might be sound judgment, or it might be merely sticking with a stop loss rule that relieves some inner pain.

Conclusion

Few professions are subject to the scrutiny and measurement applied to portfolio management. Yet little is really known about investment skill—what it is, who has it, and how to get more. Other performance-driven professions make clear that the only way to improve skills is deliberately. This means really knowing your current strengths and shortcomings at a granular level, setting out to eliminate one weakness at a time, and receiving regular feedback on how well you are implementing your change for the better.

The industry's preoccupation with short-term returns has not served capital sources or managers well. It's time for a fresh look at what everyone proclaims is of paramount importance—skill. Perhaps this refocusing can help managers to improve while also providing capital sources a greater level of knowledge about those they hire. Then we'll be able to distinguish the real stars from the asterisks.

Notes

1. Quoted in Frank Voehl, ed., *Deming the Way We Knew Him* (Boca Raton, FL: CRC, 1995), 125.

2. Quoted in Joseph Levy, "In My Opinion," *CIO* 12, no. 23 (September 15, 1999), section 2, p. 10.

I've got a great ambition to die of exhaustion rather than boredom.
Sir Angus Grossart[1]

Love may make the world go round, but psychic energy is what makes portfolio performance rock. It is essential for making critical judgments—the
kind that guide buy, sell, and sizing decisions. Research shows that judgment is highly dependent upon the availability of psychic energy, the same
energy that fuels conscious thinking, self-control, and perseverance. As
reserves of psychic energy swing from full to depleted, the choices we make
substantially shift, unintentionally. This essay examines the role that decision fatigue plays in investing and describes how self-awareness and process
can keep your portfolio energized.

Ego Depletion

Freud coined the term "ego" to describe the part of the psyche that negoti-
ates between intent and desire. Psychologist Roy Baumeister and colleagues
relate Freud's view of our inner battles with this story: A Victorian gentle-
man standing on the street might feel urged by his id (unconscious pleasure
center) to head for the brothel and by his superego (moral center) to go to
church, but it is ultimately left up to his ego to start his feet in one direction
or the other. In this model, it is the ego that enables you to make and implement decisions supportive of explicit goals while avoiding impulses. The
ego is the same mechanism that keeps you aligned with your strategy and
process instead of falling prey to comfortable yet uncalibrated heuristics.[2]

Freud also understood that such regulation by the ego consumes copious
amounts of psychic energy. One famous study conducted by Mark Muraven
et al. asked participants to not think about a white bear—a so-called thought
control task.[3] Those who were asked to not think of the white bear gave up

more quickly on a subsequent anagram task than did those in the control group. Engaging volition to not think about the white bear simply wore people out. Exercising self-control to override impulse, it appears, has the effect of temporarily exhausting one's psychic reserves, rendering individuals unable or unwilling to utilize their full decision-making power to resolve choices. This condition of temporary psychic exhaustion is known as ego depletion or decision fatigue.

And the Verdict Is ...

Decision fatigue plays an enormous role in determining judicial outcomes. Professor Shai Danziger et al. studied the outcomes of a year's worth of parole hearings in Israel. The findings are astonishing. An inmate's chances of being granted parole drop steadily from 65% at the beginning of a court session to nearly zero by the end—a time span of just a couple of hours.[4]

The researchers tried to find other factors that might account for the disparity in outcomes. Though they looked at the severity of the crime, the ethnicity and sex of the inmate, and other potential causations, it was the time expired in a session that offered by far the strongest correlation. Their findings suggest that mental rest and caloric intake build up psychic reserves, while the demands of exercising judgment under uncertainty deplete them. As the judges approach psychic exhaustion, they are less and less willing to grant parole—exhibiting classic status quo bias and risk aversion.

Expensive Choices

Active management is built on choices, but rigorous deliberation among tradeoffs comes with a hefty price tag. Studying the psychic effects of overcoming urges, Baumeister and colleagues set up an experiment in which people were seated in front of two snacks: one a bowl of chocolates, the other a bowl of radishes. Half of the participants were invited to eat the chocolates and the others only the radishes. Those free to eat the chocolates went on to perform better in a subsequent mental puzzle challenge. Participants restricted to the radishes depended upon willpower to avoid the chocolates, Baumeister concludes, causing them to expend psychic energy and reducing their puzzle-solving ability.

In another study, Baumeister and team investigated the effects of ego depletion on active decision-making. Of two similar groups recruited for the experiment, one group was exposed to a mentally fatiguing task and the other was not. Then both groups were asked to view an intentionally boring video. The participants were told they would not have time for the entire video, but should watch enough to understand what was happening and be prepared to answer a few questions afterward. Half of all participants were assigned an active control, requiring they push a button to stop the video. The others were assigned a passive control, requiring depressing the button to view the movie and releasing it to stop. In other words, half stopped the video by pressing the button, while half did so by releasing it. Stopping was further motivated by the promise that after the initial video they would see a second video of funny skits from *Saturday Night Live*.

Baumeister et al. found that among the non-ego-depleted participants there was no difference in the duration of video watching as a function of active or passive control. That is, when fully rested and energized, the participants were just as likely to actively or passively end an unpleasant task—viewing a boring video. In the group of ego-depleted participants, the results were starkly different. After first using up psychic energy, participants with the passive controls were as quick to end the video as their non-ego-depleted counterparts, while those with the active controls took considerably longer to stop their viewing. Baumeister and colleagues believe this data supports the notion that mental fatigue inhibits active decisions while favoring passive ones. From this we might conclude that mental fatigue can cause you to pass on a buy or to hold on to a position that should be sold or to make other nonactive choices.

Without a Net

While your intuition and judgment may be spectacular, they rely on a limited and easily depleted reservoir of psychic energy, and this presents serious risk that most managers do not factor into their decision-making. Baumeister et al. bring this point home with the following: "The ease with which we have been able to produce ego depletion using small laboratory manipulations suggests that the extent of the resource is quite limited, which implies that it would be seriously inadequate for directing all of a person's behavior, so conscious, free choice must remain at best restricted to a very small proportion of human behavior."[5]

For portfolio managers the lesson is clear: Your best may be terrific, but you can't count on being your best at every junction without help. And the support top managers employ is their investment process. Knowing when to slow down, think twice, benchmark to outside views, and seek independent input are some of the process elements that guard against ego depletion, as well as a host of other emotional and cognitive biases.

Conclusion

The need to make a decision while managing a portfolio can come about at any moment. What precedes the moment of decision-making, we now better understand, can dramatically alter the choices made. Mental fatigue may seem like a minor issue, but it is determining the fate of prisoners and may be affecting your returns.

Experience enables managers to develop judgment and self-awareness that can help counterbalance the effects of ego depletion. Adherence to a well-calibrated investment process can guide decisions toward choices that more often reflect intention, consistency, and quality and that help generate stronger returns. Ignoring the need to manage psychic energy may have the adverse effect of leading you toward tired performance.

Notes

1. Quoted in Bill Swainson, ed., *The Encarta Book of Quotations* (New York: St. Martins, 2000), 395.

2. Roy F. Baumeister, Ellen Bratslavsky, Mark Muraven, and Dianne M. Tice, "Ego Depletion: Is the Active Self a Limited Resource?," *Journal of Personality and Social Psychology* 74 (1998), 1252–1265.

3. Ibid.

4. Shai Danziger, Jonathan Levav, and Liora Avnaim-Pesso, "Extraneous Factors in Judicial Decisions," *Proceedings of the National Academy of Sciences* 108 (2011), 6889–6892.

5. Baumeister et al., "Ego Depletion."

Further Reading

Veronika Job, Carol S. Dweck, and Gregory M. Walton, "Ego Depletion—Is It All in Your Head? Implicit Theories about Willpower Affect Self-Regulation," *Psychological Science* 21 (2011).

Many a man thinks he is buying pleasure, when he is really selling himself to it.
Benjamin Franklin, *Autobiography*

Owning winners is not always what it's cracked up to be, especially if you
have the tendency to hold them well past their productive lives. Interestingly, it is fear more than greed that can motivate holding winners well
after they have given their best. This essay examines the theory underlying
this behavior and discusses new findings on the prevalence and cost of this
tendency.

Primal Drives

Over a century ago, Sigmund Freud observed that most human behavior is
related to seeking pleasure and avoiding pain. The wisdom of this idea continues to unfold, especially regarding investment behaviors. In the 1970s
psychologists Daniel Kahneman and Amos Tversky introduced "prospect
theory," their groundbreaking insights into decision-making under uncertainty.[1] Among its tenets, prospect theory suggests that the emotional displeasure experienced from the loss of a dollar may be two to three times
greater in magnitude than the pleasure experienced from the gain of a dollar. Due to this asymmetry in emotional experience, individuals generally
prefer taking gains quickly and avoiding realizing losses. This latter tendency is known as loss aversion and seems to reflect Freud's expectation of
pain avoidance.

It's Mine, All Mine

Perceptions of gain and loss can be stimulated in unpredictable ways. For
example, psychological research demonstrates that the act of buying is
often experienced as a gain, while selling is perceived as a loss. Once we

own an item, we feel as if our wealth or endowment has grown—even if a market price was paid and actual wealth did not change. Likewise, liquidating an item from our endowment can elicit twinges of loss even when the trade is fair. According to Kahneman et al., these emotional tugs interrupt rational decision-making: "An implication of this asymmetry is that if a good is evaluated as a loss when it is given up and as a gain when it is acquired, loss aversion will, on average, induce a higher dollar value for owners than for potential buyers, reducing the set of mutually acceptable trades."[2] This overvaluation of possessions and subsequent difficulty in selling is termed the "endowment effect."

Can't Win for Losing

As paradoxical as it sounds, the same emotion that makes individuals hold on to their losers can also cause them to cling to their winners. How's that possible? It's because the prospect of a loss is ever present. You buy a stock and it goes up. That's good of course. But now you believe that the stock still has further to climb and you wait, and wait, and wait. The stock that delivered alpha for 13 months has now been in the portfolio for close to 24 months. Fortunately it hasn't round-tripped, but for the entire back end of your owning it (11 months), it has delivered zero in the form of additional alpha. It's been dead money. And it is your fear of selling without getting what you believe is the full price that causes you to hold a winner far too long. This practice might seem benign, but when it becomes a persistent tendency, it can really hurt performance.

Uncertainty Premium

Price ambiguity enhances the potential for the endowment effect. For example, if $5.50 in quarters were offered for a $5 bill, the seller would have no fear of losing and, therefore, no feelings of loss aversion and no endowment effect. Because the intrinsic value of a financial asset is not known in any absolute manner, the seller must use imperfect information to decide at what price to sell. The use of judgment to arrive at what is commonly termed the release price, full value, or target price brings with it a nagging sense of uncertainty—fueling fear, hesitation, and the endowment effect.

Survey Says

The endowment effect is by far the most common behavioral tendency affecting professionally managed portfolios, according to the more than

$600 billion of equity assets studied by Cabot Research. Our results indicate that more than one in five managers hold winners well past the time they cease generating alpha. The cost of this behavior typically exceeds 100 basis points of incremental alpha annually. Mitigating such a negative tendency, if it is present, is proving to be one of the surest paths to capturing greater performance from existing skills and processes.

Our research also points to process shortcomings as a key contributor to the ineffective management of older winners. Unlike buying, where process tends to be highly intentional and well developed, the process for reviewing the theses of older winners typically lacks adequate rigor. As a result, names that had to fight their way into the portfolio are held to much lower standards once the stock has performed. In practice, managers find that bolstering discipline around thesis reconfirmation is often the preferred means for eliminating the endowment effect.

Endowment RX

Behavioral tendencies are difficult to identify accurately, yet the solution for correcting them can be straightforward. If you are concerned about your management of older winners, here are a few ideas to consider:

• Age histogram. Take a look at the data. Plot out the percentage of winners that you typically sell after 3 months, 6 months, 9 months, etc. This simple investigation can shed light on potential selling biases that may warrant further investigation.
• Sampling. Pick a random group of winners that have been held longer than your average holding period. Compute how they performed from the average holding length up to the time you actually sold them. Observe whether they outperform the rest of the portfolio during this time period. While far from a definitive result, this sample might help you think through your management of these positions overall.
• Get tough. As winners get older, ratchet up your standards for holding them in the portfolio. Escalation of thesis confirmation can counterbalance the natural tendency to be more forgiving the longer a position is held.

Conclusion

The endowment effect reflects the unconscious desire to avoid experiencing the negative feelings associated with taking a loss. Unlike the difficulty sometimes experienced in selling an asset for less than its purchase price (i.e., what is typically thought of as loss aversion), the endowment effect reflects the fear of selling winners for less than their full value, particularly when intrinsic value is ambiguous. Although the role of the endowment effect on professional investors has not been studied widely by academics, it is proving to be a common and costly affliction among portfolio managers.

Determining whether you may engage in this behavioral tendency is close to impossible using conventional portfolio analytics. They primarily analyze holdings over time, not specific skills like buying, sizing, and selling. Further limiting any self-assessment for this behavior is the fact that these positions are winners—and it's common to be forgiving of assets once they have delivered excess performance. What a growing number of managers are learning, however, is that greater scrutiny of how well you manage older winners may endow your portfolio with just the extra return you're looking for.

Notes

1. Daniel Kahneman and Amos Tversky, "Prospect Theory: An Analysis of Decision Making under Risk," *Econometrica* 47 (March 1979).

2. Daniel Kahneman, Jack L. Knetsch, and Richard H. Thaler, "Experimental Tests of the Endowment Effect and the Coase Theorem," *Journal of Political Economy* 98, no. 6 (December 1990).

Never put off till to-morrow what you can do day after to-morrow just as well.
Mark Twain, "The Late Benjamin Franklin"

Procrastination can boost portfolio performance. This is one of the unorthodox conclusions found in new research into the interplay among skill, process, judgment, and time. In a world increasingly measured in milliseconds, the thought of delaying may hit you as either heresy or a siren song. But we're not talking about good old-fashioned loafing. Rather, the research suggests that knowing when to go fast and when to go slow is how top professionals achieve their personal best. This essay considers how building time into your process to slow down at critical moments can speed you toward higher performance.

Tortoise and Hare

Speed does not always win the day. But its judicious use can increase your likelihood of success, according to the research compiled by Frank Partnoy in his book *Wait: The Art and Science of Delay*. One compelling example he shares concerns elite tennis players. In describing Jimmy Connors's ability to return high-speed serves, Partnoy explains: "By becoming extremely skilled and fast at actually hitting a service return, Connors was able to have more time to watch the ball and anticipate its trajectory, speed and bounce."[1] In becoming really fast at execution, Connors was able to reallocate his time and go slow when evaluating incoming shots. Consequently, he was on top of more incoming serves than his competitors were, and became one of the greatest service returners in tennis history.

Even high-frequency trading can benefit from slight delay. The stock-trading firm UNX embarked on reinventing itself in 2006. With new algorithms and technology, UNX soon leapfrogged to become the lowest-cost trading platform and garnered huge flows in the process. Believing that their edge came strictly from speed, the company decided to ship their technology 3,000 miles from L.A. to New York in order to be closer to the exchanges, hoping to shave even more time off each trade. Trading times did speed up substantially, but the cost of trading (i.e., market impact) got worse. In delivering their trades more quickly, they now were ahead of information that previously had informed the markets and facilitated more effective pricing. By slowing down their trades to the pre-New York time frame, they lowered their costs and regained their overall execution advantage. UNX learned that they needed to go slow enough to allow the market to become primed and then they could use their speed to execute fast and cheaply.

When Not to Blink

Malcolm Gladwell's well-received book *Blink* is often misinterpreted as the unabashed endorsement of instant decision-making. A more careful read shows that Gladwell was, in fact, cautioning that quick judgments, or what he described as "thin slicing," only work when the decision maker is a highly seasoned expert working within his or her narrow domain of expertise.[2] Adding to Gladwell's contributions, Partnoy offers: "The toughest part of the expert-novice distinction is that we can be experts in an area, with years of seemingly relevant experience, but then be confronted in the same area with a new twist on a decision that turns us into a novice." He adds, "Not very many experts will admit, or even see, when they are novices."[3]

For example, even successful value managers may do poorly when buying deeply discounted assets. Their expertise in assessing value opportunities simply does not extend to analyzing turnarounds. They may need to slow down to sort out when they are stretching outside of their expertise and intentionally decide if they really want to proceed. Severe and rapidly changing market conditions offer another example that can shift even great portfolio managers into periods of novice ability, where going slowly can avoid costly mistakes. "Adding in speed bumps to slow down the decision process can enable managers to stay with their proven strengths and avoid situations that feel familiar but lead them astray," Partnoy advises.

It's Relative

Fast and slow are concepts that get their meaning from the world in which you perform. High-velocity trading systems are clocked in milliseconds; hedge funds are commonly measured in days or weeks; and for traditional long-only managers, strategic choices may take months or years to play out. Within each of these time frames, there are some decisions that need to take place quickly and others that can be implemented at a more measured pace. The amount of time available to effectively make and implement decisions Partnoy has termed the "time world in which you operate."[4]

Partnoy suggests that you can harness the most from your investment process by understanding when to go fast or slow across the small and large decisions that comprise your time world. For example: If your typical new buy takes off soon after purchase, then moving quickly to full position size is essential to capturing the alpha you've identified. Alternatively, if new names tend to be somewhat sluggish for weeks, then you have more time to build up position size—enabling you to benefit from an elongated thesis confirmation period and greater liquidity. Likewise, if most of the losers in your portfolio fail to bounce back, then pushing them out quickly can significantly help performance and vice versa.

Conclusion

Technology is unalterably changing our relationship with time. In the not too distant past, "long-term investing" meant years, not months; and the close of the local market initiated the commute home, not shifting one's focus to faraway time zones. Add in the 24/7 deluge of electronic information and daily squaring up of net asset value, and life can feel like an endless effort to catch up.

Faced with too many decisions and too little time, portfolio managers can use their process to guide them toward the right use of fast and slow. Moving decisively within your expert zone and taking extra care when you are being nudged into temporary novice status can help you avoid behavioral investing and the disappointment it brings. When your intuition suggests that you may be moving outside your domain of expertise, remember the sage advice of Aesop's turtle: "Slowly does it every time!"

Notes

1. Frank Partnoy, *Wait: The Art and Science of Delay* (New York: Public Affairs, 2012).

2. Malcolm Gladwell, *Blink: The Power of Thinking without Thinking* (New York: Little, Brown, 2005).

3. Frank Partnoy, exclusive interview with Cabot Research LLC, November 14, 2012.

4. Ibid.

One of the painful things about our time is that those who feel certainty are stupid, and those with any imagination and understanding are filled with doubt and indecision.
Bertrand Russell, "If We Are to Survive This Dark Time"

Having a sense of conviction about decisions we've made, assets we own, or theses we manage is generally viewed as positive. Yet it is not easy to distinguish well-reasoned conviction from mere bluster. Chief among the biases that can nudge professional managers and analysts toward the latter is overconfidence. This small spark of emotion can turn a potentially great idea into a disappointing folly. In this essay we examine the impact of overconfidence on investment decision-making and steps that can be employed to reign it in.

Overdoing It

According to psychological research, individuals tend to be overconfident about their skills, their knowledge, and the outcomes of future events. In one study, 81% of new business owners thought their businesses had a 70% or better chance of succeeding, but only 39% thought a venture comparable to theirs and managed by someone else would have a similar chance of success. In a survey of college professors, 94% described themselves as above average in their work—a Lake Wobegon type of reality. And when asked, 42% of engineers at one employer believed their work ranked in the top 5% among their peers. In short, we're predisposed to be overly optimistic about our own ability and prospects.

Overconfidence appears innate, perhaps reflecting an evolutionary bias toward individuals who confronted unfavorable odds rather than meekly accepting certain defeat at the hands of a foe or predator. Such behavior is proving to be less helpful when confronting investment choices.

Psychologists suggest that overconfidence is strongly linked with the need to avoid the discomfort that can accompany doubt, anxiety, and fear in a world that demands certainty. In our haste to sidestep cognitive disso- nance, we easily become entangled in self-affirmation—assigning favorable outcomes to our actions while dismissing unfavorable outcomes—which, in turn, elicits and reinforces the use of overconfidence. This behavior has obvious drawbacks, as expressed by psychologist Cameron Anderson et al.: "The propensity for overconfidence is puzzling because being able to accu- rately place one's abilities relative to those of others is clearly useful."[1]

Blundering Ahead

"Overconfidence is greatest for difficult tasks, for forecasts with low pre- dictability, and for undertakings lacking fast, clear feedback," say finance professors Brad Barber and Terrance Odean.[2] These qualities precisely define the critical challenges of active portfolio management and offer a glimpse into why behavioral tendencies abound. Simon Gervais et al. suggest: "Our notion of overconfidence captures the idea that individuals overestimate the precision of their information or their ability to interpret that informa- tion when making economic decisions."[3] In studying this behavior among thousands of individual investors, Barber and Odean observe: "Overcon- fident investors also perceive their actions to be less risky than generally proves to be the case."[4]

In one of their studies, Barber and Odean examined excess trading as a measure of overconfidence. They found that overconfident investors do, in fact, trade excessively and that this practice hurts performance. Not sur- prisingly, this study also found that men exhibited greater overconfidence than women. They conclude: "We document that men trade 45% more than women. Trading reduces men's net returns by 2.65 percent a year as opposed to 1.27 percentage points for women."[5] Research points to over- confidence as closely related to, or possibly acting as a catalyst for, other behaviors—premature dismissal, confirmation bias, hindsight bias—which all act to satisfy emotional needs while dulling decision effectiveness.

Ignorance Is Bliss

The least capable tend to be the most overconfident, according to the work of psychologist Joyce Ehrlinger and colleagues. They find that self-perception of capability is poorly correlated with actual ability. Ehrlinger et al. compared the self-assessments of individuals to their achievements across a variety of tasks. Their research results show that excess optimism is greatest among the incompetent, as they refer to underperformers. Highlighting the proclivity of poor performers toward overconfidence, Ehrlinger et al. offer this illustration: "For example, students performing in the bottom 25% among their peers on tests of grammar, logical reasoning, and humor tended to think that they are performing above the 60th percentile."[6]

Reversing the twin scourges of overconfidence and poor ability is no mean feat. Describing the dilemma found among poor performers who may desire to improve, Ehrlinger et al. point out: "Their incompetence produces a double curse. First, their lack of skill, by definition, makes it difficult to produce correct responses and, thus, they make many mistakes. Second, this very same lack of skill also deprives them of success at the metacognitive task of recognizing when a particular decision is a correct or an incorrect one."[7] Sorting out successful from unsuccessful choices, therefore, seems a necessary condition in order to beat back overconfidence while strengthening skills.

Man in the Mirror

The antidote to overconfidence is simple—facts. For surely in the absence of facts, the brain will select just the right fragments of information to construct a narrative that keeps us happy and ignorant of our actual strengths and shortcomings. This defensive process bolsters emotional energy and keeps us in the game—just like the early man facing down a lethal predator. But it does nothing to support improving.

Deliberate improvement, on the other hand, wrests control from the emotional processes and shifts the act of self-development squarely into the objective part of your brain. It builds upon three essential inputs: the deliberate intention to become better, the isolation of specific repeatable tasks (e.g., executing buys, sells, or sizing decisions) and unambiguous feedback that allows you to know how well your improvement efforts are working. It helps dissipate the fog of memories and develop appropriate confidence in what is working and what is not. This approach is far superior to other methods of debiasing, such as the use of financial incentives or presenting how conclusions were developed to peers or supervisors. Ehrlinger's research indicates that such traditional methods often have the perverse effect of increasing overconfidence rather than reducing it. Management companies that have investment committees would be wise to consider this caution: Having a committee is not enough; committees can even increase the occurrence of ineffective behaviors. It is the process used by the committee in presenting and discussing ideas that can promote greater objectivity and reduce behavioral tendencies.

Conclusion

Realistic confidence or self-efficacy helps propel professional investors toward doing their best. Overconfidence, in contrast, can make you feel good in the short run while eroding your chances of long-term success. Not only is overconfidence commonplace, but it is more likely to afflict us when our skill is inferior to the task at hand.

Willpower alone is no defense against overconfidence. For the conscious effort to be more objective can, ironically, evoke feelings of angst—which your brain may try to reduce by making you feel more capable or in control than is realistic. Engaging in deliberate improvement can help by substituting facts and rigorous feedback in place of inaccurate opinions and faulty recollections. Collecting and analyzing data about specific investment skills might help you avoid a long string of underperformance enabled by overconfidence.

Notes

1. Cameron Anderson, Sebastian Brion, Don A. Moore, and Jessica A. Kennedy, "A Status-Enhancement Account of Overconfidence," *Journal of Personality and Social Psychology* 103, no. 4 (October 2012).

2. Brad M. Barber and Terrance Odean, "Boys Will Be Boys: Gender, Overconfidence and Common Stock Investment," *Quarterly Journal of Economics* 116, no. 1 (2001), 263.

3. Simon Gervais, J. B. Heaton, and Terrance Odean, "Overconfidence, Compensation Contracts, and Capital Budgeting," *Journal of Finance* 66, no. 5 (2011).

4. Barber and Odean, "Boys Will Be Boys."

5. Ibid.

6. Joyce Ehrlinger, Kerri Johnson, Matthew Banner, David Dunning, and Justin Kruger, "Why the Unskilled Are Unaware: Further Explorations of (Absent) Self-Insight among the Incompetent," *Organizational Behavior and Human Decision Processes* 105, no. 1 (2008).

7. Ibid.

Culture eats strategy for breakfast.
Peter Drucker[1]

Discussions about company culture often have the effect of a sleep-induc-
ing hypnotic. It is one of the softest aspects of business and the one regularly given the shortest shrift. Yet the behaviors, actions, and reactions that
are encouraged or discouraged within a company have a profound impact
on how individuals feel and perform. In the fast-paced, high-energy, sometimes heated discussions that surround investing, a thoughtless comment
can leave its recipient feeling hurt, isolated, and disengaged. The result is
lowered self-esteem, diminished creativity, and disappointing performance.
This essay looks at the importance of fostering vulnerability within teams
and why reducing opportunities for inciting shame is in the best interest
of your portfolio.

That E-Word Again

Daniel Goleman coined the phrase "emotional intelligence" to describe
types of awareness needed to understand and manage one's own emotions and to work successfully with other individuals.[2] Although extensive
research now connects emotional intelligence with corporate success, it
is not a topic commonly discussed within professional investing. In fact,
the money management industry is reluctant to even acknowledge that
its practitioners possess emotions at all. This point is driven home by emotional finance pioneers David Tuckett and Richard Taffler, who write: "Barring a very few exceptions, such as passing references to greed and fear and
more extensive discussions of the wish to avoid loss, emotions in investment have tended to be treated as dangerous signs of weakness, embarrassment or anxiety in both academic and professional circles."[3]

Some management companies are beginning to understand the importance of emotions within team performance, and more specifically the detrimental effects of provoking negative emotions like inadequacy, blame, and shame. Self-described former skeptic CIO Jason Hsu offers this perspective: "Over the past five years, Research Affiliates has engaged outside experts to learn about the transformative power of a positive and healthy corporate culture. As a quant, I initially approached this new age touchy-feely voodoo magic with a great deal of suspicion. Over the years, I have come to understand and deeply appreciate the enormous impact that culture can have on the individuals who come together as a collective to drive organizational success."[4] And stamping out blame and shame as management tools is a great start.

Blame and Shame

"We feel shame when we think poorly of ourselves. It is our sense of our own incompetence or powerlessness," says team innovation expert Leland Beaumont.[5] Shame can be ignited by many common practices observed within professional investing, particularly the use of finger-pointing blame. Speaking to the detrimental effects of this corrosive management tactic, Hsu suggests: "Whether it is the board blaming the investment staff at a pension fund, or the client facing team blaming the portfolio management group at an asset management firm—the modus operandi is often righteous indignation seeking to assign fault. The logical moves for the investment professionals, in this environment, are either to get defensive and deflect blame onto others or to proactively hide poor results."[6]

As terrible as a blame culture sounds, the fallout from the resulting shame is the real problem. "Shame kills inquisitiveness; showing you I don't know makes me vulnerable; and if you use it to shame me then I stop," writes shame researcher Brené Brown in her book *Daring Greatly*. Brown further points out: "Shame can only rise so far in any system before people disengage to protect themselves. When we're disengaged, we don't show up, we don't contribute, and we stop caring. On the far end of the spectrum, disengagement allows people to rationalize all kinds of unethical behavior including lying, stealing, and cheating."[7]

Risks of Returns

Finding excess return involves seeing opportunities ahead of the crowd. Consistently doing this well requires using both your analytic brain and your intuition to identify possibilities before they become apparent to others. Scaring up lots of ideas that go nowhere for every one idea that works is the rule. Engaging fully in this high-stakes, low-probability activity can be fun when the cost of poor ideas is low, but it can be a scary and emotionally crippling experience when imperfection is scorned or ridiculed. Moreover, a low tolerance for mistakes tends to permeate the organization well beyond the stock selection process, inhibiting the kinds of emotional risk-taking desired throughout the business.

Brown traces the fear of mistakes, false starts, and minor failures within organizations right back to shame: "The secret killer of innovation is shame. You can't measure it, but it is there. Every time someone holds back on a new idea, fails to give their manager much needed feedback, and is afraid to speak up in front of a client you can be sure shame played a part. That deep fear we all have of being wrong, of being belittled and of feeling less than, is what stops us taking the very risks required to move our companies forward."

Let's Get Vulnerable

High-performance teams solve problems and identify new ideas with collaborative, highly creative thinking. Creativity also requires trusting that you'll be valued for your engaged participation and not tagged with your worst idea. The more vulnerable individuals can be, the more they will dare to take appropriate risks, and the more powerful the group will be. To this end, Brown encourages us to "[s]upport those who dare to be vulnerable and engage in honest conversations. Teach everyone how to give and receive feedback in a way that fosters growth and engagement."

She also points out: "We can't control the behavior of individuals; however, we can cultivate organizational cultures where behaviors are not tolerated and people are held accountable for protecting what matters most: human beings." A big part of that cultivation is rewarding the desired behaviors and vigilantly encouraging the shifting of any corrosive behaviors toward more appropriate ones.

In her book, Brown provides practical advice for assessing and reshaping cultural norms. A strong initial step is to ponder the following questions:

• What rules and expectations are followed, enforced, and ignored?
• What stories are legend, and what values do they convey?

Answers to these basic questions may provide helpful initial feedback about your organization and its encouragement of taking creative risks.

Conclusion

Maximizing creativity requires making your culture shame-resilient. The more vulnerable individuals can be, the more their intuitions can make novel connections that might lead to good ideas. Central to encouraging this type of culture is reinforcing the notion that creativity is a process and not an outcome, and that mistakes and missteps are expected and even encouraged along the way. As Brown summarizes: "Creativity requires the room to fail; when failure is not accepted then it is replaced with shame; innovation ceases."

Culture is the residual of how individuals act and treat each other, or as Brown defines it: "Culture is the way we do things around here." Nudging the way your company does things toward encouraging vulnerability and creativity and away from ridicule, blame, and shame takes work, particularly overcoming inappropriate behaviors that have become habits. Of course, if you find the corrosive aspects of your culture just too difficult to take on, you can probably find someone on whom lackluster portfolio performance can be blamed.

Notes

1. As quoted in Andrew Smart and James Creelman, *Risk-Based Performance Management: Integrating Strategy and Risk Management* (Hampshire: Palgrave Macmillan, 2013), 233.

2. Daniel Goleman, *Emotional Intelligence: Why It Can Matter More Than IQ* (New York: Bantam Books, 1996).

3. David Tuckett and Richard J. Taffler, *Fund Management: An Emotional Finance Perspective* (Research Foundation of CFA Institute, 2012).

4. Jason Hsu, "Does Blame Predict Performance?," Research Affiliates, March 2013, http://www.researchaffiliates.com/Our%20Ideas/Insights/Fundamentals/Pages/F_2013_March_Does-Blame-Predict-Performance.aspx.

5. Leland R. Beaumont, "Shame," EmotionalCompetency.com, accessed April 5, 2014.

6. Hsu, "Does Blame Predict Performance?"

7. This and the following quotes are from Brené Brown, *Daring Greatly: How the Courage to Be Vulnerable Transforms the Way We Live, Love, Parent, and Lead* (New York: Gotham Books, 2012).

Part Three: Improving Right Away

Be a King. Dare to be different, dare to manifest your greatness.
Jaachynma N. E. Agu, *The Prince and the Pauper*

Knowing that you can become a better portfolio manager is just the first step toward becoming more self-aware and enhancing skills, refining processes, and eliminating behavioral tendencies. Now you need to take action. This will, of course, involve building upon what you've learned in Parts One and Two about using the scientific method to capture and analyze information and then improve deliberately.

Some of you may choose to approach deliberate improvement strategically, designing and implementing a series of improvement plans throughout your companies. Others may prefer to move ahead in a more measured fashion, testing and learning about deliberate improvement initially in one activity within a single investment team. Whatever your approach, you may find it helpful to learn about methods for improving that are working today, supporting individuals at money management companies and in other high-performance professions as they strive to deliver their best.

The projects that follow are intended to assist you in getting started. They include applying the scientific method to sharpen intuition, introducing basic decision-support tools like checklists and diaries, refining skills, retooling processes, and overcoming ineffective behaviors.

Project 1: Embracing the Scientific Method

Background

Active portfolio performance reflects choices—what to buy, how much to own, and when to sell. How those choices come about involves both deliberate processing (conscious thinking) and intuitive processing (unconscious thinking). At any moment, you're unlikely to be aware of which type of thought process is most influencing a choice—it just happens. Consider winnowing down a list of potential buy candidates to a short list that will go on to receive in-depth analyses. Part of this screening involves the deliberate processing of current and historical data, including company revenues, income, cash flow, leverage, and other financial information. Simultaneously, you are forming intuitive assessments of management's capabilities, the company's market potential, competitive position, likely revenue growth, and so forth. The result is that in short order you've eliminated many companies and identified a handful or so of promising candidates that you continue to analyze.

Along the way, you've formulated a preliminary thesis for each stock that has passed the initial screening. Each thesis is a story or narrative that briefly encapsulates why the stock may be a source of excess return. And while each preliminary thesis contains your analytic assessment of the opportunities and risks for a company, it also reflects your intuitions of what is and what might be. This use of intuition in sorting out possibilities is more than unavoidable; it is fundamental to making choices. The better your intuitions at stock screening, the better the outcomes—you'll surface a higher proportion of names that deserve further analysis, and more of those that you ultimately analyze fully will go on to outperform. The bottom line is this: Name selection reflects both deliberate and intuitive processing; and the better your intuitions, the better your buy process. The same goes for the use of intuition in selling and sizing.

Deliberate Intuitions

Can intuition be honed? Brain researchers who study intuitive processing and how it is acquired say it definitely can be improved. In his book *Educating Intuition*, Robin Hogarth summarizes decades of research about intuition and postulates a framework for making it better.[1] His work reflects three critical facts about intuition:

It's Irrepressible

Intuition helps guide our thinking even when we're performing what might be considered deliberate processing, like working a math problem. Your intuition may play a limited role when adding up a column of five-digit numbers but it will be working at breakneck speed as you try to find the solution to an algebraic expression. The first manipulation you consider, the subsequent steps you try, and the way you back out of blind alleys and test further approaches are all driven by your intuition, with deliberate processing providing the computational power along the way.

The same is true for everyday activities like walking down a corridor. You mostly walk down the hall on automatic pilot, allowing your intuition to guide you forward and to avoid your getting lost, perhaps while you're daydreaming about something completely different. But occasionally your conscious brain will be called upon to evaluate directions or to help operate an unfamiliar door knob. Whether you are solving a tricky math problem or just taking a stroll, the back-and-forth between intuitive and deliberate processing is instantaneous, fluid, and imperceptible.

It's Indiscriminate

Your intuition is learning all the time, mostly automatically. It collects information, outcomes, and connections (content) that it then stores in long-term memory without your knowledge or approval. This content is later recalled in varying combinations to support intuitive thinking, responding to various cues and connections that are perceived by the unconscious. A major drawback in this intuitive process is that your unconscious brain is far from perfect in determining which information to make a part of long-term memory and which to discard. Some of what is stored is helpful, while other content can cause you to jump to inaccurate conclusions or make regrettable decisions.

Sometimes weak or erroneous content that you passively learned is later called upon as part of an intuitive moment, resulting in choices that may feel right but produce undesirable outcomes. Types of weak content include misperceptions, falsehoods, biases, uncalibrated heuristics, unsubstantiated beliefs, and conditioned inappropriate emotional responses. This last type of content can motivate your intuition to seek pleasure or avoid pain rather than serve up facts that can help. Because your intuition accesses and relies upon weak and strong content with equal ease, it is impossible for you to know whether you're proceeding toward your intention or being waylaid.

It's Manageable

Useful intuitions are formed when they are learned in environments that provide clear, unambiguous, and timely feedback. Hogarth refers to these as "kind learning environments" and to their opposites as "wicked learning environments."[2] Consider skipping a stone across a pond. It doesn't take long to learn that flat, smooth stones work better than irregularly shaped ones and that tossing the stone with the flat side parallel to the surface delivers the best results. In contrast, how do you know if your selling works? Do you tend to sell losers too quickly or to hold winners too long? Feedback on such questions is not readily available. Stone skipping is, therefore, a kind learning environment, whereas investing is clearly wicked—this latter observation applying literally and figuratively.

Nevertheless, you must rely on your intuition to help guide you to successful choices. Honing intuition is thus one more skill you need to develop to deliver your best performance. It is done through the application of what is termed the scientific method or, as has been described in Parts One and Two, deliberate improvement. Using the scientific method, you can make aspects of portfolio management kinder learning environments. This will allow you to find out what's working and what's not and then implement small refinements to your process that enable you to improve deliberately. Here's how it works.

Improving Scientifically

Improving intuition requires training your automatic responses so that they propel you toward intended outcomes, not unintended ones. That way both your deliberate and intuitive processing will nudge you toward doing your best. Since you can't consciously probe your intuitions, the next best thing is to infer what they might be, using information that is relevant and available. A general model for using the scientific method to build stronger investment intuitions is presented below.

Scientific Method Adapted for Portfolio Management

1. Delineate choices. Improving intuition starts with understanding when it is being used, which is essentially whenever an idea or choice is required. This clearly includes decisions about buying, selling, and position sizing. Of course, the more granular your focus is, the better. For example, thinking about overall sizing decisions is helpful, but isolating adds made to either winners or losers is even better. The reason is twofold: first, granularity provides the clearest feedback, establishing kind learning environments; and second, you are more likely to fully implement your improvement plan if you keep the required change small.

2. Capture data. Data collection needs to be simple or it won't be sustained. Some information is available from accounting, trading, and performance measurement systems, but it will not be sufficiently specific to help with connecting intuition to skills or choices. Instead, a growing number of managers are turning to diaries to provide supplemental information. The key is to make the added information highly pertinent and simple to capture. For example, when making adds to existing positions, you might jot down answers to the following questions: Is the position currently a winner or loser? Prior to the add, is it small, mid-sized, or large relative to your typical full weight? How is it performing relative to the two or three basic attributes you use to gauge a stock's alpha potential (e.g., ROE, price-to-value, etc.)? How is the portfolio performing relative to benchmark? How are you feeling—optimistic, pessimistic, confident, fearful, etc.? You might periodically jot down the cumulative returns for positions from the date you make an add on through to the next quarter, or the next two or three. Before you know it, you will have developed the type of information that supports a kinder learning environment.

3. Analyze. There are many ways to evaluate the choices you've made, the most rigorous being the use of the new framework described in chapter 3. Some other, less analytic approaches will also provide useful insights for understanding your current skills, identifying where intuition may be going astray, and establishing your improvement plan. You can start by constructing visualizations that depict choices and outcomes together. For example, to look deeper into your adds to winning positions, you might create a graph with an x-axis indicating time and two distinct y-axes, the one on the left indicating cumulative return, and the one on the right indicating the size of the adds. An example of this type of graph is provided in the figure below. Once you identify which adds produced positive results and which didn't, you can then turn to your diary to learn more about

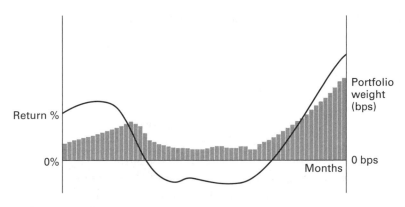

Adds versus performance over time

each type of add decision. This can lead to one or more insights into when your intuitions for adding work and when they don't. From here you can construct an improvement plan that helps you do more of what is working and retool what's not.

4. Draw up an improvement plan. A good improvement plan attempts to reflect four key characteristics. The first is simplicity: Your plan should focus on one change at a time and that change should be easy to remember and compelling. Second, your plan should be fact-based, reflecting rigorous and granular data, affording a kind learning environment. Third, since emotions are ever present, your plan should use them to help motivate the intended change. Lastly, the plan needs to remind you of when you have to invoke the changed behavior, and then provide feedback on how successful you've been.

   An example of how a portfolio team would approach adding more to younger winners might look like this:
• We have a highly achievable opportunity to improve through a small change in our process.
• Success in implementing our plan can lead to better performance, stronger client relationships, and higher AUM.
• We are going to build younger positions to full weight within three months of initial purchase if they begin to confirm their thesis.
• Thesis confirmation will include both the stock outperforming its sector during the initial 90 days and the company's forward earnings growth estimate remaining among the top 25% of its industry peers.
• To make this happen, we will review the weights of all young positions every Monday, as part of the standard portfolio review.

• The only time we will deviate from this process improvement is when, as a group, the team determines that a stock's fundamentals have deteriorated.
• We will review the success of this process improvement every quarter.
• We will communicate this improvement activity to our clients, and use it in our pitch book, once it has been in operation for at least 18 months and proven to be successful.

5. Implement the plan. Successful implementation requires equal parts of two essential elements: process and internal fortitude. Refinements to process can be as basic as the use of checklists. Developing checklists for critical decision points, especially those where improvement actions are being implemented, is a powerful way of shifting a wicked learning environment into a kind one. To the extent that the must-do's on the checklists result from capturing data as described above, the lists will help you ingrain the scientific method as an intuitive aspect of your portfolio management. Lots of internal fortitude is needed to implement change successfully, particularly at the beginning. Each time you encounter the type of choice that you are attempting to change, you can expect to be flooded with intense feelings of discomfort and to readily identify several good reasons why this time the new improvement rule should be overridden. This is precisely where the rubber hits the road: Do you go with the choice that is analytically shown to be more effective, or do you succumb to the one that has been emotionally satisfying? Real-world experience involving scores of managers makes clear that change can and does happen. The chances shift in your favor when you use the scientific method to make a kind learning environment, collecting and analyzing unambiguous and granular data, formulating an improvement plan that is focused and impactful, and harnessing your emotional drives to propel you toward your improvement goal instead of allowing them to thwart your efforts. The lesson is to make sure that you spend sufficient time gathering and analyzing information so that when you hit your own moments of truth, you'll have the inner strength to do what you intend and work at building stronger intuitions.

Notes

1. Robin M. Hogarth, *Educating Intuition* (Chicago: University of Chicago Press, 2001).

2. Ibid., 89.

Project 2: Maintaining a Diary

Background

Memories can be vivid, detailed, and regularly recalled, but they are almost useless in helping you to understand investing skills or to establish an improvement plan. The reason is twofold, having to do with how memories are created and how they are recalled. Most memories are created passively, without conscious intent or purpose. Your unconscious chooses to collect an impression of an item or event, which is often far from totally accurate or complete. When memories are recalled, they are not fixed images like photographs, but instead are the recombination of some or all of the bits about the item or event that your mind is resurrecting. Exactly which bits are recalled and how they are recombined often changes with each recollection, making memories malleable if not fictitious.

Conventional portfolio management tools like accounting, performance measurement, and risk management provide feedback about outcomes but say nothing about the decisions that produced the outcomes. So when managers endeavor to look back to discern why performance was either good or bad, they are drawn to use the only source of contextual information that is commonly available: their memories. This constitutes a wicked learning environment (see project 1) and leads to both faulty self-awareness and ineffective improvement efforts. One helpful step managers can take to substantially improve this situation is to maintain an investment diary.

Chronicle and Learn

Individuals have been keeping written journals of their thoughts, observations, and actions for thousands of years (the writings of Emperor Marcus Aurelius in the second century A.D. are among the earliest known examples). While serving many purposes, these written accounts enable the journal keeper to look back over his experiences and remember more accurately what happened, when it occurred, and in what context it took place. Other examples include explorers who used text and drawings to document and narrate their travels over land and sea. Scientists have used notebooks for centuries to capture and store detailed aspects of their experimental investigations and results. More recently doctors, lawyers, elite athletes, and other professionals have maintained journals or diaries to record activities and then link them carefully with their performance outcomes in an effort to support learning and improving.

While far from universally embraced, investment diaries are being used today by a growing number of professional portfolio managers. The content and use of these diaries are as varied as are the managers themselves. Although essentially a catalog of thoughts and decisions, the diary serves several functions that can support better investing. First, the simple act of establishing what items you'll jot down when buying, sizing, or selling helps to clarify your process. The items you choose to record will reflect key information related to important decisions.

Second, the act of making the entries can enhance mindfulness, causing you to think about what you are doing and why. Third, the information you write down is as close as you can get today to knowing what you were thinking and feeling when you made past decisions. While perhaps not perfect, this information is far superior to recollections alone. Fourth, a diary offers a safe place to unload uncertainty, angst, and fear, and serves a particularly useful purpose in business cultures that do not deal well with personal vulnerability. Finally, the diary allows you to analyze information about buying, selling, and sizing across numerous actions, upgrading your self-assessment from mentally flipping through anecdotes to computing averages and trends. Investment diaries are, therefore, an important tool for implementing the scientific method of improvement.

Diary Entries

The information contained in your diary should help you accurately recall how and why you made certain choices. Entries can be terse or verbose, bare bones or annotated with charts and graphs; they can focus purely on analytic and fundamental information, or include comments about your physical and emotional state. Some diaries even collect lifestyle information, such as how much sleep you received the night before, how much you've been exercising, your mood, and so on. Initially, however, we recommend a highly pragmatic approach that includes keeping your entries on the short side and including a few common data points for each decision. This will increase the chances that you will keep up with the entries and that they will contain information that you can put to good use later. Examples of useful, scaled-down entries are presented below.

A new buy

On Thursday, July 10, 2013, we purchased 300,000 shares of XYZ at $37.50 per share, achieving a portfolio weight of 90 bps. This stock has the three years of consecutive dividend growth we look for, backed up with strong forecasts for revenue and earnings, a defensible pricing strategy, and a solid management team. We expect the price to approach $60.00 within 18 months as the company's new product launches and sales shift from 80% U.S. to at least 40% non-U.S. Our biggest concern is a delay in the launch of the new product, or that it encounters a weak reception by the market. Conversations with management, customers, and suppliers have mitigated these concerns, but they will be watched carefully. Otherwise, all six new stocks purchased so far this year are performing well; the portfolio is currently 15 bps below the benchmark.

An add to an existing position

On Tuesday, January 24, 2014, we finally purchased the additional 200,000 shares of MNO, bringing it up to full position weight (65 bps). The stock has been in the portfolio for just over four months and has had an unrealized gain for over two months. The company's ROE is well above the average of its sector peers. We should have built it up when it began to confirm its thesis 45 days ago, but we hesitated, an unproductive tendency we are working to overcome. Fortunately, there is still plenty of headroom between today's price ($18.35) and our estimate of fair value ($25.00). I think we are getting better at moving into these young winners, but time will tell. Our biggest concern remains the availability of raw materials used in the company's manufacturing, a risk that management is attempting to mitigate through futures options. Overall, we've had some outflows in the recent four quarters due to the lackluster performance of emerging markets equities relative to other asset classes, although we remain slightly above our benchmark. It's a new year and the team is generally optimistic.

A sell

On Friday, November 16, 2012, we sold off our entire position in company ABC. The stock was up 65% from the initial purchase, but its price has been stagnant for the past six months. The company's forward earnings growth estimate dropped from first quartile among its industry peers to third quartile over the time we owned it. Overall, this stock achieved its thesis, but we probably held it longer than necessary. We will review our selling of older winners in December to see if this is a steady pattern or just an occasional delay in selling. The portfolio continues to beat its benchmark (recent three years), and we are experiencing retail and institutional inflows.

Practicalities

Investment diaries may be kept in notebooks (stitched, not loose-leaf) or in spreadsheets and other types of software. Use whatever is easiest for you. Capturing the information and building a set of reliable and granular data are the important initial goals. You'll be analyzing it infrequently, so even if combing through a notebook to assemble what you've recorded turns out to be a little cumbersome, recording it manually on paper may be the right tradeoff, especially if carrying the notebook everywhere enables you to keep up with your entries. Try using an investment diary for 30 to 40 market days and see how it goes. By then, using the diary should feel like a new habit and you might already begin to see interesting patterns, causing you to amend the type of information you are capturing or its frequency.

Conclusion

There's data and there's what you remember, and the differences between these sources of information can be enormous. If you are like the majority of managers, your environment is not set up to capture the *why*s that back up the *what*s moving into and out of your portfolio. This lack of contextual material regarding the choices you make severely limits how much you can learn from your own past. A tool as basic as an investment diary can dramatically enhance your self-awareness and ability to improve by substituting facts for poor recollections and guesswork.

As you begin to use an investment diary, keep it simple but capture enough information so that you can begin to learn more about how you buy, sell, and make sizing decisions. Do your best to make diary entries regularly—every time you make an investment decision, when the ability to register what you are truly thinking and feeling is greatest. For, as Stephen Horan of the CFA Institute notes, "If you have ever kept an investment diary and then gone back and revisited that diary a year later, you will have had a very humbling experience because the diary lays bare your own faulty recollection of how good and how reliable your decisions are."[1]

Notes

1. Stephen Horan, quoted by Lauren Foster, "Helping Financial Advisers and Clients Avoid 'Financially Dysfunctional Behavior,'" CFA Institute, January 3, 2013, at www.cfainstitute.org.

Project 3: Accounting for Skill

Background

Direct measures of skill have long been absent from equity portfolio management, as discussed in chapter 1. Conventional portfolio analytics primarily measure outcomes, which, while the *result* of skills, are not *measures* of skill itself. The absence of true measures of investment skill has greatly inhibited the ability of managers to improve. Assessing skills requires a new analytic framework, one that identifies specific actions that a manager executes and then quantifies how these actions affect portfolio performance. The three basic skills managers use to generate excess return are buying, selling, and position sizing. Quantifying the strength of these three skills fosters greater self-awareness and enables portfolio managers to engage in improving deliberately.

This discussion provides a step-by-step process for computing the returns generated by each of the three skills. These measures provide feedback about strengths and shortcomings that is superior to that provided from traditional metrics like return, relative return, hit rates, attribution analysis, and so on (see chapter 2). The measures presented are readily computable using basic portfolio information and a spreadsheet. Alternatively, accounting and/or performance software may be your preferred means of computation. The sooner you begin to integrate the scientific method into your thinking process, the quicker you'll be on the path to improvement.

Skill Accounting

The analyses described here are based on the data contained in your portfolio, plus two assumptions that reflect the way the portfolio is managed. The two assumptions need only be established once, as you customize this process to fit your portfolio. The analytic steps are to be completed at the end of each analysis period, as explained. Before beginning the analysis, you need to choose values for two analytic assumptions.

Investment Horizon

The performance of a buy needs to be measured over some period that reflects how long you typically expect to hold positions or how long they tend to deliver excess returns (see "Information Advantage" in chapter 3). This discussion uses an investment horizon of eight quarters.

Analytic Period

The more frequently you compute incremental skill values, the more granular the results. Portfolios with very low name turnover (less than 20%) might obtain acceptable results if you compute the incremental skill measures semiannually or even annually, whereas for portfolios with higher name turnover, it may be desirable to compute the incremental skill measures quarterly or even more frequently. An analytic period of quarterly frequency is used in this discussion.

Analytics

At the end of each analytic period (i.e., quarter), complete the following steps to compute the skill measures as indicated.

1. Identify names. Identify all positions in the portfolio that as of the first day of the current quarter had an active portfolio weight (i.e., portfolio weight is above its benchmark weight). This group of positions will be used to compute the rolling one-year name return, sizing skill, and sell skill, described below.

2. Identify new buys. New buys consist of all positions in the portfolio that as of the first day of the current quarter had an active portfolio weight but did not have an active weight on the first day of the previous quarter.

3. Establish the buy portfolio. At the end of any quarter, the buy portfolio includes all stocks whose names appear in any of the new buys (see step 2) in the current quarter or any of the prior seven quarters (i.e., a rolling eight-quarter investment horizon). For example, if the current quarter ended on June 30, 2014, then the buy portfolio as of that date would include all stocks whose names appeared in any of the new buys identified, beginning Q3 2012 through Q2 2014.

4. Compute the quarterly name return. Compute the total return for the names identified for the current quarter (see step 1) with all positions

equally weighted on day one of the quarter. This quarterly name return is used to compute the rolling one-year name return, as described below.

5. Compute the quarterly buy return. Compute the total return for the buy portfolio (see step 3), with all positions equally weighted on day one of the quarter. This quarterly buy return is used to compute the buy skill and sell skill, as described below.

6. Compute the rolling one-year benchmark return. This is done by linking the current quarter benchmark return with the three prior quarter returns.

7. Compute the rolling one-year actual portfolio return. This is done by linking the current quarter portfolio return with the three prior quarter returns. Then convert this to an active return by subtracting the rolling benchmark return.

8. Compute the rolling one-year name return. This is done by linking the current quarterly name return (see step 4) with the three prior quarterly name returns. Then convert this to an active return by subtracting the rolling benchmark return.

The rolling one-year name return is an intermediate value that represents a portfolio containing the manager's active buy and sell decisions but no active sizing decisions. Instead, sizing within this portfolio is accomplished using a simple passive rule. The rolling one-year name return is used to compute the sizing and selling skills.

9. Compute the buy skill. This is accomplished by linking the current quarterly buy return (see step 5) with the three prior quarterly buy returns. Then convert this to an active return by subtracting the rolling benchmark return.

The buy return includes only the manager's active buy decisions and none of the active sizing or sell decisions. The manager's sizing and selling decisions have been replaced with passive rules (i.e., equal weighting and the investment horizon).

10. Compute the sizing skill. The sizing skill equals the rolling one-year actual portfolio return minus the rolling one-year name return. This value is already an active return, since both the actual return and the name return are active returns.

The actual portfolio return includes all of the manager's active decisions. The name return includes all of the manager's active buy and sell decisions but no active sizing decisions. The difference between these two returns is the return due to active sizing.

11. Compute the sell skill. The sell skill equals the rolling one-year name return minus the buy skill. This value is already an active return, since both the name return and the buy skill are active returns.

The name return includes only the manager's active buy and sell decisions but no active sizing decisions. The buy skill includes only the manager's active buy decisions. The difference between these two returns is the
return due to active selling.

Discussion

Although streamlined to facilitate easy data collection and computation
in comparison to the more detailed new analytic framework presented in
chapter 3, the skill measures described above provide considerably more
insight into skills than is available from conventional analytics. These
measures isolate and quantify the actions taken by the manager into buying, selling, and sizing skills. The rigor and granularity of this analysis can
be enhanced little by little to meet your desires or needs. A few ideas for
enhancing the analysis are presented below, with further discussion regarding each skill, its analytic insights, and suggestions for additional analyses
provided in projects 4, 5, and 6 immediately following this discussion.

Modifying the Investment Horizon

The period chosen as the investment horizon influences the result computed for the buy and sell skills. The longer the investment horizon, the
more of each holding's performance is allocated to the buy skill and vice
versa. The reason is that the buy portfolio, as constructed here, holds stocks
in the portfolio for roughly the investment horizon (i.e., eight quarters).
The fewer positions whose actual holding period exceeds the investment
horizon, the more the return generated from the actual portfolio is then
attributed to the buy skill. In other words, the longer the investment horizon, the longer the implied information advantage (see chapter 3).

Likewise, the length of the investment horizon affects the sell skill.
For example, positions that were held in the actual portfolio for less than
the investment horizon are effectively held longer in the name portfolio.
Consequently, when the sell skill is computed (name return minus buy
skill) with a relatively long investment horizon, it tends to say more about
whether stocks are being sold too quickly. Conversely, when the investment horizon is shorter than the actual holding period of most positions,
this is more likely to measure whether stocks are being held too long. (See
project 5 for more details on this analytic point.)

Choosing the Analytic Period

The analysis period controls granularity. The shorter it is, the more granular the analysis and vice versa. Analytic periods between one month and one week seem to offer the right tradeoffs between high granularity and analytic robustness for the majority of managers (i.e., using a somewhat manual process to collect data and calculate results, with annual turnover between 35% and 100%). More robust implementations of the analytic framework, such as suggested in chapter 3, often use a daily analytic period. The analytic period can be tied to portfolio name turnover, as mentioned above. It may be helpful to test one or two analytic periods initially to provide feedback on the tradeoffs in your analyses between frequency of analysis and insight gained.

A potential shortcoming of the analysis presented above is that buys and sells are assumed to occur at the beginnings and ends of analytic periods, respectively. Thus, a buy made on day 3 of a quarter and another made on day 70 of the same quarter are weighted equally in computing the name return and buy skill in the subsequent quarter, because both are assumed to have been initiated on the first day of the following quarter. Therefore, the longer the analysis period, the greater the chance that such differences may impact the results. The same concerns are present, only in reverse, when analyzing the sell skill.

Project 4: Learning about Buying Skill

Background

A common belief among managers and their clients is that successful portfolio results are invariably built on strong buys. This belief is so ingrained that it has become an industry tautology: Buying is what makes great performance, and therefore great managers must be great buyers. The folklore that exists around buying as the driver of top performance is reinforced by conventional portfolio metrics. The single most common use of hit rates, for example, is to assess a manager's buying (the shortcomings of this approach are spelled out in chapter 2). Likewise, although performance attribution measures the returns earned from holdings, its results are regularly misinterpreted as suggesting that lots of relative return coming from stock selection is the same as having a strong buy skill. In fact, the opposite might be the case, with the relative return from stock selection perhaps being mostly attributable to strong sizing or selling skills (also discussed in chapter 2).

To improve deliberately, you need to push beyond convention and work with information that measures skill directly, instead of merely inferring it. That means quantifying your buying skill by using the method for measuring skills presented in project 3. This method enables you to isolate name selection to understand how good it is, and to begin to think about ways you can improve it.

Insights from Analyses

The buy skill is a rigorous way to think about how well you pick names that deliver excess performance, independent of how you size them or sell them. This discussion examines how you can better understand your buy skill, and its strengths and shortcomings, by using skill accounting.

Buying over Time

The buy skill, as defined in project 3, is the rolling one-year active return of new buys executed over the trailing investment horizon, where the one-year active return is the result of linking the current and prior three quarterly buy returns and subtracting the rolling benchmark return. This information alone becomes more useful simply by graphing these values over several years—let's assume 20 quarters. The shape of the curve provides valuable insight into your buy skill. Is it generally positive or negative? Is it consistent or erratic? Is it improving or on a decline? Is it at all similar to what you believed it would be before completing the analysis?

Answers to these and other questions form an important initial step in moving from hunches, guesses, and uncalibrated intuition toward deep self-awareness. Studying these initial results and discussing them with colleagues and mentors is likely to spur you on to designing and performing further analytic investigations into your buying.

Investment Horizon

The length of the investment horizon determines how much performance from each name is allocated to the buy skill. Consider this illustration.

Stock ABC was purchased by two different portfolios on the same day. As it is being included in the calculation of buy skill for each of the portfolios, we learn that manager A uses a 12-month investment horizon, while manager B uses 24 months. The buy skill for manager A will include only half the number of months of stock ABC's returns than will that of manager B. If stock ABC gained 20% in the first 12 months and then lost 40% during the second 12 months, its impact on their respective buy skills will be very different. Likewise, if stock ABC took a loss in the initial 12 months and then racked up a huge gain in months 13 to 24, the impact on buy skills of owning this stock would be reversed for the two portfolios.

Naturally, the buy skill is not dependent on any single stock, but this example illustrates that the length chosen for the investment horizon can have an important impact on the resulting measure of buy skill. Although you probably have a feel for how long your typical buy performs (i.e., generates excess returns), it nevertheless may be advisable to compute your buy skill using a series of different investment horizons. For example, if you believe that your investment horizon should be 18 months (or 6 quarters), then try setting the investment horizon to 4, 6, and 8 quarters to learn how sensitive this assumption is with regard to your buy skill. Feedback like this enhances your self-awareness and enables you to think through improvement options with greater confidence.

Analytic Period

The length of the analytic period determines the granularity of your investigation. The shorter the period, the more granular the analysis, but such analytic refinement is not free. Greater granularity requires collecting and updating data more frequently and results in more calculations.

As an example, a quarterly analysis period requires compiling portfolio data every three months and performing four sets of computations (see project 3) to produce a rolling one-year buy skill. In comparison, using a monthly or weekly period would involve 3 times or 13 times the work, respectively. The question then is, When are the benefits of greater granularity worth the extra costs?

There is no simple answer regarding which level of granularity is best for you. Here are some elements to consider:

• The portfolio's average name turnover. The lower the name turnover, the more comfortable you may be with a longer analysis period. Relatively high name turnover might, understandably, push you toward a shorter analysis period.
• Your level of automation. If the data collection is essentially by hand and the calculations performed in a spreadsheet, you might be motivated to use longer analysis periods. Alternatively, if your accounting system can generate the data easily and the computations can be performed by one of the portfolio software products you have, then a shorter analytic period is warranted.

Even if your implementation of this analysis uses more labor than automation, it might be worth examining the effects of varying the analysis period on a subset of your portfolio history, just to get some feedback on how sensitive the results are to this assumption. Employing the scientific method to learn and improve means producing and analyzing rigorous feedback at every point in the process. As our clients like to say, "Knowing is a whole lot better than believing."

Information Advantage

This analytic process enables you to more clearly understand your information advantage, which equates to how well your typical buys do and how long they perform. (See the discussion of information advantage in chapter 3.) Here's how you can go about estimating your information advantage:

• Gather as much portfolio history as is reasonably possible; the more the better.
• Confirm the analysis period you want to use.

• Using the method described in project 3, compute the buy skill over a range of investment horizons. If your standard choice for investment horizon is 8 quarters, then you might consider using 2 quarters to 12 quarters in one-quarter increments as your horizon for computing the buy skill. Graphing and studying these results will provide clearer insight into what your typical buy is and does. For example, do your buys tend to take off quickly or build up over time? Do they generate excess returns for a couple of quarters or for years? Answers to questions like these not only tell you about your buying, but also inform how you may want to sell and size positions, as taken up in projects 5 and 6, respectively.

Project 5: Measuring Your Sell Effectiveness

Background

Selling is one of the least developed skills managers possess. One reason is that the majority of improvement efforts within the investment community have focused on buying. In addition, the feedback about selling effectiveness from conventional portfolio analytics is, with little exception, useless in supporting improvement. Finally, there is a dearth of academic studies on sell effectiveness, whereas buying has been studied extensively over several decades. It should be no surprise then that a skill that is all but unattended to is so underdeveloped.

Emotions may be part of the reason that selling has received such little analytic rigor or formal study. Unlike buys, which are associated with optimism (What will this new stock do for the portfolio?), sells tend to be associated with angst or downright pain (What has the stock done to the portfolio?). Far too often, the answer to this question is that the stock has disappointed, making it emotionally difficult to ponder these sells.

Defining a Sell

Among the reasons short shrift is given to selling is the fact that this skill has never been properly defined. It surely must include more than merely observing how a stock performs after it is sold. This type of post-implementation analysis is fine for measuring market impact but is much too limited for examining sell skill. For one thing, it overlooks sells not taken, the kind of behaviors that underpin loss aversion and the endowment effect. A good definition for selling might start by considering both sells taken and those that were not taken but might have been.

The new analytic framework presented in chapter 3 describes a good sell as one that occurs when a position held has outperformed up to its sell date, but underperforms the portfolio thereafter. Basic arithmetic explains the reasoning behind this definition. When a position's return is above that of the portfolio, the position is lifting the average, i.e., it's accretive. Conversely, when a position's return is below that of the portfolio, the position is dragging down the average, i.e., it's dilutive. Consequently, the method for measuring sell skill described in project 2 answers these fundamental questions: Were the sells of positions held a relatively short time effective, or would the portfolio have benefited more had they been allowed to stay in the portfolio longer? And, was it effective to keep those positions that were held a relatively long time, or would the portfolio have benefited more had they been pushed out sooner? Determining whether a position was held a relatively long or short time relates back to the portfolio's investment horizon.

Examining Sell Skill

The sell skill is a rigorous way to assess how effectively you harvest positions, independent of how well you buy or size them. This discussion examines how to better understand your sell skill, its strengths, and its shortcomings, by using the skill accounting methodology.

Arithmetic Insights

The sell skill, as explained in project 2, is defined as the difference between the rolling name return and the buy skill. This identity is used because the name return includes the effects of active buys and sells only, with active sizing replaced by a passive rule; and the buy skill reflects returns from only active buy decisions, with both active sizing and selling replaced by passive rules. Thus, active buying and selling minus active buying leaves active selling. Deeper insight into the significance of this identity is provided below, by exploring the relationship between the sell skill and the investment horizon.

Investment Horizon

The length of the investment horizon determines how each position affects the calculation of the sell skill. In general, the longer the investment horizon, the more of each position's actual performance is used in calculating the buy skill, and the less is used in calculating the sell skill, all things being equal. The converse is also true: The shorter the investment horizon, the more of each position's actual performance is used in calculating the sell skill, all other things being equal.

Example 1   Consider stock XYZ, which is held in the portfolio for a period of 12 months. Suppose the manager chooses eight quarters as his invest-ment horizon and a quarterly analysis period, just as in the example in project 3. How, within these parameters, is stock XYZ incorporated into the computation of the buy skill and the sell skill for this portfolio?

The rolling one-year name return will include stock XYZ for its actual time in the portfolio, which in this specific instance happens to equal the analysis period, or four quarters beginning in the quarter after the stock's initial purchase. The rolling one-year buy skill will include stock XYZ in its computation for the full investment horizon (i.e., eight quarters, beginning in the quarter after it is initially purchased). In this particular instance, 100% of the actual holding period of stock XYZ is used in computing the buy skill. In fact, the buy skill also includes the performance of stock XYZ for four quarters beyond its actual sell date.

The sell skill, again, is computed as the one-year name return minus the one-year buy skill. Note, however, that the name return includes stock XYZ for four quarters, while the buy skill includes eight quarters of stock XYZ. What are the analytic implications on the calculation of the sell skill resulting from the different lengths of time that stock XYZ is present in computing the name return and buy skill? When, as in this example, the investment horizon is longer than the stock's actual holding period, the sell skill examines whether the position was either sold effectively or sold too quickly. In this case, if the name return is greater than the buy skill, the sell skill is positive, indicating that had the stock been held longer, it would not have helped performance. If, on the other hand, the name return is less than the buy skill, this means that the sell skill is negative, indicating that had the position been held longer, higher performance could have been captured. The former result suggests that the stock was sold effectively, while the latter result indicates that it was sold prematurely.

Example 2   This time, let stock XYZ have an actual holding period of 30 months, or two quarters greater than the investment horizon. The rolling one-year name return will again include stock XYZ for its actual time in the portfolio, or more precisely, for ten quarters, beginning in the quarter after it is initially purchased. This means that the stock's performance is now included in the name return for six quarters longer than it was in Example 1. The rolling one-year buy return will include stock XYZ in its computa-tion for the full investment horizon (i.e., again, eight quarters, beginning in the quarter after it is initially purchased), exactly as it was computed in Example 1. What's different is that this time only 80% of the holding period of stock XYZ will be used in computing the buy skill (eight-quarter investment horizon divided by ten-quarter holding period).

The sell skill, again, is computed as the rolling name return minus the rolling buy skill. This time the name return includes stock XYZ for ten quarters, while the buy return includes only eight quarters of stock XYZ. What does this difference suggest? When, as in this example, the investment horizon is shorter than the stock's actual holding period, the sell return essentially examines whether the stock was sold effectively or held too long. If the name return is greater than the buy return, the sell skill is positive, indicating that had the stock been sold sooner, it would not have helped performance. If, on the other hand, the name return is less than the buy return, the sell skill is negative, indicating that had the stock been sold sooner, it would have helped performance. The former result suggests the stock was sold effectively, and the latter suggests the stock was sold too late.

Analytic Considerations

Computing the sell skill over a range of investment horizons is a helpful exercise. The investment horizon that provides the highest sell skill can be used as a guide for when to think about selling. Rather than using this value as a hard and fast rule, managers use this feedback to improve their process and avoid behavioral tendencies. Specifically, this information can be part of your checklist for when to confirm or challenge the theses of older positions, as follows.

If the highest sell skill from your portfolio history comes from a relatively short investment horizon, you can use this information both to begin challenging why older positions are being held and to consider whether you might be engaging in the endowment effect or loss aversion. Combining the results of your skill analyses with a review of your diary might provide helpful direction for further investigations to see whether you are engaging in one of these behavioral tendencies.

Alternatively, if the highest sell skill from your portfolio history comes from a longer investment horizon, this information can be used both to begin challenging why younger positions are being pushed out and to consider whether you might be engaging in risk aversion or the avoidance of pain. Combining the results of your skill analyses with a review of your diary might provide helpful direction for further investigation to see whether you are engaging in one of these behavioral tendencies.

Project 6: Calibrating Sizing

Background

Sizing decisions are driven mostly by judgment and intuition. Such choices typically reflect pearls of wisdom handed down from an earlier mentor, or rules that seem reasonable but have never been verified. So here you are again, enmeshed in a wicked learning environment (see project 1) where your skill level is uncertain and your investment process has shortcomings. It's not surprising that your sizing decisions are ripe for behavioral influences. Recalling concepts from emotional finance (see chapter 1), it is easy to see where the desire to seek pleasure may motivate higher active weights (and short sells), while efforts to avoid the pain associated with underperformance or excess tracking error may push you back toward the benchmark.

Managers who typically hold a large number of positions or generate high name turnover may be more likely to focus their attention on initial sizing, whereas managers with highly concentrated portfolios and/or low name turnover might be inclined to engage in lots of trims and adds. As a result, regardless of your information advantage or overall approach to managing your portfolio, you are making important sizing decisions, and you need to know whether these active choices are, on balance, helping or hurting performance.

Sizing Decisions

Sizing decisions include a host of choices about the weight given to a position while it is owned. While sizing applies equally to long and short positions, this discussion will consider only long positions for simplicity's sake. The first choice is how big to make a new position. Then there are opportunities to make it larger (i.e., adds) or smaller (i.e., trims) over its holding period, and these two activities can happen not at all, a modest amount, or frequently. By definition, active managers hold more positions with over-weights than do their more passive brethren. While I have not found any formal research on the topic of sizing as a skill, findings from portfolios analyzed using the new analytic framework indicate that roughly one-half exhibit a negative sizing skill (where poor sizing decisions actually reduce annual performance), and one in six show statistically significant measures of regret aversion (the tendency to keep young winners far too small).

Sizing Conviction

"High conviction" is the term used to denote positions with large active weights versus those with small active weights. The operating premise is that high-conviction positions are more likely to outperform other positions held and therefore deserve larger active weights. It follows then that low-conviction positions, while likely contributors of excess return, are expected to deliver less performance and thus are more suitably given lower active weights. (Positions held to increase diversification or to limit tracking error are assumed to be close to or equal to the benchmark in size and therefore to have a zero active weight.)

The fact is that managers don't know whether their sizing regimes actually add to performance. Or, if they do know, managers don't know how well they work or what to do to improve them. When analyzing sizing skill, managers need answers to several questions: Is sizing overall helping portfolio performance? Do high-conviction positions deserve their large active weights? Do the low-conviction positions in fact generate less excess return than all actively weighted names overall? Answers to these and other sizing questions can be provided using the skill accounting method in the manner discussed below.

Sizing Analyses

The skill accounting method described previously (see project 3) supports the analysis of overall sizing skill and the more granular investigations into the effectiveness of high- and low-conviction sizing choices. In discussing these three analyses of sizing skill, it is useful to begin by describing certain specific characteristics of the portfolio being assessed.

For this example, let's consider a mid-cap global strategy that generally holds about 70 to 80 positions and has a name turnover of approximately 50%. The analysis period is one quarter and the investment horizon is set at eight quarters. The analyses use many of the analytic steps described in project 3. Since this analysis focuses exclusively on sizing, the rolling one-year actual portfolio returns, the rolling one-year benchmark returns, and the rolling one-year name returns are all that must be computed. To study high- and low-conviction positions, the analysis also uses two alternate name portfolios, explained below. The steps to completing this project follow.

1. Calculate the basic or overall sizing skill. This is computed as the rolling one-year actual returns minus the rolling one-year name returns. Positive values indicate a positive sizing skill and vice versa. The actual returns reflect all actively weighted positions in the portfolio, including the manager's actual active sizing decisions. The name returns reflect the same positions on each day but with passive sizing or equal position weights. The weights of the positions are the only difference between the two sets of returns. This answers the question: Are the manager's choices of large and small active weights adding to performance relative to a portfolio of the same names given an equal weight?

More granular analysis helps, no matter what the overall sizing skill. If it is positive, then the granular analysis might show that more success is coming from high-conviction names versus low-conviction names, or vice versa. If the overall sizing skill is low or negative, then deeper analysis can lead to specific ideas for improving.

2. Calculate high-conviction sizing skill. The purpose of this second analysis is to measure whether those positions that have been given higher active weights were, in fact, the positions that also generated the highest returns among all actively weighted positions. Said differently, did the manager bet on the right positions?

This analysis begins by establishing a second name portfolio comprising only high-conviction names. Remember, the basic name portfolio above includes only those positions in the portfolio with an active weight. This step is simply filtering the list of positions down even further, to those with the highest active weights. The cutoff point for determining high conviction is subjective and will vary with each strategy and manager. For this example, the threshold is assumed to be positions that, at the beginning of any quarter, have an active weight greater than 2%. This high-conviction name portfolio is constructed in the same manner as the basic name portfolio.

Next, compute the difference between the returns of the high-conviction name portfolio and the name portfolio. If the result is positive, then the high-conviction stocks outperformed all active positions, indicating that the manager is skilled at picking the right positions to overweight.

Alternatively, if the result is negative, then the high-conviction stocks underperformed all active positions, indicating that the manager is not skilled at picking which positions to overweight.

3. Calculate low-conviction sizing skill. The purpose of this third analysis is to measure whether those positions that have been given lower active weights were, in fact, the positions that also generated the lowest returns among all actively weighted positions. Essentially, we are investigating whether the manager shied away from the right stocks.

The analysis begins by establishing a third name portfolio that is composed of only low-conviction names. This step simply filters the list of positions in the name portfolio to those with the lowest active weights. Again, the cutoff point for determining low conviction is subjective and will vary with each strategy and manager. For this example, the threshold is assumed to be positions that at the beginning of any quarter have an active weight less than 1%. This low-conviction name portfolio is constructed in the same manner as the basic name portfolio.

Next, compute the difference between the returns of the name portfolio and the low-conviction name portfolio. If the result is positive, then the average of all active positions outperformed the low-conviction stocks, indicating that the manager is skilled at picking the right positions to underweight. Alternatively, if the result is negative, then the average of all active positions underperformed the low-conviction stocks, indicating that the manager is not skilled at picking which positions to underweight.

Armed with these three results, you learn the answers to the following questions:

• Does sizing help overall?
• Are my high-conviction names typically the highest performers?
• Do my low-conviction names generally provide less excess return than my high-conviction names or typical actively weighted holdings?

Depending upon the answers to these questions, you might then go on to develop insights like these:

• Your sizing is not helping, so you should abandon sizing determined through judgment for a simpler, rule-based approach.
• Your high-conviction names are helping, so either build them up sooner and larger, make more positions high conviction, or both; or
• Your low-conviction names are as strong as most other actively weighted positions, so there is no reason to keep them so small.

Whatever your unique results, you'll have rigorous and granular feedback about your sizing skills and be positioned to improve deliberately.

Project 7: Checklists

Background

Equity portfolio management is a complex undertaking. As it has long been known, complex tasks need different approaches from tasks that are either simple or complicated. Simple challenges, like assembling knock-down furniture, require only following directions and little in the way of skill. Complicated activities, like building a house, can be broken down into smaller and more manageable subtasks and then matched to appropriate skills, wringing out considerable risk along the way. Complex tasks, on the other hand, involve learning from past successes, plus the agility to adapt quickly to an ever-changing environment, often necessitating that you go with your best judgment. Complex environments such as portfolio management are therefore best approached with a combination of process and intuitive problem solving.

The existential question then is, When do you follow your process, and when do you rely on judgment? There is, of course, no easy answer. The data shows that process can go a long way in both assuring consistency of outcomes and in establishing an ever higher floor of quality. The best approach is to use your process to sidestep avoidable mistakes while also building in speed bumps to slow down and draw into consciousness information appropriate to the immediate challenge. And one way to strengthen your process is with checklists.

Checking Things Twice

More and more top professionals are relying on checklists to achieve their best performance. Pilots are perhaps best known for their unwavering reliance on such lists. Whether flying a supersonic fighter jet or a regional puddle-jumper, the pilot goes through a checklist before taking off. In fact, pilots have scores of checklists that cover every routine decision they can expect to encounter, plus guidelines for assessing and making choices across a host of unlikely and even potentially catastrophic circumstances. Their vigilant use of checklists comes from decades of experience, which has taught pilots that while human judgment is phenomenal, it works best when guided by rules.

Checklists surface naturally within professions where critical judgments are regularly made and where mistakes are expensive. Highly engineered construction projects use checklists to confirm that the right materials and the correct procedures go into building power plants, suspension bridges, skyscrapers, etc. Doctors around the globe have also begun to use checklists to improve surgical outcomes. And each and every flight into space is managed with a series of checklists, from preflight to takeoff to space walks, right back to reentry and landings. While far from high-tech tools, checklists are helping to improve outcomes in complex environments by strengthening processes and supporting mindfulness when judgment is required.

Making a List

Effective checklists have several common characteristics.

Purposeful

Good checklists are precise and offer reminders that help professionals stay focused and mindful when making judgments. Bad checklists are vague or contain overly detailed instructions. Good checklists are inspiring and elevate your game; bad checklists are mind-numbing and tend to be ignored or engender passive compliance.

Simple

Good checklists contain five or so items, and each task is readily understood and its importance is obvious. Bad checklists are too long and require steps that are inflexible, or that the professional cannot easily relate to a successful outcome.

Collaborative

Good checklists are developed with all members of the performing group involved, reflecting what the group knows about success, rather than one person's understanding of what should happen. Bad checklists are imposed on groups and represent an idealized approach, rather than codifying what's been effective.

Evolving

Good checklists use feedback to add, delete, or emphasize steps; bad checklists are written, printed, distributed, and rarely if ever evaluated. Helpful checklists both reinforce what's been working and steer you clear of known pitfalls. Consequently, when you gather the appropriate data from which to construct checklists (see project 1), you want to focus on understanding when mistakes occur, in addition to what leads to success. Since reflecting upon mistakes can easily bring about negative feelings, it is common to avoid thinking about them. Extra care is needed to examine mistakes thoroughly and objectively, in order to learn from them.

Samples

Key to building a useful checklist is that it is bespoke, reflecting your strategy, processes, strengths, and shortcomings. The following examples are offered not as blueprints, but instead as ideas to help jump-start your thinking.

Buying

If you are a value manager whose process involves using a quality model to rank stocks and then a deep dive to understand the fundamental characteristics of a company, a basic checklist might include the following.

1. Confirm that the stock has a quality ranking in the top 20%; otherwise, explain why you are considering it.
2. Confirm that the stock's attributes fall within the portfolio's sweet spot (see chapter 4); otherwise, explain why you are considering it.
3. Confirm that the analyst covering the company has provided a strong buy recommendation; otherwise, explain why you are considering it.
4. Identify the key assumptions related to the stock's success, and discuss how these assumptions might be incorrect. If they are incorrect, what will the impact be on intrinsic value?
5. Write down the stock's thesis, including answers to the following questions: Why do we like the stock? What is the catalyst or driver for its price to increase? What early milestones are being looked for to confirm that the stock is achieving its thesis? What will trigger building this position to full size?
6. Make a diary entry about this purchase the moment the initial buy order is sent to the trading desk.

Sizing

If the data show your adds to losers hurt rather than help performance, you might consider a checklist that includes these questions:

1. Does the position under discussion have an unrealized loss? If yes, then continue.
2. Has the stock generally been realizing its thesis as originally stated?
3. Is the stock's current go-forward thesis different from the one originally described? Is the change opportunistic or just drift?
4. Has the stock's quality ranking dropped?
5. Does the covering analyst recommend this stock as a strong buy today?
6. What are outsiders such as street analysts and independent research companies reporting?

Selling

If you tend to sell young winners well before they have delivered their full alpha, you might consider these ideas:

1. Does the position being discussed have an unrealized gain?
2. Has it been in the portfolio less than my information advantage horizon?
3. Is it still ranked among the top 20% in quality?
4. Has it fully realized its original thesis?
5. Is the current price at or above our estimate for fair value?
6. Has the thesis changed, or are we just taking gains off the table?

Thinking Twice

As a final example, if the data indicate that you often overreact when stocks drop in price by more than a few percent, then you might want to consider reining in those unproductive urges with the following questions:

1. Is the position we're discussing down by more than 10% from its recent high?
2. Other than price, have the company's fundamentals weakened, or has the thesis been disproven?
3. Is there a valid reason for the price to have dropped that does not reflect a deterioration of the company's fundamentals or market position?
4. If we didn't own this stock, would it be a buy today?

Notice that these sample checklists mainly ask questions, the kinds you might want answers to before making a decision. They certainly represent the types of questions that add speed bumps to your deliberations, helping bring to mind the change you are trying to implement and pointing out information that can aid in overcoming old, ineffective behaviors.

Conclusion

"The volume and complexity of what we know has exceeded our individual ability to deliver its benefits correctly, safely, or reliably," says Atul Gawande, author of *The Checklist Manifesto*.[1] This explosion in the volume of information and its complexity is readily observable within equity portfolio management. It helps explain why process has become such a critical topic among professional investors and their clients.

There are many ways to improve process, with the prosaic checklist being one of the most effective tools available. Following the guidelines above, you can construct your own checklists that will enable you to improve deliberately.

Notes

1. Atul Gawande, *The Checklist Manifesto: How to Get Things Right* (New York: Metropolitan Books, Henry Holt, 2009), 13.

Epilogue

It's a sunny autumn day in Boston, and Joy, the lead manager of a successful emerging markets portfolio, is about to meet with a large university endowment that is considering a $200 million allocation to this category. She is pleased to be among the three finalists vying for the award. Joy knows that the other managers have been vetted by the same selection consultant, and therefore they have comparable track records and overall qualifications. At this point Joy needs to demonstrate that her services are different and that the differences are valuable to the prospective client. In the past she would go into similar meetings focusing on her presentation skills, hoping to spark just the right interpersonal chemistry with the prospective client team. Although this strategy felt comfortable and allowed Joy to employ her exceptional emotional intelligence, it put too much faith on results outside of her control. It even came to feel a little desperate.

Today Joy is going to take a more powerful tack. She will focus on her work at deliberate improvement and how it has strengthened her team's skills and processes, and how it will continue doing so going forward. So, after the usual pleasantries, Joy shifts into delivering her message clearly, persuasively, and with just the right amount of analytic backup. She begins by explaining how her primary skills each contribute to the portfolio's performance. She supports this claim by presenting three numbers that quantify the alpha generated annually from the team's skills, a simplified version of which is depicted below.

Joy explains that a big reason for the team's success in buying is due to their process. The team is very effective at identifying strong names with lots of potential alpha. She adds that their buy skill has been consistently strong over the past ten years, which she can explain in more detail if desired. Next, she discusses her sizing skill, which is not quite as strong, but has improved significantly over time. Until about three years ago, Joy tells the audience, her position sizing was based on the team's judgment

Sources of Alpha
Past 3 Years

Buying: 255 basis points per year
Selling: 45 basis points per year
Sizing: 97 basis points per year

and resulted in lots of sizing adjustments to positions. Now she has only three active weights for positions held, enabling her to avoid most trims and adds, except to manage risk. Her once modest sizing skill (double-digit basis points) is now approaching 1% annually. This is a handsome increase in skill and performance that is directly related to her deliberate improvements.

At this point, Joy allows the conversation to slow down, coming almost to a complete stop. Her purpose is to capture the full attention of her audience before explaining what she believes will be a defining moment for this meeting. She looks directly at each member of the client team and says, "You can see that our selling skill is positive, but that has not always been the case. For a number of years, we had the habit of holding our winners for too long. These positions did well for a while, of course, but instead of pushing them out when they started to get tired, we were a little too forgiving. Perhaps we were hoping that these great names would give just a little more alpha to our portfolio. They usually didn't, and this habit of hanging on to them was unproductive. It actually hurt performance."

She then elaborated, "I'm pleased to say that this behavior is no longer a part of our management process. It's gone, completely. Here is how we did it. A couple of years ago, we began to analyze our decision-making more carefully. We looked hard at our skills, process, and potential behavioral tendencies. The result of this effort is that we became a lot more self-aware of our real strengths and shortcomings. We were able to build on our already strong buying and sizing, as I mentioned. And when we found that our selling was not up to par, well, we went at it with everything we had. We pinpointed exactly what aspect of our selling was hurting performance the most. It turned out to be holding winners too long. This behavior is, by the way, consistent with a behavioral tendency known as the endowment effect."

Then Joy described how rigorously developed knowledge was turned into stronger performance: "We implemented process changes to eradicate this problem. First we started challenging older winners more seriously. Instead of allowing them to hide in the portfolio, getting sort of a free ride, now they must pass increasingly stringent reviews the longer they are held. If we can't agree that an older winner is still very vital, then out it goes. This was a hard transition to make. It required us to change how we approach these older winners. We needed to change an old, unproductive habit, and we did it."

She concluded with this statement of payoff: "Now we are selling the older winners sooner. Not all of them, mind you, but more than in the past. And here is what I want to emphasize: As we get better at pushing out these positions, it is freeing up capital that can be used to fund new buys or to build up young positions. Since our buys generally work, this reallocation of capital from tired names to energetic names is helping us do better and stay at the very top of our peer group."

The senior member of the client team was obviously engaged by this discussion. He then asked, "How did you learn all this about yourself and your portfolio? I don't hear details like this from many other managers I meet with." This was the opening that Joy was hoping for. She leaned into the conference table and said, "Let me tell you about how we analyze skills and processes around here." After another 90 minutes of discussion, Joy knew that she had won both the respect of her newest client and a welcome allocation.

Final Take-Away

Scenes like this are playing out every day around the globe. Managers are using the new science of improving to become more self-aware and to strengthen their investing. They also are gaining the ability to communicate more effectively with current and prospective clients about how they invest, why their process supports consistent results, and just how they are going about improving. This ability to improve scientifically matches up perfectly with clients' increasing demands on managers to both deliver strong performance and explain exactly how they do what they do.

The question you may be considering at this moment is: Am I ready to stretch beyond traditional analytics and begin to improve more deliberately? If your answer is yes, then I trust that you'll find the ideas and tools presented in this book helpful on your journey. Should you have questions about deliberate improvement or want to discuss your implementation plans, I hope that you'll reach out to me. Speaking with professional investors is always a pleasure, and so is making new friends.

Glossary

Active share: A concept developed by Cremers and Petajisto that quantifies how significantly a portfolio veers from its benchmark, with higher levels of active share indicating that the portfolio's position weights deviate more from benchmark weights. *(page 10)*

Adjusted portfolio: An analytic concept used to isolate and measure skills and behavioral tendencies. *(pages 42, 57)*

Alpha: A term commonly used to describe the amount by which a portfolio's returns exceeded (or fell short of) its benchmark; but this measure is more correctly referred to as excess return or benchmark spread. As used within this book, alpha refers to a portfolio's performance relative to its benchmark, adjusted for the portfolio's comparative riskiness. *(pages 8–11)*

Anchoring: The tendency to stick with an initial value even if it is no longer relevant or helpful; for example, not wanting to sell a stock today because its current price is below its purchase price. *(page 95)*

Attribution analysis: Attempts to disaggregate the returns of a portfolio into its contributing sources. The most common type involves attributing how much performance was derived from stock selection and how much from sector selection. A useful tool for confirming some aspects of style, attribution analysis falls short of helping a manager understand his strengths and shortcomings. *(page 26)*

Authers, John: A reporter for the *Financial Times* who covers mutual funds and investing. *(page 7)*

Avoidance of pain: Selling off losers prematurely, only to have them rebound after the manager has locked in a loss. *(page 61)*

Bogle, Jack: Founder of The Vanguard Group and a pioneer of index funds. *(pages 5, 6)*

Bragg, Sanford: Founder of buy-side research consulting company Integrity Research LLC. *(page 6)*

Buy candidates: Stocks within a manager's investable universe that are well matched to the sweet spot of his or her investment process. *(pages 56, 177)*

Buy skill: Quantified by a method presented in Project 4. *(page 249)*

CAP-M: The capital asset pricing model developed by William Sharpe, generally considered the first successful means of quantifying how much risk a specific portfolio has taken to achieve a particular level of return: the so-called single factor risk model. *(page 8)*

Carhart, Mark: Added price momentum as a fourth factor to the Fama-French model. The resulting four-factor risk model is used extensively within industry and academia to measure portfolio riskiness and alpha. *(page 9)*

CFA survey: A survey conducted by the CFA Institute and Cabot Research LLC in June 2007 regarding the sell disciplines of institutional portfolio managers. *(page 87)*

Change, behavioral: Difficult to effect, but necessary for improvement. There are well-tested ideas that can make the process easier. *(page 179)*

Checklists: A valuable addition to virtually any investment process. *(page 261)*

Choice: An essential adaptive behavior. Research shows that having too many choices can make choosing difficult and reduce satisfaction in the final choice. *(page 175)*

Cohen, Randy: Author (with Christopher Polk and Bernhard Silli) of "Best Ideas," a paper that examines outperformance among the largest positions held in portfolios. Their conclusion is that most managers own at least a few high-conviction positions that outperform year after year, pointing to at least a modicum of persistent skill across the industry. *(page 10)*

Context analysis: Provides a visualization of which attributes most influence key decision points within a manager's investment process. *(page 53)*

Conviction: A colloquial term that refers to the level of active share associated with a single position, and sometimes used to describe aggregate portfolio holdings. *(page 10)*

Counterfactuals: The mental process of conjuring up "what might have been" or "if I had only"; while it can relieve feelings of disappointment or provide fantasy successes, it can also produce painful self-recrimination. *(pages 97, 135)*

Cremers, Martijn, and Antti Petajisto: Researchers who developed the concept of "active share" as a measure of active management and then linked levels of active share to long-term outperformance. *(page 10)*

Deliberate improvement: Methods of deliberate practice to achieve top performance in a field. There is growing evidence that top performers in all fields are not born great but learn to be great through years of deliberate practice. *(pages 35, 62, 75, 225, 231)*

Diary, investment: Notes kept regularly for one's own use relating to buy, sell, and sizing decisions. *(page 239)*

Ego depletion: The loss of mental energy needed for decision making. Research points to mental energy as a rapidly exhaustible resource; when this resource is depleted, it can have a profound effect on analytic thinking and decision making. *(page 211)*

Emotional finance: A new field, based on a psychoanalytic look at what can motivate financial decisions, suggesting that human emotions are a more dominant force than is expressed within behavioral finance, the latter often focusing on cognitive errors rather than emotions as the cause of faulty choices. *(pages 12, 78, 147)*

Endowment effect: The tendency to hold on to winners well past their ability to generate excess returns. *(pages 62, 81, 93, 131, 159, 216)*

Equilibrium accounting: A concept formulated by Fama and French that argues that most active equity managers are destined to underperform, after recognition of fees and expenses. *(page 9)*

Fama, Eugene, and Kenneth French: Developers of the three-factor risk model (commonly referred to as the Fama-French model) that is widely used to measure portfolio alpha. *(page 9)*

Fear and anger: Everyday emotions that can alter one's mental state from risk aversion to risk seeking. *(page 171)*

Flow: A mental state characterized by high energy, creativity, the desire to enhance skills, and enjoyment of the activity being performed. *(page 191)*

Flow of funds: The shift by investors (institutional and individual) of a substantial portion of their equity allocations from active management to passive products (index funds and ETFs). *(page 5)*

Framework: The new method for quantifying skills, investment process, and behavioral tendencies presented in this book. *(page 39)*

French, Kenneth. *See* **Fama, Eugene**

Group performance: An important area for behavioral analysis. Studies show that high-performing groups can outperform the strongest individual within the group, if they effectively interact. *(page 183)*

Heuristics: The rules of thumb employed to help make decisions throughout the day; they tend to be acquired without the benefit of rigorous confirmation, and thus they often feel good while producing poor results. *(pages 52, 108)*

Hit rate: Ratio of the number of successful outcomes to the total number of attempts. Within equity portfolio management, this metric is more confounding than enlightening. *(page 20)*

Industry scorecard: The S&P Indices Versus Active Funds (SPIVA) scorecard, a compilation of mutual fund performance that details the proportion of actively managed funds that underperform their respective benchmarks over time. *(page 4)*

Information advantage: The excess returns generated from a manager's average new buys. The greater the excess returns generated and the longer they last, the greater the information advantage. *(pages 39, 69, 144, 159, 251)*

Introspection: Often produces weak and inaccurate insights, as the brain's defense mechanisms work to build self-confidence at the expense of honest assessment. *(page 187)*

Kahneman, Daniel, and Amos Tversky: Scholars who were instrumental in developing the relatively new field of behavioral finance. Their pioneering work includes the formulation of prospect theory, for which Kahneman was awarded the Nobel Prize. *See also* **Outside view.** *(pages 12, 108, 215)*

Loss aversion: The tendency to hold on to losers well past any chance that they will rebound, in order to avoid the psychic pain of realizing a loss. *(pages 61, 159, 215)*

Mauboussin, Michael: Academic and investment practitioner who has written several well-received books on investing, including *The Success Equation. (pages 11, 145)*

Mediocre metrics: Conventional portfolio analyses measuring performance outcomes but not the skills that go into generating those outcomes. Metrics like return, relative return, attribution analysis, and hit rates are variations of portfolio performance, and are limited in their ability to help portfolio managers improve. *(page 19)*

Memory: A necessary support for experience, judgment, intuition, and deliberation. Commonly thought of as a collection of fixed factual recollections, memory is nonstatic and can be different each time an idea or image is recalled. *(pages 108, 153, 165, 208, 234)*

Motivated reasoning: One model that helps explain how emotions sometimes run roughshod over objective analysis when making choices. *(page 123)*

Narratives: The stories people tell themselves and others that make sense out of what they believe or want to believe. Differentiating sound theses from narratives is a constant challenge for managers. *(page 202)*

Outcomes: The results, observed over time, of one or more investment decisions. Outcomes include portfolio return and many of the metrics derived therefrom (hit rates, win/loss ratio, attribution analysis, etc.). Outcomes quantify the results of skill, not the level of skill itself. *(page 39)*

Out-of-sample analysis: A type of portfolio analysis used to identify persistent behavioral tendencies. *(page 58)*

Outside view: Shorthand for the process of benchmarking one's assumptions against what can be observed by examining the average results from similar undertakings by others. *(page 145)*

Overconfidence: The tendency to overestimate one's ability. *(page 223)*

Petajisto, Antti. *See* **Cremers, Martijn**

Phantastic object: A term coined by Tuckett and Taffler to describe the loving or hating of an asset, where such feelings are unconsciously driven by the need to meet an emotional desire. *(pages 77, 147)*

Priming: Exposure to information or emotional stimulation just prior to being presented a decision; this can substantially alter the choice made. *(page 165)*

Process: Referring to the methods and activities usually employed as one prepares for and makes an investment decision. *(page 158)*

Prospect theory: A new theory of financial decision making that challenges many of the bedrock assumptions of neoclassical finance; it suggests that individuals experience gains and losses asymmetrically, with losses being more intensely felt. This seemingly simple concept is at the heart of behavioral finance and underpins most well-known behavioral tendencies, such as loss aversion, the endowment effect, and regret aversion. *(pages 12, 61, 96, 127, 215)*

Reference point: An initial or prior asset price used as the basis for decision making rather than that asset's go-forward potential. Referred to as anchoring, this tendency can be overcome if one is able to accept an updated value or reference point from which to assess the asset's potential. *(page 137)*

Regret: A powerful emotion that can be triggered by either an action taken or one not taken. *(pages 127, 135)*

Regret aversion: The tendency to not build up young winners sufficiently. *(pages 59, 127)*

Risk aversion: The tendency to sell winners prematurely, before they deliver their full alpha to the portfolio. *(pages 60, 128, 159)*

Scientific method: A deliberate approach to capturing and analyzing information in order to develop greater self-awareness and improve skills. *(page 233)*

Sell discipline: An industry term referring to the formal and informal rules used by a manager to identify when it is time to sell a position. *(pages 87, 91)*

Sell skill: Quantified by a method presented in Project 5. *(page 253)*

Sharpe, William: A legendary financial academic who received the Nobel Prize for his pioneering work in portfolio risk measurement (capital asset pricing model or CAP-M). *(page 8)*

Sizing skill: Quantified by a method presented in Project 6. *(page 257)*

Skill accounting: A step-by-step process for computing returns generated by buy, sell, and sizing skills. *(page 243)*

Skills: Referring to the three basic skills used in equity portfolio management: buying, selling, and position sizing. *(page 42)*

Skill versus luck: Alternative ways to attribute outperformance by equity portfolio managers. The inability to effectively differentiate luck from skill is one of the essential shortfalls of conventional portfolio analytics. *(pages 7, 11)*

Skill versus outcome: Two ways of measuring equity management. Traditional forms of portfolio analytics measure outcomes, not skill; this shortcoming is hampering portfolio managers globally. *(pages xii, xx, 8, 11, 21)*

Sleep deprivation: One cause of increased behavioral decision making and poorer choices. *(page 119)*

Stress and eustress: Twin consequences of the release of hormones that prepare individuals for action. When feeling challenged in an area of competence, this results in eustress or a positive mental state; when the ability to succeed is doubtful, the unnerving feelings of stress can severely curtail creativity and decision making. *(page 111)*

Taffler, Richard. *See* **Tuckett, David**

Thesis: The short explanation of why a stock is owned and what events are likely to lead to its price increasing. *(pages 59, 69, 115, 149, 201, 233)*

Time world: The amount of time available in which to formulate and execute decisions; highly variable across different situations. *(page 221)*

Transaction cost analysis (TCA):   Also known as market impact analysis; it measures the impact of individual buy and sell trades. Underlying this type of investigation is the understanding that ineffective or expensive transactions are those where the manager's buys push the market price up and result in a higher effective purchase price, or her sells push the market price down and result in a lower effective liquidation price. While important for studying portfolio net return, this metric measures trading skill and not skills associated with the more strategic decisions of buying, selling, and position sizing. *(page 28)*

Tuckett, David, and Richard Taffler: Developed the new study of emotional finance; their books include *Minding the Markets* (Tuckett) and *Fund Management: An Emotional Finance Perspective* (Tuckett and Taffler). *(pages 12, 77, 82, 147, 201, 227)*

Tversky, Amos. *See* **Kahneman, Daniel**

Unconscious thinking: Source of the majority of choices made by all people, including portfolio managers. *(pages xxi, 105)*

Vacation report: Measures the difference between a portfolio's actual performance over a period of time and that of a comparable portfolio that includes all of the same positions at the beginning of the analysis period but none of the manager's subsequent buy, sell, or sizing decisions. It essentially investigates how the portfolio would have done had the manager gone on vacation and left the portfolio alone. *(page 25)*

Visual illusions: The brain's visual recognition of something not there. The visual cortex is constantly guessing about what images are coming next; visual illusions occur when the patterns it infers don't match reality. *(page 195)*

Vulnerability: An aspect of emotional intelligence. Research demonstrates that team cohesion and performance are linked to mutual trust, and that this quality is enhanced when individuals feel they can be vulnerable and share their ideas and suggestions. *(page 227)*

Win/loss ratio: Ratio of the number of successful outcomes to unsuccessful outcomes. Similar to the hit rate, this ratio offers an interesting view on outcomes, but little useful insight about skill. *(page 23)*